# DINING IN

# DINING IN

Highly Cookable Recipes

**ALISON ROMAN**

Photographs by Michael Graydon and Nikole Herriott

CLARKSON POTTER / PUBLISHERS
NEW YORK

For Jen, Finn, and Theo

Copyright © 2017 by Alison Roman
Photographs copyright ©2017 by Michael
Graydon and Nikole Herriott

Published in the United States by Clarkson
Potter/Publishers, an imprint of the Crown
Publishing Group, a division of Penguin
Random House LLC, New York.
crownpublishing.com
clarksonpotter.com

CLARKSON POTTER is a trademark and
POTTER with colophon is a registered
trademark of Penguin Random House LLC.

Library of Congress Cataloging in
Publication Data is available upon
request.

ISBN 978-0-451-49699-7
Ebook ISBN 978-0-451-49700-0

Printed in China

Book and cover design by
Elizabeth Spiridakis Olson
Cover photography by Michael Graydon
and Nikole Herriott

10 9 8 7 6 5 4 3 2

First Edition

**Burrata with Tangerines, Shallots, and Watercress**
**PAGE 95**

# CONTENTS

# INTRODUCTION

**When I was twenty,** I told my mom I was going to take a break from college to cook food for a living. She gave me a special look, reserved only for mothers about to ask a question in a half cry, half yell: "You're going to quit school so that you can go work at Hot Dog on a Stick?" Not exactly. It was, in fact, a really nice restaurant, James Beard award and all. No corn dogs, no hand-pressed lemonade. It wasn't that I didn't like school (I did), or that I wasn't good at it (I was!), but more just that I didn't feel anything for it, and I was really all about following my feelings at that time. Eleven years later, I'm still on that break from college.

Over time, in and out of restaurant and editorial test kitchens, I've cultivated my own personal cooking style, which is hard to classify. I wouldn't call it lazy—I prefer the term *lo-fi*—but to give you some insight into my life as a home cook, I don't own a blender, and up until a few months ago, I didn't even own a food processor (my love for good bread crumbs finally broke my resolve). I use the same stainless-steel skillet to cook nearly everything, a cast-iron one for everything else, and when I inevitably misplace my rolling pin, I take pleasure in rolling piecrust with an unopened wine bottle. The ingredients I keep in my kitchen are mostly familiar (herbs, lemon, olive oil, salt) with only a few that aren't (yuzu kosho, lime pickle), but all have certainly earned their place among the chaos that is my kitchen cupboard. I prefer my steak seasoned with only salt and pepper and believe that my chipped, fire-orange Dutch oven scavenged at a flea market does the job of ten electric slow cookers.

The recipes in this book follow my general approach, in that I would never ask you to toast nine different hard-to-locate spices on a Monday after work, and I'd never suggest you make something that takes 2½ hours if there were a simpler and equally delicious way to do it in one. I've been calling these recipes "highly cookable," meaning they're easy to shop for, simple to execute, and a joy to eat. They prove that casual doesn't have to mean boring and simple doesn't have to be uninspired and that more steps or ingredients don't always translate to a better plate of food.

In most cities it's easy to eat every meal out at a wonderful restaurant if you want. From $1 plates of dumplings to $26 avocado salads, you can truly have it all. And don't get me wrong, I love the experience of eating out, being served, ordering things I would never cook or make myself, like roasted bone marrow on toast with a perfect martini or 36-hour ramen. But for everything else, I prefer dining in. Sure, there's the grocery shopping (a task I actually love), the chance that your oven will stop working halfway through roasting a chicken slathered with anchovy butter (finish it on the stove!), and yes, there are dishes to clean (that can wait until tomorrow). But for me, there's nothing more special or satisfying than cooking for your friends, family, lovers, or, perhaps most important, yourself. Maybe it's because I have cultivated unrealistically high standards for my food tasting exactly as I would prepare it: pork chops almost too salty, salad almost too lemony, bacon so crispy most would call it burnt. Or maybe it's that cooking, dining in, is truly a whole other experience from eating at a restaurant or ordering takeout. Your kitchen isn't meant to compete with the hottest restaurant in town, but there is no reason that the food cooked in your own home should be any less fabulous or bring you any less joy.

Here you'll find a collection of recipes that are neither obnoxiously aspirational nor so obvious that you'd wonder why you bought this book, but fall somewhere delightfully in the middle, full of advice that will help you to become a better cook along the way. These recipes are meant to inspire you to adapt, encourage you to riff, and empower you to maybe not follow the recipe. My hope is that you'll use this book so much that you'll never have to look at it again, cooking from it until each page is covered in olive oil and splattered with tomato, loving it until the pages fall out; the well-worn *Velveteen Rabbit* in your kitchen.

To buy a book and cook from it is an extremely personal experience. You're trusting someone you don't know with your birthday dinner, your housewarming party, your date night, your desk lunch. It's really quite intimate, and I want you to know that we (this book and I) don't take this responsibility lightly. I promise that we will never ask you to make something in two skillets if it can be done in one. We will never ask you to buy an ingredient you've never heard of unless I can defend it with my life and tell you 20 other things to do with it. I promise that we will never require you to remove all the leaves off the parsley stem because that takes FOREVER and I think you'll like the stem anyway. I promise that if you read this book, you will learn at least one thing that will make you a better and more independent cook for the rest of your life.

Table for one? Yes, please. Weekend dinner party? You got this. There is no occasion too big or too small to decide that tonight, you're dining in.

# THE PANTRY

**Try as I might, I am not the keeper of a well-organized kitchen.** My ingredients are not stored in antique Ball jars, and they're certainly not arranged alphabetically, by color, or even by size. A can or package of something spills out of my cabinet nearly every time I open it, and my Ikea metro shelf is bursting with half-filled plastic bags from the bulk bins at Whole Foods. Maybe one day all of this will change, but I don't count on it. I have no system, and that is my system.

Among the chaos are the things I can't imagine cooking without: the can of tomatoes hiding behind the bottle of apple cider vinegar, my box of flaky sea salt precariously perched on top of a very small jar of capers. These staples most influence my food; they are the ingredients that make me a better cook, organized or not.

The pantry list is not a mandate, but if you have most of these things, it'll make cooking the recipes in this book much easier. I also respect that certain things aren't for everyone. You might buy a tin of anchovies and write an angry letter asking me to refund your $8.99. Or they might change the way you make tomato sauce and roast a chicken, and you'll heap mountains of praise onto me for suggesting you give them a try. I'm hoping for the latter, but if not, you know where to find me.

While some of these ingredients might be unfamiliar, nearly everything on this list can be found at a regular grocery store in any major city. For everything else, there's the Internet.

# Salty Stuff

## ANCHOVIES

Anchovies have come a long way since their *Teenage Mutant Ninja Turtles'* smear campaign in the '90s, but more often than not, it still takes some convincing to get people excited about them. And I get it—they are a small, very oily fish with a rather "aggressive" flavor. Not helping their cause, they also come in a tin or a jar. "Fish in a jar? No thanks." I hear you! There was definitely a time when I had to pretend to like them in an effort to keep my "cool young person in the food industry" membership. But once I realized their primary use was not to be eaten like potato chips (note: anchovies are very good on potato chips), I really came around. This is an instance where, kind of like high-thread-count sheets, the quality of the ingredient is directly related to how much it costs. There are no secret "bargain" anchovies, and while the cheap ones will do in a pinch, a good, high-quality jar of anchovies will turn on all the lights for you, so to speak.

I like to put anchovies on just about everything. Thing is, they smash into a fine paste with minimal effort and dissolve almost immediately in a hot skillet, making it all too easy to reach for a jar, pull out a few plump fillets, and sizzle them with garlic as the base of an extraordinarily easy pasta, Caesar-y salad dressing, or crazy-flavorful butter to slather all over a chicken (page 246). Once you start cooking with them, you'll go from cautiously adding one fillet to wrecklessly dumping an entire jar into your next batch of tomato sauce.

## CAPERS

Capers are little bursts of joy, with all the briny, salty, lightly tangy flavor of a pickle without the obvious crunch. When I was growing up, Sunday bagels did not exist without the Costco-sized jar on the table (the 4-ounce jar that capers normally come in is tragically small), my brother and sister and I arguing over who took more capers, all of us worried that we might, one day, run out. Understandably, I like to use them in everything: finely chopped in salsa verde, popped and lightly crisped in browned butter, sautéed and softened in garlic and tossed with vegetables, and, yes, covering every visible inch of my well-toasted bagel.

## FISH SAUCE

This is something I use sparingly but frequently. Often times, I use it as a sort of liquid salt with added . . . umami (a word I told myself I wouldn't use in this book), which to me really means flavor without taste. It's an acceptable substitute for anchovies from time to time, like in pasta sauce or salad dressing, but it's also great used as a secret ingredient in stews, braises, and soups, just like people used Worcestershire sauce in the '50s. When buying a bottle, this is another place where it'll behoove you to splurge on a good bottle, which still won't cost a ton (especially when you consider it'll likely last you forever). Look for fish sauce made with 100% fish—usually anchovies—with no additional ingredients, other than salt, of course. Red Boat makes a good one.

## FLAKY SEA SALT

It feels very 2002 for me to wax poetic about my love for flaky sea salt, but trust me, it's not a trend, it's a way of life. There is something about an ingredient that delivers both salt and crunch at once that speaks to me, and because french fries are so popular, I know I'm not alone. One time I ran out of kosher salt and had to use a box of pricey flaky sea salt to season pasta water, and it felt very luxe, kind of like using expensive face cream all over your body. While it did technically work, I would recommend you save it for things like seasoning beautiful salad greens, finishing your steak, or sprinkling on top of cookies. I love recommending Maldon because it's so widely available, but I also stock my kitchen with Jacobsen, which is made in the good ol' US of A outside of Portland, Oregon.

## KOSHER SALT

It's a given how important salt is on basically everything, and since you asked (did you ask?), my preferred salt is kosher. Kosher to salt my pasta water, kosher to season my chicken, kosher to use in every baked good. Once I realized that the perfectly and consistently shaped flakes were ideal for just about everything, I stopped buying fine sea salt. It should go without saying that regular table salt has never even seen the inside of my apartment, because it has a funny metallic taste and it's too salty, even for me.

## OLIVES

Oil-cured or brined, green or black, Castelvetrano or kalamata, I am an equal opportunity olive enthusiast, making any grocery store olive bar my idea of heaven. Even those black ones from a can that you can wear on your fingers—I like those, too. I put olives out for snacking when I have people over, but I also cook with them frequently, thrown into stews or braises for pops of salt, sautéed in pan drippings to spoon over chicken, or chopped raw and sprinkled over pastas or grilled fish. I prefer to see them crushed, mostly because to get the pit out, it's easiest to crush them with the side of a knife—the pit pops right out—but also because sliced rings of olives remind me of an illustrated drawing of pizza.

The thing with olives is that each variety really is unique, so olives are not always interchangeable. That's why when I call for an olive, I'm pretty specific. Some, like Castelvetrano, are fruity and less salty; some, like kalamata, are briny and taste more like a pickled vegetable. Depending on where they come from and how they're treated, olives will have different amounts of tang and salt, as well as unique textures, so it's best to try them all to see which ones you like the most for pasta, which you prefer in salads, and which are best reserved for your very impressive and fancy cheese plate.

### PARMESAN CHEESE

If I had to pick one cheese to eat for the rest of my life, it would be Parmesan (followed closely by Kraft Singles). I love it because it's cheese, of course, but really it's a true workhorse in the kitchen, doing more than just picking up the slack for underseasoned pasta. To be clear, I find pre-grated, pre-shredded, pre-crumbled Parmesan to be drastically inferior to a hunk of the stuff. I use a Microplane to grate a hunk of Parm over vegetables before roasting or after steaming; a peeler to shave it over salads into long, thin ribbons; and my knife to crumble it into pea-sized nuggets to sprinkle over soups, stews, and warm grains.

### PRESERVED LEMONS

Just when I thought I couldn't love a lemon more, I tasted a preserved lemon. Salty as hell, tangy beyond my wildest dreams, and the color of sunshine, what's not to be absolutely obsessed with? Preserved lemons are significantly softer with less bitterness than a regular lemon, so it's the perfect gateway to using the whole thing. They're good finely chopped into a relish, thinly sliced into half-moons for punchy salads, left whole and simmered with stews, or smashed into butter to spread on radishes. A little goes a long way, so when experimenting with them in the kitchen, start by adding a small amount at a time (for example, a quarter of a lemon). While good-quality preserved lemons are actually not that easy to find, they are worth seeking out. Better yet? Make your own (check out page 27 to see how).

# Spicy Stuff

### BLACK PEPPER

Freshly cracked black pepper is incomparable to the pre-ground stuff, which I'm pretty sure might be just ground-up old newspapers, because it really has no taste. Freshly cracked pepper, on the other hand, is actually remarkably spicy (dare I say piquant?), with a kind of floral vibe that is so special there's a reason nearly every recipe in the world calls for it.

So, please, if you don't already own one, get a pepper grinder (and some black peppercorns!), because it's worth it. I promise.

### DRIED CHILES

My mom went into labor on a night she craved spicy Thai food, and while I'm sure that's probably pretty common, I'll go ahead and say that it's the reason I feel the need for nearly everything I eat to be just a little spicy. Rather than reach for a bottle of too-sweet or too-tangy hot sauce, I like the fruity, toasty flavors of dried chiles. Whole chile de árbol, crushed red pepper flakes, and Aleppo pepper all have their own jars right next to my salt and olive oil, which means, more often than not, I'm reaching for at least one of those things. Each has its own flavor, heat level, and texture, making for different and unique applications.

I use chile de árbol when I want a suggestion of heat without committing to eating the actual chile (I often pick them out), as in soups or braises. Fiery crushed red pepper flakes are for sprinkling on a dish, either before or after cooking, to make it spicy and fruity. They are especially good sautéed in olive oil that has already had garlic or shallots added to it. I use sweet and smoky Aleppo pepper like crushed red pepper flakes, but also for finishing a dish as I would use flaky salt, or in things that never get cooked, like salsa verde or gremolata. Aleppo pepper isn't really all that spicy, which means you can use a lot more of it than crushed red pepper flakes.

### HARISSA

Harissa is a spicy paste made from hot chiles, garlic, and spices. Its texture ranges from a tomato paste to a thick sauce, and it lacks the sweetness often found in many store-bought hot sauces. It's one of the few "hot sauces" used for cooking, rather than as a straight-up condiment, which makes sense because (like tomato paste) the flavor really does get better when it's caramelized in a skillet, roasted onto meat or fish, or fried in olive oil. While harissa is certainly becoming more popular, there still isn't one standout brand that I've found in the States. Harissa comes in a tube, in a can, or in a jar. Some harissas are sweeter, some have no spices at all, some are unbearably spicy, some you can eat by the spoonful. My advice is to sample the ones you can find and always try a little before proceeding with the recipe to make sure you like it. For what it's worth, I have found harissas that come in tubes to be the spiciest, whereas the ones in jars are typically tempered with tomato or roasted red peppers.

### YUZU KOSHO

Yuzu kosho is not as popular as it should be, and I have no idea why. A fermented paste made from Japanese yuzu fruit, green chiles, and salt, it's got funk and flavor for miles. If crushed red pepper flakes are my white clogs, yuzu kosho is the pair of pink Rachel Comey patent leather platform heels I bought on a whim and wear twice a year, but when I do, I am *so* glad I bought them. Because the yuzu flavor (think sour lemon meets floral grapefruit) is so pronounced, it's a little less all-purpose than some of the other things in this category (like crushed red pepper flakes or black pepper), but it's got this charming heat that really sneaks up on you when you least expect it and just the most unique and delicious salty, citrusy flavor. I whisk it into dressings for cold noodles (page 162) and shaved vegetable salads, massage it onto cabbage for slaws, and dollop it into pots of braised vinegar chicken (page 221).

# Crunchy Stuff

### BREAD CRUMBS

Overwhelmingly pleasing in their small, concentrated delivery of crunch and salt, bread crumbs add unbridled happiness to whatever you're eating. If they were a person, they'd be the kind you always want at your party because they know to bring the good wine and also a case of seltzer. Of course they are invited to your summer squash gratin (page 63),

and when you're making a heaping pie of mustardy bitter greens (page 79), you'd better believe they are on your guest list. I always keep a box of panko around for emergencies, but really, nothing compares to the not-too-small, never-sandy, perfectly textured homemade bread crumb.

For more on how to make your own (and why you should be making your own), see page 24.

### NUTS

With their toasty, buttery crunch, nuts really are nature's crouton. It would be hard for me to pick a favorite, so I end up keeping most varieties on hand, always stored in the freezer (the natural oils inside tend to go rancid when left at room temperature). While I do bake with them a considerable amount, I use them with equal frequency in savory applications, replacing actual croutons in salads with chopped almonds (page 90), using crushed walnuts instead of bread crumbs for pasta (page 147), or just finishing tender roasted vegetables with a confetti of roasted pistachios (page 84) to replace some of that lost crunch. And while it may be annoying to toast the nuts every time you want to use them, please know that it is most definitely worth it. Those natural oils? Well, that's where all the flavor is, and they need to be coaxed out by a trip to the oven. Think of how much better toast is than regular bread, and you'll understand.

For more on the how and why of toasting, head to page 50.

### SEEDS

Depending on the type (poppy, sesame, fennel, or cumin), seeds are great for lending crunchy texture, flavor, or sometimes both. Since each serves a unique purpose, I like to keep them all on deck, even if that means my

freezer looks like I might own more than a few pet birds (seeds, like nuts, contain high amounts of oils, so they tend to go bad when left at room temperature for a couple of months). I prefer the texture of biting into a cumin seed rather than hoping your ground cumin from 1998 is still potent enough to make a difference, and I think that freshly toasted sesame seeds are good on just about everything, including buttery shortbread, a savory granola (page 143), and for tossing on vegetables before throwing them in the oven (like the carrots on page 52) so they toast as the vegetables roast. I create seasoning blends with seeds for my lamb chops (page 225) and also for my avocados (page 119), really making it a mission to use seeds whenever and wherever I can.

# Fatty Stuff

### COCONUT OIL

Coconut oil is definitely on the higher end of the price spectrum, and it's not something that you just have to have, but it is something that you really should have. I recommend using virgin unrefined coconut oil, which has a more pronounced (yet still pretty mild) coconut flavor (compared to the refined version, which is very neutral in flavor with almost no coconut taste to speak of) and lends a slightly nutty, tropical vibe to whatever it touches. Coconut oil started gaining popularity for its purported health benefits, and while that's not what draws me to coconut oil, I can say that if you haven't popped popcorn in the stuff, you haven't lived (it also makes a great hair conditioner, for what it's worth). Unlike olive oil, it solidifies at room temperature but liquefies when warmed, making it especially great for key lime piecrust (page 270), but its almost buttery richness makes it a remarkably good match for simple dishes like sautéed greens with garlic or chicken soup with mushrooms and celery (page 219).

### OLIVE OIL

Next to salt, olive oil is probably the most-used ingredient in this whole book. I use it to sauté food at high heat and roast at high temperatures, and I've even been known to use it for grilling (on a hot grill). I generally keep one nicer bottle on hand for finishing salads or fresh vegetables, and one more workhorse kind for actual cooking. Since I use a lot of olive oil, I'm willing to spend a little bit more on it, even for the one I cook with. The good news is that these days, you don't have to use your whole paycheck for a reasonable bottle. While I am picky about the flavor (I avoid anything that tastes super bitter or seems too "grassy"), I am not picky about where it comes from, although I do think California Olive Ranch makes some really great stuff.

### YOGURT

If it were up to me, every recipe in this book would either be drizzled, dolloped, served, or made with yogurt. There is always a tub of full-fat Greek yogurt in my fridge, waiting to be used the way most people would use mayonnaise or sour cream, and even in some ways they wouldn't. I find myself reaching for yogurt just as much for breakfast (with savory granola, of course) as I do for dinner, grating fresh garlic into a bowlful of the stuff, or seasoning with plenty of salt and a squeeze of lemon for swooshing under spicy, crispy chickpeas (page 126) or vinegar-roasted beets (page 33). It always seems to be the kind of tangy, fatty, rich-but-not-too-rich

ingredient that goes with everything, making lean foods feel more substantial and richer foods somehow cleaner.

# Tangy Stuff

### CANNED TOMATOES

While fresh tomatoes are a sure bet in July and August, canned tomatoes are around 365 days a year, making them a true kitchen miracle. Especially come March, when I feel like I might never see a fresh vegetable ever again, they come through in a major way, providing bright, juicy acidity to soups, stews, braises, and, of course, pasta. I prefer to buy my canned tomatoes whole, even if I'm crushing them later, because I like to control the size of the crush—do I want larger, chunkier pieces for a stew? Smaller, more pureed pieces for a silkier sauce? Or leave them whole to roast alongside a bird in the oven—having options makes me feel like the possibilities are endless, and when it comes to canned tomatoes, they really are.

### CITRUS

I say citrus, but what I really mean are lemons and limes. Don't get me wrong, I *love* grapefruits, oranges, kumquats, tangerines—all citrus, really. But lemons and limes are the real heroes here. Since they have different flavors and levels of acidity and juiciness, they are not always interchangeable—the milder lemon would never be able to perk up a taco *al pastor* (page 208) quite like a lime, and a lime would certainly be too aggressively bitter for roasting alongside paprika-rubbed chicken (page 227). But I still like to have both on hand at all times. Their acidity and sweetness are quieter than any vinegar, which means they play

nicely with just about everything (which is great, since I do put citrus on just about everything).

Aside from just taking advantage of the well-balanced juice of the lemon and lime, I never ignore their floral, peppery zest. It's great to finish just about anything that needs a pick-me-up. And as for just lemons, they are also great used whole, and eating them raw or roasted, thinly sliced or finely chopped, is a revelation in just how good bitter flavors can be.

### VINEGAR

I sometimes think vinegar is still recovering from its association with raspberry vinaigrettes and too-sweet fake balsamic, which for a time was drizzled over literally everything. Good vinegar is not cloying, and it certainly isn't made with caramel coloring. Instead, it's tangy, funky with hints of things like apple, white wine, or sometimes nothing at all (while most white distilled vinegars are made from corn, the flavor is removed to just get pure acidity).

I like to keep several kinds on hand because they really all do serve their own purposes: apple cider vinegar punches up the acidity in apples and cabbage while they roast next to pork (page 244), intensely acidic white vinegar pickles just about everything (page 23), and the more mild rice vinegar dresses quick kimchi (page 70) or cold soba with cucumbers (page 162). While I do believe each vinegar is worth having for its own unique flavor profile and acidity level, many of the recipes in this book allow for lots of flexibility and swapping in one variety if you don't have the other.

# CONDIMENTS

**Part of the reason New Yorkers subject themselves to insanely high rent,** crowded subway cars, and grocery stores that don't sell wine is because it is a city where you can truly get anything you want, whenever you want (except for wine at a grocery store). Specialty spots like the Middle Eastern haven Sahadi's in Brooklyn ensure that you never have to learn how to preserve your own lemons, because theirs are so good. You can always head to a small, unassuming store in Chinatown to buy some authentically MSG'd chili oil, so why bother making your own? Well, not everyone lives in New York, and even taking the train to Sahadi's is too much for me, which is why I've included recipes for some of my favorite condiments, even if I'm spoiled enough to never have to make them myself.

While these recipes appear as a component or sidekick to other dishes throughout the book, I would recommend making extra batches just to keep on hand to use in whatever way you like. Think of making your own condiments as a way of doing your future self a favor. Once you start dressing up takeout with your Crunchy Chili Oil (page 20), rescuing the saddest of salads with Lemony Tahini Dressing (page 22), or just eating those beet-pickled turnips (page 23) straight from the jar, you'll never look back.

# Crunchy Chili Oil

*Makes about 1½ cups*

Just as you can tell a good deli by its rye bread, I think the quality of a Sichuan restaurant is revealed by its chili oil. The best ones have small pots of the fiery stuff on every table, the salty oil glowing neon orange and floating with flaky, seedy bits, almost too hot to eat. While I have no intention of opening a Sichuan restaurant, I do think that this Crunchy Chili Oil is pretty damn good.

The peanut oil is the real hero in this recipe; since it arrives roasty and toasty, you're already halfway to something really delicious. You can also use another neutral oil with a high smoke point, such as grapeseed, vegetable, or canola, if you don't want to use peanut oil, adding a splash of toasted sesame oil for more flavor.

I really enjoy the crunchy, flaky, almost gritty (in a good way) texture that the sizzled seeds and flakes bring to the table, and I really think that's what makes this one so special. During the cooking process, a lot of the heat in the actual chile flakes and peppercorns is tamed, meaning you can stir up the settled bits and eat them with wild abandon. That said, if you're not accustomed to the mouth-numbing tingle of the Sichuan peppercorn, start with less and work your way up to more.

There's always a large jar of this oil in my fridge so I can put it on nearly everything I eat, in the way most people use Sriracha. I toss it with cold buckwheat noodles, spoon it over lackluster takeout, and drizzle it into soups like the one with chicken, celery, and mushrooms on page 219. It's especially good as a dressing for cold, crispy vegetables like kohlrabi and cucumbers (page 61), whisked into tahini and soy sauce for an insanely delicious dressing, or simply mixed with rice vinegar and tossed with steamed greens.

**¾ cup unrefined peanut oil (grapeseed or vegetable oil will also work)**
**¼ cup crushed red pepper flakes or Aleppo pepper**
**¼ cup black or white sesame seeds, or 2 tablespoons of each**
**2 to 3 tablespoons Sichuan peppercorns, chopped**
**4 garlic cloves, thinly sliced (optional)**
**Kosher salt**

Heat the peanut oil, red pepper flakes, sesame seeds, Sichuan peppercorns, and garlic, if using, in a small pot over the lowest heat possible. Let it come to a simmer (all the bits in the pot will start to sizzle) and cook until the red pepper flakes are a dark brick red and the sesame seeds are golden brown and toasted (if using black sesame seeds, you will start to smell them toasting), 15 to 20 minutes. Remove from the heat and add several generous pinches of salt. Let cool completely before chilling.

**DO AHEAD:** Chili oil can be made 1 month ahead and stored in a (preferably glass) jar in the fridge.

# Everything Seed Mixture

*Makes about ½ cup*

There are so many "everything" puns to be made here, but I will spare you. While perfect on a just-opened avocado, this Everything Seed Mixture can be used to doctor store-bought pita or lavash (brush with oil, scatter over, and bake till crispy), sprinkled over whipped ricotta for dipping, or serve dusted on top of roasted vegetables. I like to toss these seeds into salads for a salty crunch and pops of flavor from the caraway, and to top baked potatoes with sour cream. Point is, keep it on hand and you'll find a way to use it … on everything (get it?).

**3 tablespoons white sesame seeds**
**3 tablespoons black sesame seeds**
**2 tablespoons caraway seeds**
**1 tablespoon poppy seeds**
**2 tablespoons granulated or dehydrated onion (optional)**
**1 tablespoon flaky sea salt**

Place the white sesame seeds, black sesame seeds, caraway seeds, and poppy seeds in a small skillet. Toast them over medium heat until the sesame seeds are golden brown and the caraway is fragrant, about 3 minutes (don't walk away here; sesame seeds burn super quickly, especially around the edges of the skillet). Remove from the heat and add the onion (if using) and salt. Let cool completely before storing in jars.

**DO AHEAD:** This can be made 1 month ahead and stored at room temperature.

# Fresh Za'atar

*Makes about ½ cup*

Za'atar is a Middle Eastern spice blend made of thyme, sesame seeds and, more often than not, ground sumac. Because the quality, texture, and type of za'atar will vary depending on where you buy it, I find it useful to just make my own (especially should I have extra thyme on my hands—literally), keeping it next to flaky sea salt as a part of my seasoning arsenal. The salt and sumac act as a sort of salty/sour dream team together in any circumstance (like with the melons on page 99), but thyme brings the fresh herbiness and toasted sesame anchors the whole thing with a deeply savory, nutty flavor.

Use this as you would use the store-bought stuff, which is to say, use it on everything. It'll be your best friend come summer (it's perfect on raw tomatoes and nearly all grilled produce during the hotter months), but it's also great as a winter pick-me-up, dusted over roasted chicken or seared fish, sprinkled over smashed root vegetables, and, of course, served with butter-tossed radishes (page 58) any time of year. While the thyme will dry out (this is not a bad thing), this fresh za'atar will keep for up to a month at room temperature stored in an airtight container.

¼ cup raw white or black sesame seeds
¼ cup fresh thyme leaves, coarsely chopped
2 tablespoons ground sumac
Kosher salt

Toast the sesame seeds in a small skillet over medium heat, tossing constantly until they're fragrant and golden brown, about 4 minutes. Remove the skillet from the heat and add the thyme and sumac, tossing to combine. Season with salt and let cool completely before transferring it to a storage container.

# Another Salsa Verde
*Makes 2 cups*

With all the salsa verde recipes out there, it seems silly to contribute yet another one to the world, I know. However, I would be remiss not to include a recipe for this one, since it truly is my favorite condiment. It's the perfect confluence of zesty, herby, salty, and oily that seems to be the answer to the question you might ask of almost any dish that's not quite hitting all the notes for you: "What is this missing?" It makes boring fish exciting, dry meat edible, and leftovers (like the cold garlicky pasta on page 161) delicious again. It can be thinned with more lemon juice or vinegar and used as a makeshift salad dressing, or spread onto overly crusty bread to become the ultimate sandwich savior (not all heroes wear capes).

While the concept of salsa verde is basically the same wherever you go (chopped herbs, olive oil, some form of acid, and maybe shallot or another allium), there are endless ways to customize it. Mix up the herbs depending on the season and whatever you have in abundance, make it spicy with fresh or dried chiles, use garlic instead of shallot, add some salty anchovies or Asian fish sauce. Go wild. While I prefer the rustic look and coarser texture of everything chopped by hand, this is definitely an instance where a food processor comes in handy, so feel free to use that instead of going the old-school route (just know you'll get a more emulsified, finely chopped salsa verde).

½ small shallot, finely chopped
2 tablespoons fresh lemon juice, red wine vinegar, or white wine vinegar, plus more as needed
Kosher salt and freshly ground black pepper
2 cups tender herbs, such as parsley, cilantro, chives, and/or mint (pick one or mix them), finely chopped (see Note)
¾ cup olive oil

Combine the shallot and lemon juice in a medium bowl and season with salt and pepper. Let it sit for 5 minutes or so (this slightly pickles the shallot and takes a bit of the oniony edge off). Stir in the herbs and oil, and season again with salt, pepper, and lemon juice, if needed. If you like, add anything from the following list, or keep it simple, keep it classy.

**NOTE:** If using a food processor, leave the herbs whole. Process them until they're finely chopped, then pulse a few times with the olive oil, salt, and pepper. Transfer to a bowl and stir in the shallot-lemon mixture, season again with salt and pepper, and adjust the lemon juice, if necessary.

**THINGS TO STIR IN AT THE END, IF YOU LIKE**
4 anchovy fillets, finely chopped
½ lemon, seeds removed, finely chopped
1 serrano chile, with or without seeds, finely chopped
2 teaspoons Aleppo pepper (if you have it—and you should have it) or 1 teaspoon crushed red pepper flakes or hot smoked paprika
1 or 2 garlic cloves, finely grated
1 tablespoon soy sauce or Worcestershire sauce

**DO AHEAD:** This can be made 5 days ahead and refrigerated in a glass jar or resealable container.

# Green Romesco
*Makes 2 cups*

For all you romesco purists out there with pitchforks, yes, I know this can't possibly be a real romesco because it lacks both tomato and red pepper, but I use this garlicky, paprika-y sauce just like I would a "real" romesco: dragging thin slices of steak through it, topping crispy-skinned salmon and radishes (page 175) with it, thinning it with olive oil to toss with beans (page 141), and eating it with every grilled, steamed, or roasted vegetable possible (but it's especially great with the Olive Oil–Roasted Spring Onions, Leeks, and Shallots on page 38). I prefer to make this sauce by hand for the coarse, uneven texture of the herbs and chopped nuts, but if you like a finer, paste-like consistency, it's also easy to make in the food processor.

2 cups parsley, tender stems and leaves, finely chopped (see Note)
¾ cup olive oil
¼ cup skin-on almonds or walnuts, toasted and finely chopped
2 garlic cloves, finely grated
1 jalapeño pepper or serrano chile, without seeds, finely chopped
1 tablespoon red wine vinegar
½ teaspoon smoked paprika
Kosher salt and freshly ground black pepper

In a bowl, combine the parsley, olive oil, almonds, garlic, jalapeño, vinegar, and paprika. Season with salt and pepper.

**NOTE:** If using a food processor, you don't need to finely chop the parsley, almonds, jalapeño, or garlic. First, process the almonds until they are coarsely chopped, about the size of a grain of rice. Add the parsley, garlic, and jalapeño and process until you've got a coarse paste. Add the olive oil and pulse just to blend. Transfer the mixture to a bowl and stir in the vinegar and paprika (I find adding the vinegar and paprika outside the food processor keeps the colors more vibrant), seasoning it again with salt and pepper.

**DO AHEAD:** This can be made 5 days ahead and refrigerated in a glass jar or resealable container.

# Lemony Tahini Dressing
*Makes about 1 cup*

I've considered buying those little plastic cups that come with takeout salad just so I can carry this dressing with me wherever I go. There's not much that wouldn't be improved by it, and while using it to pour over a salad (like the Little Gem lettuce with pickled turnips and cabbage on page 80) is an obvious choice, it's also the kind of thing you'll want to dip raw vegetables into, serve as a side sauce for roasted chicken, and generally bathe in. Even with just the one clove of garlic, this dressing gets at the point, screaming, "Garlic lovers, this one's for you!"

¼ cup tahini
¼ cup fresh lemon juice, plus more as needed
3 tablespoons olive oil
1 garlic clove, finely grated
Kosher salt and freshly ground black pepper

Whisk the tahini, lemon juice, olive oil, garlic, and ½ cup water together in a small bowl and season with salt and lots of pepper, adding more lemon juice if you like it especially tangy. This dressing can be refrigerated for up to a week, so take advantage of that and make a double batch.

**DO AHEAD:** This dressing will keep for up to 1 week in the refrigerator.

# Lemon Relish with Leftover Stems
*Makes 1½ cups*

I go through a lot of big, leafy greens; I use them wilted in soups, with scrambled or fried eggs, or sometimes just on their own with lots and lots of crispy garlic. But that's not the point. The point is that sometimes I just want the leaves, which means I'm left with lots of perfectly edible stems. While they are good tossed into stir-fries or sautéed alongside the leaves, I prefer to celebrate their crunchiness rather than tame it. This relish can be made with any greens, but it's especially striking with the vibrant red stems from Swiss chard.

1 bunch Swiss chard, kale, or mustard greens, leaves and stems separated
1 small shallot, finely chopped
½ lemon, seeds removed, finely chopped
1 tablespoon white wine vinegar or red wine vinegar, plus more as needed
Kosher salt and freshly ground black pepper
¼ cup olive oil

Reserve the chard leaves for another use. Finely chop the stems and combine them in a small bowl with the shallot, lemon, and vinegar. Season with salt and pepper and let sit 5 minutes or so. Add the olive oil and season again with salt, pepper, and more vinegar, if you like.

**DO AHEAD:** This can be made 5 days ahead and kept in the fridge.

| **Pickled Stuff** | While I was growing up, my grandmother used to say to me, "You eat so many pickles, you're going to turn into one." And it's true. I've always had a very aggressive pickle habit, keeping at least three types in my fridge at any given time, eating them straight out of the jar, slicing them and putting them in salads, or serving them with other raw vegetables as a party starter (if pickles don't say "let's get this party started," I don't know what does). I | order them as a side to my matzo ball soup at Jewish delis, order extra when eating Nashville-style hot chicken, and always set out a bowl full of them when serving really fatty cuts of meat as a respite from all the richness. Luckily, once I run out of pickles, I still find a way to keep their spirit alive, using the liquid left behind to brine chicken or as the base of a really good Bloody Mary.

Realistically, it would be insane to give a recipe for | just one type of pickle when there are so many options out there, so here are three of my favorite brines, which can be mixed and matched depending on what you're trying to pickle. You should know that none of these brines are sweet (I think bread-and-butter pickles should be illegal), and they are highly customizable, with just the right amount of salt and vinegar to go with almost any vegetable under the sun. |

# Basic Salt and Pepper Brine

*Makes 3 cups brine*

Sure, this brine is as basic as they come, but it's the perfect blank canvas for adding complementary herbs (dill with cucumbers!), spices (fennel seed with carrots!), or other aromatics (crushed garlic with green beans!), depending on what you're pickling and the flavor you're looking for.

**1 cup white distilled vinegar**
**2 tablespoons kosher salt**
**1 tablespoon black peppercorns**

**USE WITH:** cucumbers, carrots, green beans, radishes, jalapeños, onions

**1** Bring the vinegar, salt, peppercorns, and 2 cups water to a simmer in a small pot, stirring to dissolve the salt. Remove from the heat and pour over a large jar of vegetables. Place a lid on top and let the brine cool completely before refrigerating. Let sit at least 1 day for smaller or sliced vegetables and up to 3 days for larger ones left whole.

**2 TO MAKE THE PICKLES:** Prepare 1 pound of vegetables however you please. Different vegetables will

want different treatments (e.g., slice the fennel, quarter the turnips and cucumbers, cut the carrots into sticks, leave green beans whole, cut cauliflower into small florets, quarter the onions), but whatever you choose, the idea is that they are all cut the same size.

**3** Pack the vegetables into either two 8-ounce glass jars or one 16-ounce glass jar, adding any aromatics you like. Think sliced lemons, fresh bay leaves, sprigs of dill. Bring your chosen brine to a simmer and pour it over the prepared vegetables. Seal the jars and let them come to room temperature before refrigerating (no need to process; this is not a canning book).

**4** Even without processing or canning (something you do when you want these to last literally forever), these "refrigerator pickles" will keep for up to 2 months.

# Beet Brine

Aside from turning it a stunning, vibrant fuchsia color, adding a sliced beet to your brine will lend some of its sugar to whatever you're pickling, great for adding some natural sweetness without being cloying. Oh, and did I mention the vibrant fuchsia color?

To make the beet brine, peel and slice 1 large red beet and add it to the Basic Salt and Pepper Brine before simmering.

**USE WITH:** turnips, carrots, radishes, hard-boiled eggs, cauliflower, onions

# Turmeric Brine

Adding fiery orange turmeric will give you a brine that not only looks like it is made of sunshine, but has a lightly spiced, earthy taste that's especially great with hearty root vegetables and even hard-boiled eggs.

To make the turmeric brine, add 1 teaspoon ground turmeric or 2 tablespoons peeled and chopped fresh turmeric to the Basic Salt and Pepper Brine before simmering.

# Fresh Bread Crumbs

There are plenty of things out there that call themselves "bread crumbs," but often what you're purchasing resembles the sawdust on a dive bar floor more than anything that came from a crusty loaf of bread. More powder than crumb, they are hardly deserving of the name.

Proper bread crumbs do not get soggy and turn to mush when doused with olive oil or melted butter (and you must douse them). When toasted or browned, they offer rich, dimensional texture with mind-blowing crunch. Think of the perfect bread crumb size as very, very small croutons. Now, doesn't that sound delightful? Sure does.

The good news about the impending hassle of dragging your food processor out to make these is that it's literally the most complicated part of the whole ordeal. Make a large batch, store them in ziplock bags, and freeze them until the next time you're in need (they'll keep up to a month if well sealed).

Start with a loaf (or two) of some delicious-looking crusty bread, such as sourdough or ciabatta—even baguettes work. I prefer using fresh bread, since it's softer and easier to break down in the food processor, but day-old or just-stale bread works, too.

Cut the bread into 1- to 2-inch cubes (I leave the crust on, unless the crust is *very* dark). Fill the food processor about halfway with the bread cubes and pulse until you've got really small, tiny pieces of bread (future bread crumbs!). Pick out any large pieces that didn't quite get the memo to break down and place your bread crumbs in a bowl if you're using them right away or in a large ziplock bag to freeze them plain for later use (like for the trout on page 191). Repeat until you've used all the bread.

These bread crumbs are called "fresh" because they are not dried. Fresh bread is porous and spongelike, primed to absorb fat in a way that dry bread crumbs cannot, and if they aren't absorbing the fat, what's the point? (Yes, sometimes fresh bread crumbs get toasted, but those are a different thing than "dried" bread crumbs, which are just fresh bread crumbs that are left out to dry.)

# Toasty, Garlicky Bread Crumbs

*Makes 2 cups*

While Fresh Bread Crumbs are a blank slate, these are prepared bread crumbs—a complete situation, ready to go, waiting to be sprinkled over a leafy salad like the perfect little croutons they are, folded into cheesy pasta, or scattered on top of a carved roasted chicken for additional crunch. This basic version features garlic, but there are lots of ways to customize your bread-crumb experience by sautéing something along with the bread as it toasts (anchovies, dried chiles, grated cheese) or adding it after they've been toasted (lemon zest, fresh herbs).

¼ cup olive oil
2 cups Fresh Bread Crumbs (opposite)
Kosher salt and freshly ground black pepper
4 garlic cloves, finely chopped

Heat the oil in a large skillet over medium heat. Add the bread crumbs and season with salt and pepper. Cook, stirring pretty frequently, until the bread crumbs start to turn golden brown, about 4 minutes. Add the garlic and toss to coat. Continue cooking and tossing until the bread crumbs are a deep golden brown (think graham crackers) and crisped, another 2 to 3 minutes. Transfer to a small bowl and let cool before using.

**DO AHEAD:** These bread crumbs can be made 5 days ahead and refrigerated. Rewarm them in a skillet before using.

# Salty Anchovy Bread Crumbs

*Makes 2 cups*

When you need a salty, punchy crumb to stand up to aggressive salads, like the chicory salad on page 79, or to liven up otherwise simple roasted vegetables, especially brassicas like cauliflower or broccoli, look no further than these bread crumbs. Don't worry about chopping up the anchovies; they'll dissolve right into the olive oil, just like magic. Use more or fewer anchovies, depending on the kind you're using and how much you love the little guys.

¼ cup olive oil
6 anchovy fillets
2 cups Fresh Bread Crumbs (opposite) or panko bread crumbs
Kosher salt and freshly ground black pepper
1 garlic clove, finely chopped

Heat the oil in a large skillet over medium heat. Add the anchovies and, using a wooden spoon or spatula, move them around in the oil until they've dissolved into a delicious paste; this will happen almost immediately. Add the bread crumbs and season with salt and pepper. Cook, stirring pretty frequently, until the bread crumbs start to turn golden brown, about 4 minutes. Add the garlic and toss to coat. Continue cooking and tossing until the bread crumbs are a deep golden brown (think graham crackers) and crisped, another 2 to 3 minutes. Transfer to a small bowl and let cool before using.

**DO AHEAD:** These bread crumbs can be made 2 days ahead and refrigerated. Rewarm them in a skillet before using.

# Spicy, Herby Bread Crumbs

*Makes 2 cups*

Sometimes those long-braised pots of meat or almost-too-tender stews need not only a little texture but also a little herby freshness and maybe a bit of heat—enter Spicy, Herby Bread Crumbs, which do both wonderfully. Parsley is used as a lion's share of the herbage here, adding most of the freshness and a vibrant green color, but for extra flavor, feel free to mix it up, depending on what you're making. Finishing roasted spring vegetables? Go tarragon. Looking for something to sprinkle onto a bowl of beef stew? Maybe choose thyme.

¼ cup olive oil
2 cups Fresh Bread Crumbs (opposite)
1 teaspoon Aleppo pepper or ½ teaspoon crushed red pepper flakes
Kosher salt and freshly ground black pepper
¼ cup finely chopped tender parsley leaves and stems
2 tablespoons finely chopped herbs, such as thyme, oregano, marjoram, and/or sage

Heat the oil in a large skillet over medium heat. Add the bread crumbs and Aleppo pepper and season with salt and black pepper. Cook, stirring pretty frequently, until the bread crumbs are a deep golden brown (think graham crackers) and crisped, 5 to 7 minutes. Remove from the heat and add the parsley and other herbs. Transfer to a small bowl and let cool before using.

**DO AHEAD:** These bread crumbs can be made 5 days ahead without the herbs and refrigerated. Rewarm them in a skillet, then stir in the parsley and other herbs before using.

# Cheesy, Peppery Bread Crumbs

*Makes 2 cups*

If you, like me, fantasize about a cheese that is also crispy to top pastas, sprinkle over crunchy, lemony lettuce, or just eat by the spoonful, might I recommend cheesy bread crumbs? Adding grated Parmesan or Pecorino Romano cheese (using a Microplane yields the best results) to the bread crumbs doesn't quite melt the cheese; rather, it toasts and browns along with the crumbs, giving you another layer of texture and toasty flavor. To me, this stuff is better than the cheese that melts and browns on the skillet when you're making a grilled cheese, which is very high praise.

¼ **cup olive oil**
2 **cups Fresh Bread Crumbs (page 24)**
½ **teaspoon coarsely ground black pepper**
**Kosher salt**
½ **cup finely grated Parmesan or Pecorino Romano cheese**

Heat the oil in a large skillet over medium heat. Add the bread crumbs and pepper and season with salt. Cook, stirring pretty frequently, until the bread crumbs are turning golden brown, about 4 minutes. Add the cheese and toss to coat. Continue cooking and tossing until the bread crumbs are a deep golden brown (think graham crackers) and crisped, another 2 to 3 minutes. Transfer to a small bowl and let cool before using.

**DO AHEAD:** These bread crumbs can be made 2 days ahead and refrigerated. Rewarm them in a skillet before using.

# Mayonnaise for People Who Hate Mayonnaise

*Makes 2 cups*

My dad refuses to eat eggs unless they are scrambled, and that's because every other type of egg (hard-boiled, fried, poached) reminds him of mayonnaise, the "worst thing on the planet." Pretty much the only downside to being my father's daughter is that, growing up, I, too, was taught to hate mayonnaise, that it was my enemy, not to be consumed under any circumstances. As a result, for nearly twenty-five years, I ate my tuna sandwiches with only mustard and celery, endured very dry BLTs, and always ordered my In-N-Out without special sauce.

All that changed the day I learned to make my own mayonnaise. Of course, it wasn't called mayonnaise, it was called "aioli," but let's be real: they are nearly the same thing. I found the action of slowly drizzling oil into eggs, creating a thick, smooth, velvety sauce that was yellow with egg yolks, completely therapeutic. And guess what? It was also crazy delicious, tangy with lemon juice and aggressively salty. It was nothing like that bright white, gloppy, vaguely sweet stuff that came from a blue-labeled jar, and yet the process of combining egg and oil was the same, so did that mean I . . . liked mayonnaise? I guess it did. I liked this kind, anyway, and Dad, I think you will, too.

This is a handmade mayo, so put away that food processor and bust out a whisk. Like cream that is whipped by hand, I find you have a lot more control over the emulsification process when you're doing it sans food processor. Unless you're making a huge batch (here you are not), I think it's easier to do it the old-fashioned way, with better results.

2 **large egg yolks**
1 **teaspoon Dijon mustard**
1 **teaspoon fresh lemon juice, plus more as needed**
**Kosher salt**
½ **cup olive oil**
½ **cup grapeseed or vegetable oil**
1 **small garlic clove, finely grated (optional)**

**1**  Whisk the egg yolks, mustard, lemon juice, and a pinch of salt together in a medium bowl (one that is deeper than it is wide, if possible; it's easier to emulsify everything when there is more of it concentrated in one area—another reason I prefer doing this in a bowl, not a food processor). Combine both oils together in a measuring cup with a spout.

**2**  In a slow, steady stream, add the oils to the egg mixture, 1 tablespoon at a time, whisking all along, making sure the oil is completely incorporated before whisking more in. Add all the oil, thinning with water or more lemon juice, as needed, to keep the future mayonnaise from becoming too thick (note that the ideal mayonnaise thickness is extremely personal, but when you know, you know).

**3**  Whisk in the garlic, if using, and season with more salt and lemon juice, as desired.

**IF YOU'RE FEELING SASSY, YOU CAN ADD ANY OR ALL OF THE FOLLOWING TO THE MAYO**
1 **tablespoon prepared or grated fresh horseradish**
½ **teaspoon hot or smoked paprika**
2 **teaspoons whole-grain mustard**

4 anchovy fillets, finely chopped
½ cup finely chopped fresh herbs, such as tarragon, dill, and/or parsley
4 cornichons, finely chopped

# Preserved Lemons

*Makes 2 cups*

Preserved lemons are essentially the love child of two of my favorite things: pickles and lemons. It's a lemon pickle, really. They're salty but never punch-you-in-the-face salty, with an addictive tanginess that gives me the same pleasure as a bag of Sour Patch Kids. I have to stop myself from putting them on everything I eat, although if I did, would it really be the worst thing?

Through the salting and preserving process, lemons soften greatly and their bitterness all but disappears, making them excellent candidates to be sliced or chopped and tossed into salads (like the Little Gems on page 80), added to vinaigrettes or sauces, or just sprinkled on top of rich, fatty stews (like the lamb stew with fennel on page 241).

I've made preserved lemons many different ways, using recipes with different ingredients and techniques, but I think this is the simplest and easiest way to get preserved lemons into your life. You could even make these without the spices and they would still be incredible (ah, the magic of lemons and salt), but I think the spices do add a little something special.

8 lemons, scrubbed
8 tablespoons kosher salt
1 tablespoon whole coriander seed
1 tablespoon black peppercorns or pink peppercorns
4 chiles de árbol or 1 tablespoon crushed red pepper flakes (optional)

**1** Without cutting all the way through, slice each lemon in half crosswise until it can open up nearly all the way. Then slice it lengthwise, again avoiding slicing all the way through. Sprinkle each lemon inside with 1 tablespoon of the salt and place them, standing up straight, in a small baking or casserole dish so that they fit all snugly (if they are not snug, find a smaller vessel). Cover this with plastic (or a lid, if available) and let it sit in a cool, dark place until the juices have run and the lemons have started to soften, about 1 week (you can also refrigerate them, but then it will take closer to 10 days).

**2** Transfer the lemons to a large, wide-mouth jar, kind of smooshing them inside to make them fit and submerging them in their own juices. Add the coriander, peppercorns, and chiles (if using). Let these sit another 3 weeks in a cool dark place (patience is a virtue!), until they're totally softened and no longer grainy or distinctly salty.

**3** They are now ready to eat and will keep in the fridge for up to 6 months.

# Preserved Lemon Labne

*Makes 1 cup*

This is the ideal two-birds, one-stone kind of condiment. It's tangy, rich, fatty, salty, and lemony, all without trying too hard. It can be thinned out with some buttermilk or even plain ol' water for dressing crunchy lettuces, or served as is in dip form to accompany things like turmeric-roasted lamb (page 235) or grilled artichokes (page 57). If you crave a super-silky texture, run this through the food processor rather than mixing it in a bowl. Oh, and the labne and preserved lemons are bringing plenty of salt to the table, so no need to add more (if using yogurt or sour cream, you might need to season with a bit of salt, but not much).

1 cup labne, Greek yogurt, or sour cream
½ Preserved Lemon, any seeds removed, finely chopped
Freshly ground black pepper
Olive oil, for drizzling
A pinch of ground turmeric, for sprinkling (optional)

Combine the labne and preserved lemon in a medium bowl. Season with lots (and lots) of pepper. Transfer it to a serving bowl and drizzle the top with olive oil and a pinch of ground turmeric, if using.

# VEGETABLES

# When I was about seven or eight, I had a thing for supermarket shoplifting.

Not toys, books, or magazines from the back of those interior aisles, but vegetables. I'd walk down the produce aisle, grabbing small fistfuls of whatever small treasures were left out in the open, vulnerable little pods of snap peas and green beans, sprouts and peanuts, waiting to be plucked from their bins and stuffed into my pockets. We'd check out and I was sure that the cashier knew, her eyes scanning the insides of my jacket for stowaways. The anxiety I suffered walking out of those grocery stores, wondering if I'd get caught, was all worth it for those few blissful bites of raw, unwashed vegetables. Nobody ever called the police, but my mom did eventually figure out where all those stray bean sprouts were coming from.

All this is to say that I really, really love vegetables. And I have a stealing problem. Just kidding—I grew out of that. The greener and leafier the better, although spicy radishes will always be my number one (especially those tossed with butter, as seen on page 58), and I'd never kick caramelized winter squash out of bed (especially topped with coconut gremolata, like on page 48).

When cooking vegetables, I'm rarely inclined to mix and match. I find throwing everything that's in season together into one dish overwhelming, and not necessarily more delicious. Letting one or two vegetables speak for themselves is infinitely more interesting to me, a better opportunity to get to know them and all their quirks a little bit better. Raw, roasted—or better yet, raw and roasted—one vegetable two different ways can be as dynamic and fabulous as five vegetables. They are my favorite little shape-shifters, often the most important item on my table for any given meal.

# Vinegar-Roasted Beets
# with Spring Onions and Yogurt

*Serves 4*

2 bunches tiny beets (about the size
    of a golf ball) or 1 bunch medium
    beets (about 1½ pounds)
2 tablespoons white distilled vinegar
    (white wine vinegar or sherry
    vinegar also work here)
3 tablespoons olive oil
Kosher salt and freshly ground black
    pepper
2 medium spring onions, quartered,
    or 4 whole scallions
1 cup full-fat Greek yogurt
2 tablespoons fresh lime juice
¼ cup fresh dill, tender stems and
    leaves

Remember back in the late '90s when everyone was serving roasted beets with arugula and goat cheese? No disrespect, but this dish is kind of like that, except better. Yogurt replaces the goat cheese with equal tanginess and better creaminess, so you won't miss it. When it comes to roasting beets, adding a splash of vinegar kind of lightly pickles them while they cook, which curbs their sweetness and seasons them from the inside out. I like white distilled vinegar for this, but the other noted types will do.

1  Preheat the oven to 400°F.

2  Divide the beets and place them on two large pieces of foil. Drizzle each set of beets with the vinegar and 2 tablespoons oil; season with salt and pepper. Wrap each bunch tightly, so that any steam created stays inside the packet. Roast until the beets are totally tender and cooked through—check them after 45 minutes; they should be easily pierced with the tip of a knife or fork (if larger than golf-ball size, they may take upward of an hour). Once they're cooked through, open the packets and let them cool slightly.

3  Using paper towels or a kitchen towel you don't mind staining forever, gently peel the beets. If they are on the larger side, halve or quarter them; otherwise, leave them whole. Place them in a small bowl with any juices from the foil packet and season with salt and pepper; just let them hang out here for a bit.

4  Heat the remaining 1 tablespoon oil in a large skillet over high heat. Once it's super hot and shimmery, add the spring onions and season with salt and pepper. Toss them every so often, until they're charred in spots and the bulbs are tender, about 3 minutes. Remove from the heat and set them aside.

5  In a small bowl, combine the yogurt and lime juice, and season with salt and pepper. Spoon it on the bottom of several (or one large) serving platters and top with the beets and a couple spoonfuls of the juices that have pooled at the bottom of the bowl. Top with the spring onions and dill.

# Blistered Green Beans with Creamy Tahini and Fresh Hot Sauce

*Serves 4*

¼ cup hazelnuts, coarsely chopped

2 tablespoons white distilled vinegar

½ red or green jalapeño pepper or habanero chile, seeds removed, finely chopped

1 garlic clove, finely grated

Kosher salt

Pinch of sugar

½ cup labne, full-fat Greek yogurt, or sour cream

2 tablespoons tahini

1 tablespoon fresh lemon juice or white wine vinegar

1 pound green beans or Romano beans, ends trimmed if you like

1 tablespoon vegetable oil

Freshly ground black pepper

**NOTE:** This creamy tahini sauce is great underneath just about any vegetable—charred, roasted, grilled, or even raw. Make extra.

**DO AHEAD:** Creamy tahini can be made 5 days ahead and refrigerated.

I find any vegetable that's been grilled to a smoky, charred, blistered deliciousness to be one of the more perfect foods, but especially when it's dragged through a creamy tahini sauce and doused with fresh hot sauce. The key to getting these beans perfectly charred without setting off your smoke alarm is cooking them as quickly as possible over high heat. Use a grill if one's available, but for those without a grill (or good weather), this indoor skillet method works extremely well to char a variety of vegetables (slabs of zucchini, coins of eggplant, bulbs of spring onions…).

I love wider, flatter Romano beans here (more surface area = more char), but they are not always available, so just know that green beans or any other summer pole bean work, too.

**1** Toast the hazelnuts in a small skillet over medium heat, shaking the skillet pretty frequently, until they're golden brown and starting to smell like browned butter, about 5 minutes; set aside.

**2** Combine the distilled vinegar, jalapeño, and garlic in a large bowl; season with salt and sugar, and set aside.

**3** In another bowl, combine the labne, tahini, and lemon juice, and season with salt. (I like this sauce on the thicker side—better for dipping—but if you like, you can thin it out with a bit of water to get a more drizzly consistency.)

**4** Heat a large cast-iron or stainless-steel skillet over high (yes—high!) heat. Toss the green beans with the oil and season with salt and pepper. Throw them into the hot skillet and cook, tossing frequently, until the green beans are lightly charred on all sides but still bright green and with some snap to them (army green = soft beans), about 4 minutes.

**5** Remove the skillet from the heat and, using tongs, add the beans to the bowl with the jalapeño mixture, tossing to coat. Let them sit in this for a minute or two to absorb some of that vinegary heat.

**6** Spoon some of the creamy tahini onto the bottom of a serving platter and top with the green beans and hazelnuts.

# Spring Peas with Anchovy, Lemon, and All the Radishes

*Serves 4*

## DRESSING
**3 anchovy fillets, finely chopped**
**2 stalks green garlic or scallions (white and light green parts only), thinly sliced**
**½ lemon, seeds removed, finely chopped**
**1 tablespoon fresh lemon juice, plus more as needed**
**Kosher salt and freshly ground black pepper**

## SALAD
**½ pound snap peas, halved lengthwise, stringy pieces removed**
**2 cups thinly sliced radishes, preferably a mix of watermelon, French breakfast, and regular**
**2 cups pea tendrils or shoots**
**½ cup tender tarragon leaves and stems**
**3 tablespoons olive oil**
**Kosher salt and freshly black ground pepper**
**Fresh lemon juice**

When it comes to spring produce, I prefer my peas raw and my radishes plentiful. These crunchy, flawless vegetables are only made better by salty, funky anchovy and an aggressive amount of lemon. Because the peas and radishes are so sturdy, they can be dressed a bit in advance. When you're ready to serve, add the more delicate tendrils and herbs, seasoning once more before it hits the table.

**1 MAKE THE DRESSING:** Combine the anchovies, green garlic, chopped lemon, and lemon juice in a small bowl and season with salt and lots of pepper; this dressing should taste assertive in every way possible: salty, tangy, garlicky, peppery.

**2 MAKE THE SALAD:** Toss the snap peas and radishes together in a medium bowl. Add the anchovy dressing and let sit a few minutes (this will soften them slightly and give them a chance to get to know the dressing). Add the tendrils and tarragon, and toss to combine. Drizzle with olive oil and season with salt, pepper, and more lemon juice, if you feel like the salad needs a touch more tang.

**NOTE:** This anchovy dressing is great spooned over all leafy things and most green things. Despite what I said about asparagus on page 71, it is especially good spooned over those electric green spears. Make extra and tell all your friends.

# Olive Oil–Roasted Vegetables

Slow roasting vegetables—any vegetable—in obscene amounts of olive oil is a two-part love story. In part one, the vegetables sizzle along in their luxurious bath, the water inside them evaporating so that the flavors intensify and the natural sugars are coaxed out, little bits caramelizing along the edges. Delightfully rich and tender, they are ready to be plopped directly into your mouth, but they are also incredibly versatile: perfect for topping Sour Cream Flatbread (page 137), adding to a skillet of garlicky anchovies for mind-blowing pasta, or using as part of a spread, accompanying roast chicken and a big knife-and-fork salad (pages 75–85).

In part two, there's the wildly flavorful leftover olive oil. This is dreamy stuff. Because the oil will be infused with whatever aromatics you've previously roasted in it (herbs, garlic, shallots), it's a real two-for-one kind of deal. Sure, you can use it to store the vegetables if they're not used immediately, or you can save it to roast even more vegetables, cook greens, fry eggs, or even just dip bread in.

To store these vegetables, keep them in a container that is deeper than it is wide, so the vegetables stay submerged in the oil. They (along with that oil) will keep up to 2 weeks in the fridge.

### OLIVE OIL–ROASTED SPRING ONIONS, LEEKS, AND SHALLOTS

Preheat the oven to 400°F. Halve 3 pounds of any combination of spring onions, leeks, and shallots lengthwise and place them in a 3-quart baking dish. Cover with 1½ cups olive oil and season with salt and pepper. Roast until the onions are caramelized and starting to char lightly at the tips, 30 to 40 minutes. Let cool before storing in their oil in the fridge, or eat them right away with roasted chicken.

### OLIVE OIL–ROASTED MUSHROOMS

Preheat the oven to 400°F. Tear or cut 2 pounds of mixed mushrooms (maitake, oyster, shiitake, button, chanterelle—you name it) into largish pieces and place them in a 3-quart baking dish. Cover with 1½ cups olive oil and add a few halved shallots or heads of garlic, along with a few sprigs of fresh rosemary or thyme. Season with salt and pepper, and roast until the mushrooms are caramelized and deeply browned, 35 to 45 minutes. Let cool before storing in their oil in the fridge, or eat them right away on top of the Sour Cream Flatbread on page 137.

### OLIVE OIL–ROASTED TOMATOES

Preheat the oven to 325°F. Halve 3 pounds of smallish, medium tomatoes (such as hothouse or vine-ripened) crosswise and place them in a 3-quart baking dish, cut-side up. Cover with 1½ cups olive oil and add a few cloves of crushed garlic and a few sprigs of fresh oregano or thyme. Season with salt and pepper, and roast the tomatoes until they start to caramelize around the edges of the baking dish and are totally softened and nearly shriveled, about 3½ hours. Let cool before storing in their oil in the fridge, or use them right away for the pasta on page 153.

# Raw Broccoli and Basil Salad
# with Peanuts and Shallot

*Serves 4*

⅓ cup vegetable oil

2 shallots, thinly sliced crosswise
    into rings

Kosher salt

¾ pound young broccoli (flowering
    broccoli, if possible)

2 tablespoons fresh lime juice, plus
    more as needed

1 teaspoon Asian fish sauce, plus more
    as needed

1 teaspoon light brown sugar

Freshly ground black pepper

½ cup roasted, salted peanuts

1 cup Thai, lemon, and/or purple basil
    leaves, torn if large

½ cup cilantro, stems and leaves

**NOTE:** Putting crispy, salty, fried shallots onto your salad is like taking a cab when you could take the subway. Sure, it'll cost you (some extra time), but you'll be so glad you did. They are great here, but also good on most any salad imaginable.

**DO AHEAD:** Shallots can be fried 2 days ahead and kept tightly wrapped at room temperature.

Raw broccoli is a true gift to the salad world. It takes on dressing like a champ, fully absorbing whatever it's bathed in without wilting, improving with time. This particular dish, which makes great leftovers, is the only excuse you need to seek out that really nice, young, tender broccoli you can pretty much find only at the farmer's markets or in your nearest Chinatown.

Larger, more adult broccoli is an acceptable substitute here; just make sure you cut the florets into small pieces and thinly slice the stalk (which is definitely edible and definitely delicious).

**1** Heat the vegetable oil and shallots in a small pot over medium heat. Cook, stirring occasionally. The shallots will clump at first, but this is okay. As they cook, they will start to bubble and sizzle (this is the water leaving the shallots) and then begin to turn golden brown (this is them getting crispy). After the shallots are good and golden, about 6 minutes or so, remove them with a slotted spoon, transfer to a paper towel, and season with salt. Set the oil aside and let it cool slightly so you can use it in the next step.

**2** Cut any big pieces of broccoli in half lengthwise so they aren't too large (you want longish, kind of elegant pieces, but nothing you couldn't comfortably eat) and place them in a large bowl with the lime juice, fish sauce, and brown sugar, and season with salt and pepper. Massage the broccoli so it gets all tender and well seasoned. Add the peanuts, basil, cilantro, fried shallots, and 2 tablespoons of the reserved shallot oil.

**3** Toss everything together and season with more lime juice, fish sauce, salt, and pepper as needed. The salad should be pretty assertively flavored, but also refreshing, as if you could eat the whole bowl at once.

# Roasted Broccolini and Lemon with Crispy Parmesan

*Serves 4*

1 lemon, halved crosswise, seeds removed
4 garlic cloves, smashed
2 bunches broccolini, ends trimmed, or 1½ pounds broccoli, thinly sliced lengthwise, stem and all
2 tablespoons olive oil
Kosher salt and freshly ground black pepper
½ cup finely grated Parmesan cheese

I'm not the first person to dump cheese onto something, roast it, and call it genius, but I do think it's worth mentioning how wonderful this recipe is. Maybe it's the caramelized, jammy slices of lemon; maybe it's the almost burnt, crispy, frilly bits of tender broccolini. Whatever it is, I feel the need to serve a version of this at nearly every dinner party I throw, and I think you should, too. While there is something special about the broccolini here (nothing compares to the tender stalks and those wispy, crispy ends), this technique also works with root vegetables like carrots, potatoes, and parsnips, as well as other brassicas like cauliflower and Brussels sprouts.

**1** Preheat the oven to 425°F.

**2** Thinly slice half the lemon into rounds and set the other half aside. Toss the lemon slices, garlic, and broccolini with the olive oil on a rimmed baking sheet. Season with salt and pepper, and make sure everything is evenly coated, especially the broccolini tips so they get all fried and crispy.

**3** Sprinkle with the Parmesan and roast until the broccolini is bright green and starting to char and the cheese is golden brown, 10 to 15 minutes.

**4** Remove from the oven, squeeze the other half of the lemon over the top, and serve.

# Fried Eggplant with Harissa and Dill

*Serves 4*

4 garlic cloves, finely grated
2 tablespoons harissa
1 tablespoon tomato paste
½ teaspoon ground cumin
3 tablespoons white distilled vinegar
Kosher salt and freshly ground black pepper
1 cup olive oil
1 large globe eggplant, sliced into ½-inch-thick rounds
¼ cup fresh dill, tender stems and leaves, coarsely chopped

**DO AHEAD:** Eggplant can be fried and marinated 5 days ahead and refrigerated.

There is a falafel spot near my apartment in Brooklyn that pretty much sustains me when I just can't cook another thing, but I rarely go there for the falafel. I'm really there for the eggplant, which they call Eggplant à la Yaffa, a nod to the owner's grandmother. It's fried, spiced, garlicky, tangy, and so delicious that I dream of it nearly every day. I eat it on toast, with eggs, over hummus, chopped up in salads, as a side dish for literally anything, and, probably most frequently, by itself, right out of the container.

This habit, as you can imagine, got slightly expensive, so I tried making my own. Despite being a frequent and loyal customer, the guys at the restaurant would never tell me what goes into it, and since I've never met Yaffa, I'm not sure how close I am to the original, but I'd like to think they'd all approve.

**1** Combine the garlic, harissa, tomato paste, cumin, vinegar, and 2 tablespoons water in a small bowl; season with salt and pepper and set aside.

**2** Heat ½ cup olive oil in a large skillet over medium-high heat. Working in batches (all the slices will not fit at once), fry the eggplant until golden brown on both sides, 5 to 8 minutes total. Transfer the eggplant to a plate lined with paper towels to absorb any excess oil; season it with salt. Repeat with the remaining eggplant, adding more olive oil to the skillet as needed (and you'll need it).

**3** After the last round of eggplant is finished frying and most of the oil has been absorbed (yes, it went inside the eggplant—try not to think about it!), add the harissa mixture to the skillet (it'll bubble and sizzle a bit, so stand back) and remove the skillet from the heat. Add the rest of the previously fried eggplant to the skillet and toss everything to coat in the harissa mixture. Scatter the dill over the top and serve.

## Eggplant: A Delicious, Complicated Ingredient

This vegetable has a complicated history with a lot of he said/she said about whether to salt it before cooking. Most of what made eggplants super bitter has been, for better or for worse, bred out of the common varieties. I don't salt my eggplant, and I don't think you need to either.

The best eggplant preparations involve grilling, roasting, or frying in plenty of fat. These little babies are basically like a giant sponge, and you gotta treat them right by dousing them in a luxurious amount of olive oil. Regardless of how you make eggplant, it may seem like you're adding an excessive amount of oil, and sure, maybe it is, but it's excessive and necessary, and you'll be rewarded with superlative eggplant, ready to dress with garlicky walnuts (page 68) or douse in vinegary harissa.

# Roasted Sweet Potatoes
# with Hot Honey Browned Butter

*Serves 4*

4 small to medium sweet potatoes,
    scrubbed
6 tablespoons (¾ stick) unsalted butter
2 tablespoons honey
1 tablespoon white wine vinegar or
    apple cider vinegar
1 teaspoon crushed red pepper flakes
Kosher salt and freshly ground black
    pepper
Flaky sea salt

**DO AHEAD:** The hot honey browned butter can be made 5 days ahead and refrigerated. Rewarm in a small pot before using.

Doubling down on sweet potatoes' sweetness by adding honey is like adding fuel to the fire, but the nuttiness from the browned butter, heat from the crushed red pepper flakes, and bright acidity from the vinegar all work together to bring it back from the brink. Speaking of, this hot honey browned butter is so good that I would likely make myself sick if left alone with a pot of it. It's also good on roasted winter squash, over plain oatmeal, and, if we are being honest, probably over ice cream, but that's a different chapter.

1 Preheat the oven to 425°F.

2 Poke each sweet potato all over with a fork and place them all directly on the oven rack. Roast until they are impossibly tender, with bits of sweet potato sugar caramelizing in the spots they've been poked, 60 to 80 minutes.

3 Meanwhile, melt the butter in a small pot over medium heat, swirling the pot just until the butter starts to bubble and brown, about 5 minutes. Add the honey, vinegar, and red pepper flakes, and season with kosher salt and black pepper. Remove from the heat and set aside.

4 Once the sweet potatoes are out of the oven, slit them down the middle. Warm up the browned butter mixture and pour over the sweet potatoes (alternatively, scoop the flesh out of the skins and transfer it to a bowl or serving dish, then drizzle with the browned butter sauce). Sprinkle with tons of flaky sea salt.

# A Perfect Tomato Recipe

While an obvious choice of vegetable, there's no recipe for tomato salad in this book. I've got, like, three broccoli salads, but hardly anything with fresh tomatoes. But they're the darling of the produce world! Everyone's favorite vegetable/fruit! This is not an oversight. If you've ever had a really awesome, ripe tomato, I want to know, what could possibly be better than cutting it in half, sprinkling it with salt, and eating it like an apple?

To be honest—and I know this will not be a popular opinion—I don't even think that they belong on sandwiches or in salads. So, with this in mind, you can see my frustration when, every summer, someone inevitably asks me to bring a tomato salad to their barbecue. I oblige, of course, with this tomato recipe that I think is perfect:

Slice a bunch of tomatoes that are ripe, planning on about one tomato per person. Remember to eat one slice from each tomato. (What if one is bad? You'd want to know!)

Put the sliced tomatoes on the biggest plate you have and sprinkle them with good crunchy salt. Drizzle with enough olive oil to make it look like they are kind of swimming in it. If there are good fresh herbs around (chives, basil, parsley, and cilantro are my favorites), throw some on there. There you have it: a perfect tomato recipe.

# Caramelized Winter Squash
# with Toasted Coconut Gremolata

*Serves 4*

**SQUASH**

**2 medium winter squash, such as delicata or acorn (1½ to 2 pounds)**

**3 tablespoons coconut oil, melted, or olive oil**

**1 tablespoon honey**

**Kosher salt and freshly ground black pepper**

**TOASTED COCONUT GREMOLATA**

**¾ cup unsweetened coconut chips**

**¼ cup finely chopped fresh chives**

**½ cup fresh cilantro, tender leaves and stems, finely chopped**

**1 tablespoon finely grated lemon zest**

**2 teaspoons Aleppo pepper or 1 teaspoon crushed red pepper flakes**

**Kosher salt**

**DO AHEAD:** Everything but the coconut can be made 1 day ahead; when ready to serve, toast the coconut and add it to the chive mixture (toasted coconut will start to soften once mixed with the herbs and refrigerated).

I ate a lot of squash with brown sugar and butter while growing up. This recipe is my more practical "I can't have ice cream for every meal" compromise, using honey instead of brown sugar and coconut oil instead of butter. I would probably eat this as dinner on its own, but I happen to know it's also great as a side with things like roasted chicken or pork chops.

While tender, caramelized, salty-sweet squash is magnificent all on its own, it should be mentioned that the real reason for making this dish is for the toasted coconut gremolata: chips of nutty, unsweetened coconut tossed with herbs, lots of lemon zest, and a bit of Aleppo pepper. It's wildly addictive, and there is no reason it couldn't appear over roasted carrots, sprinkled onto a curry or stew, or even over salads as a stand-in for croutons.

**1 ROAST THE SQUASH:** Preheat the oven to 425°F.

**2** Leaving the skin on, slice the squash into ½-inch-thick rings. (I roast my squash with the seeds still inside, because they get all crispy and I love the texture they bring to the table, but you can remove them if you like. Best way to do that is cut the squash in half crosswise and scoop out the seeds with a spoon, then slice into rings.)

**3** Toss the squash with the coconut oil and honey on a rimmed baking sheet and season with salt and pepper. Roast, flipping the squash once, until it is completely tender, browned, and caramelized, 25 to 30 minutes.

**4 MAKE THE GREMOLATA:** While the squash is roasting, heat a small skillet over medium heat and add the coconut. Shake the skillet occasionally until the coconut is starting to brown at the edges and smells all toasty and amazing, 3 to 4 minutes. Place it in a medium bowl to cool completely.

**5** Once the coconut has cooled, add the chives, cilantro, lemon zest, and Aleppo pepper, and season with salt. Using your fingers, mix this together until the oils in the lemon zest have released and everything is evenly distributed (especially the lemon zest, which can stubbornly clump up).

**6** Sprinkle the coconut gremolata over the roasted squash and serve.

# Why Are You Always Asking Me to Toast My Nuts?

When any recipe calls for toasted nuts, I imagine you rolling your eyes. "Honestly, do I have to?" And I hear you. But yes, you have to. Toasting brings out an entirely new (that is, better) flavor in whatever nut you're working with. Because it can be annoying to toast a small amount of nuts, I generally do a lot at a time and freeze them. Sure, they lose a little magic from a trip to the icebox, but their internal flavor will still be better than if you use them raw.

The best way to toast any nut is in the oven. Toasting them in a skillet on the stovetop is okay for small nuts and seeds like pine nuts, sesame seeds, or pumpkin seeds, but you really can't toast larger whole nuts like walnuts, almonds, or even hazelnuts the whole way through just by shaking them around a hot skillet (if they are chopped, it's okay to use this method).

**TO TOAST NUTS**, preheat the oven to 350°F. Place the nuts on a rimmed baking sheet (you could use a rimless one, but they slide off easily, so be prepared to pick up nuts off the floor for at least a few weeks). Toast, shaking the baking sheet once or twice, until the nuts are evenly and deeply toasted, anywhere from 8 to 12 minutes (closer to 8 for things like pecans and hazelnuts, closer to 12 for larger walnuts, almonds, and cashews). When you break open the nuts, they should be toasted to the core, smell like buttered toast, and be nuttier tasting than when they went in.

I love the taste and look of leaving the skins on nuts, especially hazelnuts. While the skin on the almonds will stay put, the hazelnut skins will want to kind of slip off as they toast, and this is okay. To get rid of the skins that want to shed, place warm hazelnuts in a dishtowel and just move them around like you're playing with a bag of marbles. Don't worry about getting all the skin off (I like the kind of toasty, bitter flavor it lends); just focus on the papery bits that want to fall off anyway.

# Cumin-Roasted Cauliflower and Dates with Tahini and Pine Nuts

*Serves 4*

1 head of cauliflower (including any green leaves or stems), sliced lengthwise into ½-inch-thick steaks

1 teaspoon cumin seed

5 tablespoons olive oil

Kosher salt and freshly ground black pepper

6 dates, such as Medjool, pitted and halved

3 tablespoons tahini

½ cup pine nuts

2 scallions, thinly sliced

1 cup mint leaves, coarsely chopped

½ cup tender cilantro leaves and stems, coarsely chopped

2 tablespoons sherry vinegar or white wine vinegar

The quickest and easiest way to make cauliflower delicious is to roast it fast and furiously. It's a sort of sneak-attack approach: placing it in the hottest oven possible to get the edges and bits to start caramelizing and browning before the florets turn to a total mush, which they are wont to do. In another effort to combat any potential mushiness, I always throw in the sturdy stalks of the cauliflower, as well as any of those cute little green leaves, which to me taste like a broccoli-cauliflower hybrid of sorts. Along for the ride in the oven are dates, which, when given the same treatment, get a little chewier, a little stickier, and a lot crispier.

**1** Preheat the oven to 500°F.

**2** Using your hands, break the cauliflower into smaller florets, keeping the stalks long (this way you get some well-roasted tender parts as well as smaller, crispier parts). Toss the cauliflower and cumin with 3 tablespoons of the olive oil on a rimmed baking sheet and season with salt and pepper. Roast, tossing occasionally, until just starting to brown, 10 to 15 minutes. Add the dates, toss to coat, and continue roasting until the cauliflower is deeply browned and caramelized all over and the dates are plump and starting to caramelize around the edges, 10 to 15 minutes more.

**3** Meanwhile, whisk the tahini and 2 tablespoons water together in a small bowl; season with salt and pepper.

**4** Toast the pine nuts in a small skillet over medium heat, shaking the skillet occasionally, until the pine nuts are golden brown and smell like popcorn, about 5 minutes. Remove from the heat and let cool enough to coarsely chop.

**5** In a small bowl, combine the pine nuts, scallions, mint, cilantro, vinegar, and the remaining 2 tablespoons olive oil; season with salt and pepper.

**6** Spoon the tahini onto the bottom of a large serving platter. Remove the cauliflower and dates from the oven and place them on top of the tahini. Spoon the mint mixture over and serve with any extra alongside.

# Turmeric-Roasted Carrots with Seeds and Labne

*Serves 4*

1 pound small carrots, scrubbed, tops trimmed to about ½ inch

3 tablespoons olive oil

1 tablespoon finely grated fresh turmeric or ½ teaspoon ground

2 teaspoons cumin seed

2 teaspoons fennel seed

Kosher salt and freshly ground black pepper

¾ cup labne or full-fat Greek yogurt

1 garlic clove, finely grated

2 tablespoons fresh lemon juice

3 cups spicy greens, such as mustard greens, watercress, or wild arugula

**DO AHEAD:** These carrots are actually great at room temperature and can be roasted about 4 hours ahead.

This could easily serve as a side to roast chicken or as a salad with something heavier, like a stew, but often I serve this as a sort of salad-side hybrid for when I don't want to make both. The unique earthiness of fresh turmeric really makes this dish, especially when the bits get a little too dark and crispy as the carrots roast, but ground turmeric is a totally acceptable substitute.

Roasting carrots hot and fast will give you something that is caramelized and deeply flavorful on the outside without sacrificing their snappy texture, and roasting them with seeds means you don't have to toast the seeds separately to coax out their flavor. It's really quite a good deal for all involved, and sometimes I make them sans leafy greens when I just want to take advantage of this very good deal.

**1** Preheat the oven to 450°F.

**2** If using carrots on the larger side, halve them lengthwise. Toss the carrots with the olive oil, turmeric, cumin, and fennel on a rimmed baking sheet and season with salt and pepper. Roast, shaking the pan occasionally, until the carrots are evenly browned and tender (but not totally soft), 20 to 25 minutes; if your carrots are on the larger side, this might take a bit longer. Remove from the oven and set aside.

**3** Combine the labne, garlic, and 1 tablespoon of the lemon juice in a small bowl, and season with salt and pepper.

**4** Put the greens in a large bowl along with the remaining lemon juice and season with salt and pepper. Spoon some of the garlicky labne onto the bottom of a large serving platter or bowl and scatter the carrots and greens on top, making sure to scrape any of the oily, seedy business from the baking sheet in there, too.

# Steamed Artichokes
# with Salted Garlic Butter

*Serves 2 to 4*

**2 large artichokes**
**½ cup (1 stick) unsalted butter**
**1 head of garlic, halved crosswise**
**Kosher salt**
**Lemon wedges, for serving**

My earliest memory of being in the kitchen is standing up on a chair and using (probably very dull) scissors to trim the cactus-like thorns from the tip of the artichoke leaves so that my mom could steam them. Surely there were safer tasks for an eight-year-old, but before you call child services, I'm sure it was something I did with plenty of supervision, likely more resembling arts and crafts than *Iron Chef*.

And while a recipe for steamed artichokes might seem a basic one to include here, like a classic baked potato, it's not here to give you a recipe, per se; it's here to remind you that you should be eating steamed artichokes.

Since these steam for quite a while, don't forget to check the water level—burnt artichoke water is a smell from my childhood, so I kind of like it in a weird way, but I'm pretty sure you will not feel the same.

**1**  Trim the stem of each artichoke so it's about ¾ inch long. Make sure it's even, so it stands up straight in the pot.

**2**  Using a sharp serrated knife, slice off the top 2 inches of each artichoke (you should be able to see a bit of the purple choke on the inside). Next, using sharp kitchen shears, trim the spiny ends off each outer leaf.

**3**  Fill a pot wide enough to fit both artichokes with 2 inches of water (fill it any higher and you'd be boiling, not steaming, the artichokes, which would waterlog them) and place the artichokes in the pot; no need for a steamer basket. Bring to a boil and reduce the heat to medium-low to keep the water at a weak simmer.

**4**  Steam the artichokes until you can easily release an outer leaf (it should pull right off, kinda like the leaves on a ripe pineapple), 50 to 60 minutes.

**5**  Meanwhile, melt the butter in a small pot. Remove it from the heat and add the garlic and lots of salt. Let this hang out while the artichokes cook to infuse the butter as much as possible.

**6**  Serve with the melted butter and lemon wedges and eat the artichokes with one person you love, or share them with three people you like.

# Grilled Artichokes with Preserved Lemon Yogurt

*Serves 2 to 4*

2 to 4 steamed artichokes, as prepared
    opposite (sans garlic butter)
2 tablespoons olive oil, plus more for
    drizzling
Kosher salt and freshly ground black
    pepper
Preserved Lemon Labne (page 27)
¼ cup fresh mint, dill or parsley,
    coarsely chopped

If steamed artichokes are perfection, grilled artichokes are perfection 2.0. Not necessarily better, just different and most definitely worth doing if you have the time and the warm weather. The grill imparts a smokiness that makes artichokes seem a little more meaty, while also lightly charring the outside leaves, which get crispy enough to nibble on. And, yes, although you could certainly grill artichokes without steaming them first, they will cook faster and more evenly if you do.

**1** Using a sharp knife, halve the steamed artichokes lengthwise.

**2** Heat a grill to medium-high. Brush both sides of the artichokes with the olive oil and season with salt and pepper. Place them, cut-side down, onto the grill and let them get nice and charred, about 4 minutes. Using tongs or a large spatula, flip them over and let them get equally nice and charred on the other side, another 4 minutes.

**3** Remove the artichokes from the grill and drizzle them with more olive oil. Sprinkle the labne with mint and serve alongside the artichokes.

**Artichokes** Just like tearing the shells off peel 'n' eat shrimp or ripping apart a Maine lobster, preparing, cooking, and eating artichokes (the lobsters of California, really) is also strongly rooted in ritual. There's the meticulous trimming of the thorns, then the steaming for all eternity until army green and tender.

Once they're freed from the pot, you start to tackle the thing, quickly realizing those smaller leaves toward the bottom aren't worth a damn. You move on, dipping each larger, sturdier leaf in some very garlicky, salty, warm butter, applying just the right amount of pressure with your bottom teeth to properly scrape off the "meat" from the leaves. You might think you're finished once you run out of hearty leaves—until someone shows you how to pull off the too-thin, still-pointy ones in the center (also not really worth a damn) and scrape away the fuzzy, furry choke in the center (don't eat this) to reveal your true reward: the tender, meaty heart. Depending on the size of the artichoke and how full you are at this point, the heart might be enough to share or something you save just for yourself. Personally, I've never been too full, but like all other rituals, you must decide for yourself and make this one your own.

# Butter-Tossed Radishes
# with Fresh Za'atar

*Serves 4*

2 tablespoons olive oil

2 garlic cloves, smashed

1 bunch radishes, with their tops,
    halved lengthwise

Kosher salt and freshly ground
    black pepper

1 tablespoon white distilled vinegar

3 tablespoons unsalted butter

2 tablespoons Fresh Za'atar (page 20),
    plus more as needed

Flaky sea salt

**NOTE:** I don't have anything else important to say about this dish, only that it is probably my favorite one in the whole book.

These radishes have everything I want in life—butter, za'atar, and lots of salt—and are the ultimate motivation for hunting down a nice bunch with perky green tops. Cook these guys just long enough to wilt the greens and to barely soften the outside of the radish, keeping all that spicy sass inside. This is the ideal thing to serve either as a predinner snack or with your actual dinner (especially something punchy and spiced, like the turmeric-roasted lamb on page 235 or the paprika-rubbed chicken on page 227).

**1** Heat the oil in a medium skillet over medium-high heat. When the oil is hot and shimmery, add the garlic and radishes, and season with kosher salt and pepper.

**2** Once the greens have wilted and the radishes are tender but not soft (they should still have some bite), about 2 minutes, add the vinegar and butter, swirling to melt the butter and coat the radishes. Remove from the heat and sprinkle with the za'atar.

**3** Transfer to a large serving platter, finishing with flaky sea salt and more fresh za'atar.

# Cucumbers and Kohlrabi
# in Crunchy Chili Oil

*Serves 4*

**2 hothouse or English cucumbers**
**1 medium kohlrabi, peeled**
**2 tablespoons rice vinegar or fresh
    lime juice**
**Flaky sea salt**
**3 to 4 tablespoons Crunchy Chili Oil
    (page 20)**

**NOTE:** This dish also works with thinly
sliced fennel, celery, or raw beets
(pictured).

Cold, crispy vegetables were made to be doused in hot, fiery, fatty chili oil, and no vegetables are colder or crispier than cucumbers and kohlrabi. I like to double this recipe, which is more addictive than it ought to be, even if it exceeds the amount I think anyone (including myself) could possibly eat in one sitting. These go with just about any preparation of most proteins, but they're especially good with something that would get along with a little extra fiery chili oil served alongside, like the seared short ribs on page 222, or the already spicy lamb chops with cumin salt on page 225.

**1** Using a vegetable peeler or a mandoline, thinly slice the cucumbers lengthwise into very thin ribbons and place them in a large bowl. Using a vegetable peeler, peel the (yes–already peeled) kohlrabi, creating long, thin strips; alternatively, you can slice it into very thin rounds using a mandoline or sharp knife.

**2** Place the kohlrabi in the bowl with the cucumbers, toss with the vinegar, and season with sea salt.

**3** Drizzle with the chili oil and toss again, making sure to evenly distribute all those crispy bits everywhere.

---

**Kohlrabi**

Kohlrabi, a bulbous member of the cabbage family, is a tragically underrated vegetable. Closely resembling the aliens in the vending machine from *Toy Story*, it is a little strange looking, and if you have never seen one before, you might not know what it tastes like or what to do with it. I think kohlrabi tastes like a broccoli stalk (which, to me, is the best part), but kohlrabi is even more delicately flavored. It is good cooked, softening and taking on a more turnipy vibe. Or use it raw, thinly sliced or shaved to show off its delightfully crunchy texture, which is somewhere between that of a radish and a carrot.

# Baked Summer Squash with Cream and Parmesan Bread Crumbs

*Serves 4*

1 cup coarse Fresh Bread Crumbs (page 24) or panko

½ cup finely grated Parmesan cheese

2 garlic cloves, finely grated or chopped

2 teaspoons fresh oregano, marjoram, or thyme leaves, chopped

4 tablespoons olive oil

Kosher salt and freshly ground black pepper

¾ pound small summer squash (yellow squash or zucchini), halved lengthwise (or quartered, if all you can find are large squash)

1 cup heavy cream

Summer squash is a polarizing vegetable, as in it's wildly abundant and, generally speaking, totally flavorless—unless you cook it in heavy cream, letting it caramelize and get all sticky, then top it with garlicky, cheesy bread crumbs. Then it tastes pretty damn good.

During the summer months, I like to avoid turning the oven on or eating things that are simultaneously hot and contain heavy cream, but this dish is the exception to both house rules, because, yes, it's that delicious. It's even substantial enough to hold its own, anchoring a summery Meatless Monday alongside a bowl of lightly dressed peppery greens and a plate of sliced and salted tomatoes.

**1** Preheat the oven to 400°F.

**2** Combine the bread crumbs, Parmesan, garlic, oregano, and 3 tablespoons of the olive oil in a small bowl; season with salt and pepper and set aside.

**3** Place the halved squash in a large ovenproof skillet or 2-quart baking dish. Pour the cream and the remaining 1 tablespoon olive oil over, and season with salt and lots of pepper. Sprinkle the bread crumb mixture on top of the squash and place the baking dish on the middle rack in the oven.

**4** Bake until the bread crumbs are golden brown, the cream is reduced and starting to caramelize around the edges, and the squash is tender and cooked through, 25 to 30 minutes. Remove from the oven and let cool slightly before eating to avoid roof-of-the-mouth burns.

# Raw and Roasted Carrots and Fennel with Feta and Pistachios

Serves 4

1 large fennel bulb, halved lengthwise

1 bunch smallish carrots (preferably with their tops)

1 bunch scallions, halved crosswise

5 tablespoons olive oil

Kosher salt and freshly ground black pepper

2 tablespoons fresh lemon juice, plus more as needed

1 cup cilantro, tender stems and leaves

3 ounces feta cheese, sliced into ⅛-inch-thick slabs (if it crumbles a bit, that's fine)

¼ cup pistachios, toasted and chopped (see page 50 for more on toasting nuts)

**NOTE:** If you're not familiar with carrot tops, they taste like a more assertive parsley. Next time you see carrot tops, save them and use like you would in pesto, salsa verde, or just general herbage—like in this salad.

**DO AHEAD:** This dish, sans feta and pistachios, can be made 5 hours ahead, no need to reheat. Add the feta and pistachios when ready to serve.

This salad is a good exercise in the magic that can occur when you treat one ingredient very differently, in this case, as raw and roasted. It's doing a lot with a little; caramelized, tender bits of carrots and fennel mingle with slices of their raw, crunchy former selves, and, well, there's really nothing better. This salad is also terrific at room temperature and is easily doubled, making it great for feeding a crowd, so feel free to show off this little number at your next party or potluck.

1  Preheat the oven to 425°F.

2  Slice half the fennel into ½-inch-thick wedges and place them on a rimmed baking sheet.

3  If your carrots have tops, remove and set them aside. Scrub the carrots (no need to peel) and place half of them on the baking sheet with the fennel. Add half the scallions and toss with 3 tablespoons of the olive oil. Season with salt and pepper, and roast, tossing occasionally, until the carrots and fennel are browned and the scallions begin to char, 20 to 25 minutes. Remove them from the oven and let cool to room temperature.

4  Meanwhile, thinly slice the remaining carrots and fennel lengthwise and place them in a large bowl. Thinly slice the remaining scallions on a strong bias and add to the bowl with the vegetables.

5  Once the roasted vegetables have cooled, add them to the bowl of raw vegetables. Toss with the lemon juice, cilantro, and some chopped carrot tops, if you've got 'em (if not, use more cilantro, parsley, dill, or mint—whatever you have). Season with salt, pepper, and more lemon juice, if you like.

6  Drizzle with the remaining 2 tablespoons olive oil and top with the feta and pistachios.

# Grilled Corn Salad
# with Fresh Cheese and Corn Nuts

*Serves 4*

6 ears of yellow corn, husks on

2 tablespoons fresh lime juice, plus
    more as needed

½ small red onion, thinly sliced

½ teaspoon crushed red pepper flakes,
    plus more as needed

Kosher salt and freshly ground black
    pepper

1 cup cilantro, tender leaves and stems

4 ounces queso fresco, haloumi, or
    other firm fresh cheese, crumbled
    or finely chopped

½ cup corn nuts, coarsely chopped

**NOTE:** You can also do this in the oven, although it will take a bit longer. Place the unhusked corn directly on a rack inside a preheated 450°F oven and leave it alone, except maybe to turn it a few times over the next 30 to 40 minutes. Check the corn at 30 minutes by peeling back a bit of the husk; it should be this crazy golden-yellow color with spots of char. If it isn't, give it another 10 minutes or so.

When I was in Mexico, I tasted the craziest corn I had ever had. It was huge and starchy, and even when it was doused in crema, lime, and chile, you could tell that the kernels tasted like an unborn corn nut. Corn nuts! And it was there that I made the connection to corn nuts and the fact that they came from corn. I mean, duh, of course they do, but . . . wow. If you haven't lost respect for me after reading that, thank you!

Anyway, the corn I ate growing up (white corn, boiled and served smeared with margarine, stuck with those surprisingly useful little corn holders) never got me as excited as the cool ranch corn nuts I ate from the school vending machine, so I decided to make a salad that did just that (with corn nuts, of course).

**1** Heat a grill to high (see Note). Throw the corn right on that grill and leave it alone, except maybe to turn it a few times over the next 25 to 35 minutes. Check the corn at 25 minutes by peeling back a bit of the husk; it should be this crazy golden-yellow color with spots of char from the grill. If it needs more time, I don't think your grill is hot enough, but at any rate, throw it back on the grill and check again in 10 or so minutes.

**2** Meanwhile, combine the lime juice, onion, and red pepper flakes in a large bowl. Season with salt and pepper; set aside.

**3** Once the corn comes off the grill, let it get cool enough to handle so you can shuck it and strip the kernels off the cob. The easiest way to do this is to hold the corn by the stem and place it in a large bowl. Starting at the top, using a sharp knife (a serrated knife works well, too) and getting as close to the cob as possible, shave the kernels off; they should land in the bowl, rather than scatter all over your counter and kitchen floor.

**4** Add the onion mixture to the bowl with the corn kernels and season with salt and pepper, tossing to coat. Add the cilantro, queso fresco, and corn nuts, and season with salt, red pepper flakes, and more lime juice, as needed, to make sure it's good and limey.

# Grilled Eggplant Dressed with Garlicky Walnuts and Lots of Basil

*Serves 4*

**1 pound Fairy Tale eggplant, halved lengthwise, or the smallest globe eggplant you can find, sliced into 1-inch-thick rounds**
**6 tablespoons olive oil**
**Kosher salt and freshly ground black pepper**
**½ cup walnuts, toasted and crushed**
**1 garlic clove, finely grated**
**Pinch of crushed red pepper flakes**
**½ cup fresh basil leaves, chopped, plus 1 cup whole leaves**
**Ricotta, for serving (optional)**

**NOTE:** You can also do this in an oven. No, they won't be grilled (duh), but the dish will be delicious. Roast them in a preheated 450°F oven until deeply browned and totally tender, 15 to 20 minutes. Proceed!

**DO AHEAD:** The garlicky walnut mixture can be made 5 days ahead and refrigerated. Bring to room temperature before using.

I thought I liked eggplant, then I met Fairy Tale eggplant. They are smaller, which means that not only are they adorable but also that they have less water and fewer seeds (less mush, less bitter!). And the name! I mean, come on. If you cannot find them, use the smallest globe eggplant you can find (no need to salt either of them; for more on that, see page 45).

While, yes, this recipe is called grilled eggplant, you can certainly roast them and dress them all the same (see Note). At the risk of offering too many variations, I should also mention that this recipe works astonishingly well with cauliflower (grilled or roasted).

**1** Heat a grill to medium-high.

**2** Toss the eggplant with 3 tablespoons of the olive oil and season with salt and pepper. Grill the eggplant, turning it occasionally, until it's lightly charred and totally tender, about 5 minutes per side.

**3** Meanwhile, combine the walnuts, garlic, red pepper flakes, chopped basil, and the remaining 3 tablespoons olive oil; season with salt and pepper. Spoon some ricotta, if using, onto the bottom of a serving plate and top with the grilled eggplant, the walnut mixture, and the whole basil leaves.

# Quick Kimchi

*Makes 2 cups*

1 garlic clove, finely grated

1 (1-inch) piece of ginger, peeled and
　　finely grated

2 tablespoons gochugaru (aka Korean
　　chili powder) or 1 tablespoon
　　crushed red pepper flakes

½ teaspoon Asian fish sauce

1 tablespoon unseasoned rice vinegar

1 teaspoon kosher salt

1 small head of napa cabbage,
　　halved lengthwise and cut into
　　2-inch-wide strips

1 Asian pear or crisp apple, unpeeled,
　　cored and thinly sliced

**DO AHEAD:** This can be made 1 month
ahead, packed in a glass jar, and
refrigerated.

Think of this as kimchi for beginners. It's more a spicy, refreshing slaw than the fermented bucket of funk you'll find in real-deal kimchi (for the record, I think both are great). That said, if you let it hang in your fridge for a few weeks, it'll grow funkier and tangier, which is definitely a good thing. This is the kind of clean, crunchy side dish that is great next to any sort of large piece of meat, but it goes without saying, its true destiny is meant to be shared with the seared short ribs on page 222.

**1** Combine the garlic, ginger, gochugaru, fish sauce, vinegar, and salt in a large bowl.

**2** Add the cabbage and massage it as if your life depends on it. It will shrink to about half the size, so before you start, when you think, "What am I going to do with all this kimchi?," relax; it's not actually that much. Once the cabbage is massaged and evenly coated, add the Asian pear and toss to coat. Boom! Your quick kimchi is ready.

**3** This can be eaten right away, but is also great kept in the fridge for up to about a month. The flavor will deepen, and the texture will soften, all for the better.

# Perfect Asparagus
# with Garlic and Salted Olive Oil

*Serves 4*

Kosher salt

1 pound asparagus (about 1 bunch), ends trimmed, peeled halfway up the stalk

¼ cup olive oil (use the nice stuff)

2 teaspoons Aleppo pepper

1 garlic clove, finely grated

1 lemon, halved (optional)

Crunchy sea salt, like Maldon or Jacobsen

**NOTE:** If you overblanch the asparagus, it will not only change the flavor from fresh and springy to sad and brown, but the texture will be soft and flaccid, a word that is never used to describe anything favorably, and so this asparagus will not be good and you should start over.

Asparagus and I have a complicated relationship. I don't exactly love it. I never crave it, and given the option, I almost always choose something else, even during spring, its peak season. But there is something about it that makes me pay extra-close attention when cooking it. Like, you couldn't pay me to peel a carrot. But asparagus, while fussy and completely annoying to peel (those thin, wispy strings always get caught in the peeler), gets the royal treatment every time. It's also one of the few vegetables I actually prefer blanched, which is a technique I almost always find to be unnecessary and "too much work." So why all the extra effort for a vegetable I feel just "okay" about?

Well, I gotta say, even if I'm standing pantless in my small Brooklyn kitchen, holding a perfectly blanched, electric green, delightfully snappy asparagus spear and dragging it through a powerfully flavored olive oil, I've never felt more elegant.

When shopping for asparagus, you are either a thin-spear or a fat-spear kind of person. There is no right or wrong, but what you'll likely find is something in the middle, which is actually my favorite.

**1** In a large pot of salted (salty like the sea) boiling water, blanch the asparagus until it turns bright neon green and is just barely cooked, about 45 seconds. Take a sample spear and cut off a small bite from the end; it should be pretty firm through the center but just softened around the edges (see Note). Using tongs, remove the asparagus and transfer it to a plate lined with paper towels to absorb the excess moisture.

**2** Meanwhile, heat the olive oil, Aleppo pepper, and garlic in a small saucepan over low heat, stirring until the pepper bleeds orange and the garlic is fragrant, about 2 minutes. It should never sizzle, just kind of warm through.

**3** Arrange the asparagus on a serving platter and drizzle with the warm oil mixture. Squeeze with lemon if you feel like it. Sprinkle with salt and call it a day. Best eaten with your hands.

# I Love Boiled Potatoes

One of the strangest and most useful things I keep on hand in the refrigerator is a bowl of small, waxy boiled potatoes. People ask me questions about them all the time, mainly, "What are those?" and "Are those potatoes?," followed by "Why do you have a bowl of boiled potatoes in your fridge?"

Well, I love potatoes, and I'd eat them a lot more frequently if they cooked more quickly. Boiling them in advance solves this problem. Never mind that they are the first step in creating excellent crispy smashed potatoes (page 73); they can also be halved and added to grains (like the niçoise-y version on page 134) and salads (like the breakfast salad on page 115), used to make really fast hash browns, or snacked on, simply dipped in crunchy salt, or dressed in salsa verde (page 21) with a soft-boiled egg. They can also be easily tossed in olive oil and roasted at 500°F for 10 minutes for a quick crisp-up. Or just halve them and toss in the drippings from any roasted meat.

I like waxy potatoes that are between the size of a golf ball and a quarter. Look for varieties such as "new potatoes," fingerlings, baby Yukon Golds, and German butterballs. These potatoes all have a nice thin skin and a wonderfully creamy, fluffy interior. When purchasing, choose potatoes that are all roughly the same size so they cook in about the same time. Boil 'em in heavily salted water until they're totally tender, 15 to 25 minutes, depending on the size of the potatoes. Eat them straightaway (they are especially magical piping hot, smeared with butter, and seasoned with salt and pepper) or, you know, pop them into the fridge to quietly await their destiny.

# Crispy Smashed Potatoes
# with Fried Onions and Parsley

*Serves 4*

Kosher salt

1¼ pounds new potatoes (1 to 2 inches, about the size of a golf ball) or small fingerlings

⅓ cup chicken fat, olive oil, or peanut oil

Freshly ground black pepper

2 tablespoons (¼ stick) unsalted butter

½ small yellow onion, thinly sliced into rings

1 teaspoon Aleppo pepper or ½ teaspoon crushed red pepper flakes

Flaky sea salt

¼ cup chopped fresh flat-leaf parsley

**NOTE:** Choose small, waxy new potatoes. Most new potatoes are inherently small *and* waxy, so you shouldn't have to worry too much about this, but it's worth mentioning. Some widely available varieties include fingerlings, Yukon Golds, peanut potatoes, micro creamer potatoes, and marble potatoes. If you can only find large Idaho potatoes, this recipe will not work; you should make a baked potato instead.

Some of you may be thinking, "Does the world need another crispy smashed potato recipe?" And at least some of you are saying, "*Yes*, we do!" So here you go. Plus, you're going to want something to fry up in that paprika-y, garlicky fat from the roast chicken on page 227 (yes, regular olive oil works, too). But honestly—no, seriously—these are the best. And the crispiest. Make them; you'll be so happy.

For those of you who have struggled with these in the past, I can offer you a few tips to make your life easier:

- Don't oversteam or they will fall apart, never giving them a chance to hit that oil.
- Don't understeam or you'll never be able to crush them.
- Let them cool a bit before you smash them so they also dry out a bit, making them less likely to fall apart.
- The oil must be hot. Think of this as a shallow-fry: if the oil is not hot enough, it will soak into the potato rather than crisp it up.

**1** Bring 2 inches of salted water to a boil in a large pot fitted with a steamer basket. Add the potatoes and season with salt. Cover and steam until the potatoes are tender, 8 to 10 minutes. (Check one of the smaller ones after 8 minutes to see how tender it is; you should be able to insert a fork into it easily.) If you don't have a steamer basket, boil them in a large pot of salted water until tender, 10 to 15 minutes.

**2** Remove the potatoes from the steamer and let them cool slightly. Using the bottom of a bowl or cup or the palm of your hand, smash the potatoes until they're just crushed to expose the inside, but not so much that they fall apart. You're going for maximum crispy surface area here.

**3** Heat the chicken fat in a large skillet over medium-high heat. Add the potatoes in a single layer (work in batches, if you need to) and season with kosher salt and black pepper. Cook until both sides are super browned and crispy, about 5 minutes per side.

**4** Remove the potatoes with a slotted spoon or spatula and transfer them to a serving bowl or platter. Add the butter to the skillet and let it melt and foam. Add the onion rings in a single layer and season with kosher salt and black pepper. Cook, swirling the skillet occasionally, until the onions have turned golden brown and started to crisp, 4 to 6 minutes.

**5** Remove the skillet from the heat and add the red pepper flakes, swirling the skillet a few times to combine. Pour the onions and any butter in the skillet over the potatoes and top with flaky sea salt and the parsley.

# KNIFE-AND-FORK SALADS

# In the same way I love whipping cream by hand or getting all the seeds out of a pomegranate, there is something uniquely satisfying to me about a salad that makes you work for it with a knife and fork.

I'm sure a therapist could tell me what all these things have in common, but I'm going to gloss over any implications and say that I guess I just really like a challenge.

To me, these big, leafy salads cut to the core of what this book is about. They are meant to be shared, fawned over: dramatically large halves of robust vinegared romaine hiding large dollops of sour cream (page 83) are served with the pride of someone presenting their first Thanksgiving turkey. They are elegant, punchy salads that could easily serve as a main course but also do well in a more supporting role alongside things like stews and roasts. Think of these salads as the anti-salad, so much more than anything that could possibly be contained in a bowl.

In case you decide that a knife and fork is one utensil too many for eating your salad, then yes, of course, the large leaves and wedges featured here can be chopped up for a more "traditional" approach.

# Chicories with Anchovy Bread Crumbs and Egg Yolk

*Serves 4*

3 tablespoons olive oil

2 tablespoons whole-grain mustard

1 tablespoon fresh lemon juice

Kosher salt and freshly ground black pepper

1 head of radicchio, halved lengthwise and leaves separated

1 head of Treviso or endive, quartered lengthwise

4 large egg yolks

1 cup Salty Anchovy Bread Crumbs (page 25)

I am in love with raw egg yolks. They are a creamy, luxurious, and unfussy ingredient, and if you've ever had a really good Caesar salad, you already know about their saucy magic. Without any whisking, freshly cracked and freed from the shell, separated from the watery white, rich, fatty egg yolks all by themselves are one hell of a secret ingredient. Here they're plopped onto a nest of hearty radicchio and Treviso, showered with salty anchovy bread crumbs, and broken just before serving to become the world's greatest low-maintenance salad dressing.

Like the other salads in this chapter, I'd happily eat this crunchy, mustardy little number as my main course, but the bitter leaves and punchy dressing are also the ideal companion for those more indulgent dishes like garlicky chicken confit (page 229) or citrus-braised pork shoulder (page 230).

**1** Whisk the olive oil, mustard, and lemon juice together in a small bowl and season with salt and pepper.

**2** Using your hands (yes, your hands!), rub the dressing onto the radicchio and Treviso, in between the leaves and whatnot, taking care not to crush the life out of them. Season them with salt and lots of pepper.

**3** Nestle the egg yolks somewhere in there so they are cradled by the leaves and season them with salt and pepper, too. Make sure whoever serves first breaks the yolk to create "the dressing" (alternatively, you can whisk the egg yolks together in a small bowl and drizzle over the radicchio).

**4** Scatter the bread crumbs over the top, serving any extra on the side, because you'll want them.

# Little Gems and Cabbage with Pickled Turnips and Lemony Tahini Dressing

*Serves 4*

2 Persian cucumbers, thinly sliced
    (about 1½ cups)
2 scallions, thinly sliced
½ preserved lemon (page 27 or
    store-bought), finely chopped
¼ small head red cabbage, thinly sliced
¼ cup thinly sliced pickled turnips or
    any other pickled vegetable you
    fancy (see page 23)
2 tablespoons fresh lemon juice
Kosher salt and freshly ground pepper
2 heads Little Gem lettuce, halved
    lengthwise, or 1 head romaine,
    quartered lengthwise
2 tablespoons olive oil
1 cup picked tender herbs, like cilantro,
    parsley, and/or dill, coarsely
    chopped
Lemony Tahini Dressing (page 22)

**NOTE:** Pickled vegetables are a very secret weapon that I like to sneak into salads whenever I can. They offer crunch and tang, and are a great option if you don't have any fresh vegetables lying around.

This salad was made during a particularly bad hunger emergency (code red) one day, sloppily cobbled together with the contents of my refrigerator, which at the time included half a head of red cabbage and an unopened jar of beet-pickled turnips. As I ate it, probably standing up at my counter, I realized why I loved it so much: it was like eating a falafel sandwich, without the falafel (or pita). It had the tangy, crunchy cabbage, plenty of herbs, and, of course, tahini.

While this would otherwise be classified as a kitchen sink kind of salad, I've now started intentionally buying those ingredients and keeping this lemon-tahini dressing on hand just so I can make a (refined version of) it at least once a week—with or without a hunger emergency.

**1** Combine the cucumbers, scallions, preserved lemon, cabbage, turnips, and lemon juice in a large bowl. Season with salt and pepper and let sit a few minutes.

**2** Transfer half the cucumber mixture to a large serving platter (or divide among a few plates). Top with the lettuce, drizzle with olive oil, and season with salt and pepper. Top with the remaining cucumber mixture and any juices that have accumulated. Scatter the herbs over the top and season with salt and pepper. Drizzle the dressing over the salad, serving any left over alongside for more dipping/drizzling.

# LADIES WHO KEENS

**M**ost women I know love a good steakhouse, but none more than Julia, Lilli, and me. Our favorite, Keens Steakhouse in Manhattan, is a very special place. We started a tradition of going there a few years ago when we worked at Condé Nast in Times Square, just as a way to check in with each other and celebrate our fabulous selves (it also serves as an opportunity to re-up on the matchbooks from the host stand—best matches in NYC, ask anyone). We call this event "Ladies Who Keens," as our version of "Ladies Who Lunch," which we were always too busy to do.

We like coming here because, even though one of us always gets hit on at the bar by someone old enough to be our grandfather, it's a kind of New York institution that we are proud to patronize, especially as women, because the place was made exclusively for men. Going to a restaurant that has been around since 1885 has a way of making you feel like you are connecting to a piece of city history, which in its own way is both sentimental and empowering. That, and it's an excuse to get a little fancy, a little loud, and a little tipsy.

While each time we are catching up over something different (relationships, career goals, general life anxieties), we rarely deviate from what is now known as "The Order." It starts with dirty martinis (gin, extra olives) at the bar, followed by a shrimp cocktail, wedge salad, rib-eye steak (medium-rare), side of creamed spinach, and several bottles of whatever moderately priced red wine they offer, concluding with probably an ice cream sundae and a slice of cheesecake— unless I'm picking, then it's key lime pie. Pretty standard steakhouse stuff.

Of all the things we come here for, I bet you'd never guess that the wedge salad is what excites us most, but it does. But honestly, it's never really that good. Overdressed with blue cheese, out-of-season cherry tomatoes, and undercooked bacon, there's a lot to complain about. And yet there's something about tackling a salad like you would a steak, reinforcing that, yes, we are at a steakhouse, and we will eat everything on the table as we would a steak. Steak, steak, steak!

That said, and this is not to disrespect years of tradition, but I've since made it my life's mission to improve on the wedge salad—the one at Keens and just about every steakhouse salad I've ever had. I want less dressing and crispier bacon, and if tomatoes aren't absolutely perfect, they are uninvited to this salad party. Maybe I don't even want the blue cheese, because I think it's maybe just a bit too much. So here's the version I'd be eating if it were up to me. No stinky cheese, no dumb tomatoes. Just lots of thick, crunchy romaine; salty, crispy slabs of bacon; a showering of herbs; and *tons* of sour cream.

# Vinegared Romaine
# with Sour Cream, Bacon, and Herbs

*Serves 4*

**12 thick-cut smoked bacon strips
(about 1 pound)**
**½ small shallot, very finely chopped**
**2 tablespoons white wine vinegar**
**Kosher salt and freshly ground black
pepper**
**1 cup sour cream**
**2 small or 1 large head of romaine
lettuce, ends trimmed, halved
lengthwise (or quartered if large)**
**2 cups fresh herbs, such as parsley,
cilantro, tarragon, and/or dill,
tender stems and leaves**
**Olive oil, for drizzling**
**Flaky sea salt, for sprinkling**

To me, this is the ultimate (and my favorite) knife-and-fork salad. Resplendent halves of frilly romaine lettuce; nooks and crannies that would make an English muffin jealous; perfect for dressing with lightly pickled shallots, olive oil, and, of course, bacon. Because it's a nod to the classic wedge salad, you could, of course, use iceberg (which I happen to love), but the romaine has a much better, greener flavor.

**1** Cook the bacon in a large skillet over medium heat until it's really crispy (I like it almost burnt), 5 to 8 minutes, depending on thickness. Set the bacon on some paper towels to drain the excess grease (but save the bacon grease in the skillet for another day when you're making eggs or pancakes or roasting vegetables).

**2** Combine the shallot and vinegar in a small bowl. Season with kosher salt and pepper, and let sit a few minutes so that the shallot softens a bit and lightly pickles in the vinegar.

**3** Season the sour cream with kosher salt and pepper and divide it evenly among four plates by dolloping and kinda swooshing it around, spreading it in a nice even layer. Place half (or one-quarter) of a romaine head on the sour cream and spoon the shallot vinegar over the lettuce. Season with kosher salt and pepper. Tuck the bacon in between the leaves like you're making an Edible Arrangement, scatter the herbs on top, and drizzle olive oil over everything, letting it pool in and around the lettuce's nooks and crannies. Sprinkle with flaky sea salt and eat with a knife and fork.

# Raw and Roasted Kale
## with Pistachios and Creamy Pecorino

*Serves 4*

**2 bunches Tuscan (aka lacinato) kale**
**3 tablespoons olive oil**
**1 teaspoon Aleppo pepper or**
**   ½ teaspoon crushed red**
**   pepper flakes**
**Kosher salt and freshly ground**
**   black pepper**
**3 ounces pecorino cheese, finely grated**
**   (about ½ cup)**
**1 tablespoon fresh lemon juice**
**1 tablespoon white wine vinegar**
**½ garlic clove, finely grated**
**¼ cup finely chopped toasted**
**   pistachios, almonds, or walnuts**
**   (see page 50 for how and why**
**   to toast nuts)**

To me, there is no better leafy green than kale. Honestly, I probably go through about four bunches a week. Crispy kale, raw kale, sautéed kale. Kale with garlic, creamed kale, kale in my soup. Pasta with kale, kale salad with cucumbers. I literally cannot get enough. I know, what is this, 2004? My body must know on some level that it's good for me; otherwise, why would I be constantly craving it? Sure, drowning it in olive oil and covering it with cheese might negate some of the health benefits, but at the end of the day, you're still eating half your weight in dark leafy greens, and you can feel good about that.

When it comes to preparing kale, I like to use my hands. Hands to strip the leaves from the stalk, hands to massage the oil into the leaves and soften them in the process. It's a pretty hearty and forgiving green, and you'd have to work extremely hard to destroy it, so don't worry. While the stems don't get used here, they are worth saving for some delicious lemony relish (page 22) or to toss into your next batch of pesto for some extra greenery.

**1** Preheat the oven to 425°F.

**2** Separate the leaves from the stalks of the kale (it's okay if they don't stay totally intact). Toss half the kale with 1 tablespoon of the olive oil on a rimmed baking sheet, sprinkle with the Aleppo pepper, and season with salt and black pepper. Lay the leaves flat and roast them until the kale is starting to look a little crispy, 10 to 15 minutes. (The main goal here is crispy kale, not burnt kale, so keep an eye on it.)

**3** Meanwhile, combine the pecorino, lemon juice, vinegar, and garlic in a large bowl. Add the remaining 2 tablespoons olive oil and season with salt and black pepper. Add the raw kale and, using your hands, massage the dressing into the leaves, taking care to leave the leaves whole.

**4** Arrange the raw leaves on a large plate or platter and top with the crispy kale leaves. Sprinkle with the pistachios before serving.

# FRUIT
# SALADS

# Before you skip this chapter because the idea of out-of-season berries, cubed melon, and halved grapes all tossed together really turns you off, just know that it turns me off, too.

Fruit, in all its acidic, perfectly textured glory, deserves more than that kind of treatment. Rather than always doubling down on its obvious sweetness, fruit is somehow even more perfect when it gets invited to play in the realm of the savory, letting the natural sweetness complement salty cheese or tame spicy greens. The fruit salads in this chapter are real salads, or at least fruit dressed like one, nary a halved grape in sight.

On page 99, you'll see that, showered in snipped chives, drizzled with good olive oil, and sprinkled with lots of cracked black pepper, a good melon will never be underestimated again (no prosciutto necessary), and that when paired with crunchy, licorice-y fennel and some sumac-pickled shallots, grapefruit is actually a juicy, bitter, tangy, savory salad MVP (page 103).

The success of these salads really does hinge on high-quality, perfectly in-season fruit. Even the most skilled baker would find it challenging to make underripe persimmons delicious, but when eaten raw, there's no butter or sugar to hide behind. Most fruit tends to lose acidity as it ages, so for these applications, the sweet spot is just before it hits peak ripeness.

# Apple and Endive Salad
# with Parsley and Salted Almonds

*Serves 4*

½ cup skin-on roasted almonds or raw walnuts or pecans, chopped (see Note)

3 tablespoons olive oil

Kosher salt and freshly ground black pepper

2 endives, ends trimmed, quartered lengthwise, leaves separated

1 large tart apple, such as Pink Lady, cored and thinly sliced crosswise into rounds

1 shallot, thinly sliced crosswise into rings

1 cup fresh parsley, tender stems and leaves

½ cup mint leaves

2 tablespoons fresh lemon juice, plus more as needed

1 teaspoon Asian fish sauce (optional)

My ideal salads are the ones that have tons of texture, acid, and salt. This one, in particular, hits every note: it's fresh, bitter, salty, sweet, and crunchy as hell. Yes, the bit of fish sauce is optional, but I will say that its uniquely salty, savory funkiness takes this salad from simply great to truly, impossibly delicious. Feel free to mix up the types of herbs and nuts here, depending on what you have and what you like, swapping mint for parsley or walnuts for almonds.

**1** Combine the almonds and olive oil in a small bowl. Season well with salt and pepper.

**2** Toss the endive, apple, shallot, parsley, mint, lemon juice, and fish sauce (if using) in a large bowl. Season with salt and pepper. Taste a leaf or two of endive and adjust with more lemon, salt, or pepper, if needed.

**3** Place the apples and endive on a large serving platter or bowl and top with the salted almond mixture.

**NOTE:** If using raw walnuts or pecans, toast them per the instructions on page 50.

# Persimmons and Pears
# with Blue Cheese and Spicy Pecans

*Serves 4*

1 cup pecans

2 tablespoons maple syrup

1 teaspoon Aleppo pepper

1 tablespoon olive oil, plus more for drizzling

Kosher salt and freshly ground black pepper

2 Bosc pears, cored and thinly sliced

2 persimmons, thinly sliced

1 tablespoon white wine vinegar or apple cider vinegar

3 ounces firm blue cheese, such as Valdeón or Bayley Hazen Blue, thinly sliced or crumbled

Persimmons don't seem to get the credit they deserve, and I guess that's because, at first look, they don't seem to be bringing a whole lot to the table. Not particularly sweet, there's no acid to speak of, and the texture is best described as soft. But… *I love them.* I love their bright orange color, their vaguely winter-squash-like flavor, and their slightly tannic skin. I love that they get along with just about every other fruit, and most of all, I love how their demure honey-like sweetness and velvety texture come out to play when blanketed in some funky, salty, creamy cheese.

**1** Combine the pecans, maple syrup, and Aleppo pepper in a large skillet over medium heat. Cook, stirring constantly, until the maple syrup bubbles, reduces, and crystallizes around the pecans, 5 to 8 minutes. They will look all white and fuzzy with an even layer of crystallized sugar coating each nut—this is what you want. Add the olive oil and remove from the heat; season with salt and pepper, and let cool completely before coarsely chopping the pecans.

**2** Scatter the pears and persimmons around a large serving platter or bowl and drizzle with the vinegar and olive oil. Season with salt and pepper, and finish with the pecans and blue cheese.

# Creamsicle, or the Most Delicious Thing

My Creamsicle obsession started when I was sixteen at my first job, which was at Jamba Juice. Before we go any further, yes it was as fun and also as degrading as you'd think, no I never had to wear the banana suit, and yes, I still know how to make 85 percent of the menu; e-mail me for deets.

During this very broke time, my breakfast, lunch, and/or dinner was, obviously, a smoothie. But not just any smoothie: I wasn't a Razzmatazz kind of person (frozen bananas and apple juice, no thanks), and the Strawberries Wild was basically the equivalent of ordering a Pumpkin Spice Latte (which, as we all know, is a once-a-year kind of thing). For me, it was the Orange Dream Machine, hereafter referred to as the ODM, made with soy milk, orange juice, vanilla frozen yogurt, and orange sherbet. I would occasionally add protein powder, or maybe one of those "immunity boosts," because when your diet consists of orange sherbet smoothies, you need all the help you can get.

Even beyond Jamba Juice, I was all about anything that tasted like the ODM, and I was constantly looking for my next fix. Orange Julius at the mall, Creamsicle bars at my friend's house, orange sherbet at Grandma's, orange slices in my vanilla pudding at home—you name it. Any way you slice it, when you have that rich, fatty, creamy vanilla flavor cutting through the tart acidity of oranges, you create what is undeniably the most simple and delicious craveable thing in the world.

While I've grown up and now won't sip anything through a straw if it doesn't contain at least a half bunch of kale and cashew milk, I still have a very *very* soft spot for that Creamsicle flavor profile, and I aim to slip it in wherever I can. This salad is a very good example of that.

# Burrata with Tangerines, Shallots, and Watercress

*Serves 4*

1 shallot, thinly sliced into rings
1 tablespoon fresh lemon juice
Kosher salt and freshly ground black
    pepper
1 (8-ounce) ball burrata
3 tangerines, peeled and sliced
    ½ inch thick
3 cups small spicy greens, such as
    watercress, mizuna, or arugula
Olive oil, for drizzling
Flaky sea salt, for sprinkling

Juicy, tart, tangy, and just sweet enough, perfect tangerines shine brightest when paired with something fatty and creamy, tasting of milk, simultaneously cutting through and enhancing the richness, almost like . . . a Creamsicle. Okay, this is like a Creamsicle in salad form.

But to call this a salad would be generous, because it is mostly cheese and fruit. For that reason, use the best cheese and fruit you can find, since, like I said, that's pretty much all you're eating. Sure, there's small, spicy lettuces, but you're here for the cheese and fruit, and that's okay, so am I.

The cheese here is burrata, a very, very creamy, rich cheese that is basically a ball of cheese wrapped in cheese and filled with heavy cream—sorcery at its finest. While not widely available, it is worth seeking out at specialty cheese stores and high-end grocers for its magical dueling textures: firm, almost springy on the outside (like a good mozzarella), soft and wildly creamy on the inside (like a much better version of ricotta). If you are blessed with more citrus variety than just tangerines (like kumquats or mandarins), feel free to slice those up and add them to the mix.

**1** Toss the shallot with the lemon juice in a small bowl and season with kosher salt and pepper; let sit 5 minutes, tossing occasionally.

**2** Depending on how ripe the burrata is, you can tear, slice, or cut it into a few pieces and arrange them on a large serving platter (the "riper" the cheese, the runnier it will be, making it more difficult to slice, so I recommend tearing).

**3** Scatter the tangerine slices around the burrata.

**4** Combine the shallot and the spicy greens, and season them with kosher salt and pepper. Toss to coat and scatter the mixture around the tangerines and burrata.

**5** Drizzle all over with olive oil and sprinkle with flaky sea salt.

# Watermelon and Cucumbers with Spicy Sumac Salt

*Serves 4*

2 tablespoons ground sumac

1½ tablespoons Aleppo pepper or 1 tablespoon crushed red pepper flakes

1 tablespoon kosher salt

½ small watermelon, sliced ¾ inch thick (I leave the rind on, but that's up to you)

2 cucumbers, preferably small ones such as Persian or Kirby, unpeeled, thinly sliced

Ever had Tajín seasoning? It's a Mexican seasoning made from chiles, salt, and dehydrated lime juice. It's the best on watermelon, mango, or eaten out of the palm of your hand. Sumac replaces the lime here, but damn if it's not a dead ringer for that tangy, mouth-puckery sensation. Make lots of this mixture and keep it around to sprinkle over raw fruit all summer long.

Combine the sumac, Aleppo pepper, and salt in a small bowl. Arrange the watermelon and cucumbers on a large platter, sprinkle with the spicy sumac salt, and go to town.

# Cantaloupe with Arugula
# and Black Olives

*Serves 4*

2 tablespoons oil-cured black olives, pitted, very finely chopped

3 tablespoons olive oil

1 small or ½ large very ripe cantaloupe, canary, or Charentais melon, peeled, seeds removed, and sliced ½ inch thick

2 cups wild arugula

1 lemon

¼ cup chopped fresh chives

Flaky sea salt and freshly ground black pepper

My friend Lauren and I made a version of this dish one summer, using some super-wild-looking late-summer arugula (which we both agreed is the tastiest kind) and the craziest, ripest cantaloupes we have ever had the pleasure of eating. If, for some reason, you've never had a cantaloupe at its absolute peak, it tastes like honey and squash and vanilla ice cream all at once, and it's so juicy that one bite will produce rivers of cantaloupe juice running all over your face and hands, dripping on whatever you're wearing. It will be messy, it will be sticky, it will be worth it.

Yes, cantaloupes are perfect on their own, but there is a way to make them better: blessed with salty, briny olives and the spiciest arugula you can find. If you can't find crazy-ripe melons, you might want to skip this one.

**NOTE:** Regarding the type of melon here, cantaloupe is what you'll find in the supermarket, and I'm sure that it's fine. But for a next-level melon experience, you'll need to head to a farmer's market or farmstand. This is where the real-deal, wildly flavorful melons come to be seen and purchased.

1 Combine the olives and olive oil in a small bowl.

2 Arrange the cantaloupe and arugula on a large platter.

3 Squeeze the lemon all over the top, sprinkle with the chives, and drizzle with the olive mixture. Finish with flaky sea salt and pepper.

# Blood Oranges with Crunchy Red Onion and Avocado

*Serves 4*

¼ small red onion, very thinly sliced into rings
4 blood oranges (or regular oranges), peeled and sliced ¼ inch thick
1 avocado, thinly sliced
2 tablespoons fresh lime juice
Flaky sea salt and coarsely ground black pepper
1 teaspoon nigella seed, black sesame seeds, or poppy seeds
¼ cup fresh cilantro, tender stems and leaves
2 tablespoons olive oil

Aside from going with "everything," I think the best way to eat avocado is with some citrus and raw onion. Sure, I know what you're thinking: sounds like guacamole. But guacamole this is not. Here the avocado must be sliced, not mashed; the citrus should be fat, wonderful slices, not just the juice; and the onions should be slightly silenced by a trip to an ice bath so that you may eat them in equal proportion to the other ingredients.

While the blood oranges do provide a significant amount of acid, the fatty avocados still need a boost from a bit of lime juice, which is okay. I could eat this salad for breakfast, lunch, or dinner. No toast needed.

**1** Soak the onion in a medium bowl of ice water for 10 to 20 minutes; this will soften the oniony bite and also make it super crunchy.

**2** Meanwhile, layer the orange and avocado, overlapping the slices slightly, on a large serving plate.

**3** Drain the onion and scatter it on top; drizzle with the lime juice. Season with flaky sea salt and pepper.

**4** Sprinkle with the nigella seed and cilantro, and drizzle the whole thing with the olive oil.

# Fennel and Grapefruit Salad
# with Honey and Mint

*Serves 4*

2 teaspoons fennel seed

1 small shallot, thinly sliced

2 tablespoons fresh lime juice, plus
more as needed

2 teaspoons honey

1 teaspoon ground sumac

Kosher salt and freshly ground black
pepper

2 large red, pink, or pomelo
grapefruits, peel and pith removed,
sliced into ½-inch-thick rounds,
and cut into bite-sized pieces

1 medium fennel bulb, thinly sliced
crosswise

1 cup fresh mint leaves

1 cup fresh, tender parsley, leaves
and stems

2 tablespoons olive oil

Grapefruits are a very special fruit, one of my favorite ingredients to cook with and to eat. With acidity that's tamer than that of a lemon or lime and an aggressive bitterness an orange could only dream of, they have a certain mystique—do they want to be savory or sweet? Should I shower you in sugar or eat you with salt? Well, I asked. To reach the fullest expression of itself, the tangy, floral, bitter grapefruit wants to be more savory than sweet. It likes lightly pickled shallots, olive oil, lots of salt, and just a touch of honey, and gets along with potent spices like toasted fennel seed and tangy sumac.

The color and flavor of pink or ruby red grapefruits really can't be beat, but pomelos (a larger variety with a yellowy-green skin and flesh that can be either pale yellow or a salmony pink) have a quiet bitterness and an incredible juiciness that make them another great option. They do tend to be less sweet and tangy than the ruby reds, so adjust the honey and lime accordingly.

**1** Toast the fennel seed in a tiny skillet over medium heat, swirling the skillet frequently, until they have turned a light golden brown and smell super fragrant, about 2 minutes. Transfer them to a cutting board and let them cool slightly. Using the side of a chef's knife, crush the seeds (or you can chop them) and combine them in a small bowl with the shallot, lime juice, honey, and sumac. Season with salt and pepper, toss to combine, and let sit a few minutes.

**2** Toss the grapefruit, fennel, mint, and parsley together in a medium bowl and add the shallot and any liquid. Mix everything together and season with salt and pepper. Drizzle with the olive oil before serving.

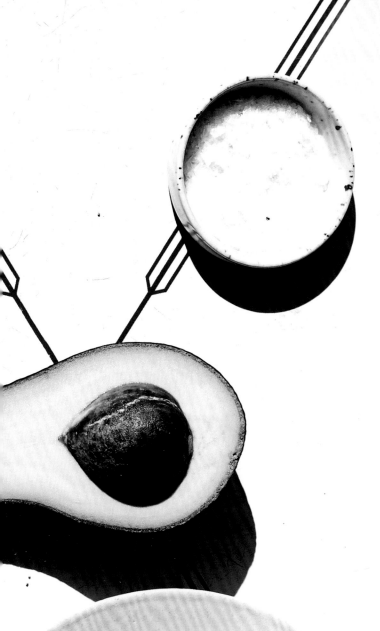

# SAVORY
# BREAKFASTS

# Generally speaking, I am a savory-over-sweet kind of gal, but especially when it comes to breakfast.

I already have a hard time focusing, but eating a bowl of sugar first thing in the morning would just send me into an immediate directionless tailspin. Even yogurt with berries and honey is too high octane for me. My body knows this, and so it craves a hard-boiled egg dipped in salt, crispy chorizo with a can of chickpeas (page 110), or a kimchi and Cheddar omelette (page 109)—which, by the way, if you haven't tried that combo, is fantastic. There's something about starting the morning with something a little heftier and saltier (and sometimes cheesier) that makes me feel emotionally and physically better prepared to face the day.

But savory breakfast doesn't have to be an oversized bacon, egg, and cheese sandwich (aka B.E.C.) from the bodega, a stamp of overindulgence. It can be savory granola loaded with good-for-you seeds and nuts sprinkled over smashed cucumbers and Greek yogurt (page 112) or a pile of lemony greens and eggs crisped in chicken fat with hot sauce (page 116)—as light as it is satisfying.

While I say breakfast, please know that there is no reason these things couldn't be cooked for lunch, dinner, or a snack somewhere between. There's also a magical thing called second breakfast, where you wake up after a weekend nap and decide that maybe it's breakfast time again, wherein these dishes would be most appropriate.

# Savory Barley Porridge with Parmesan and Soy

*Serves 4*

2 cups chicken broth, vegetable broth,
   or water
½ cup barley
¼ cup millet
Kosher salt and freshly ground black
   pepper
¼ cup buckwheat groats
1 tablespoon white distilled vinegar or
   white wine vinegar
4 large eggs
½ cup grated Parmesan cheese, plus
   more (optional) for topping
2 scallions, thinly sliced
2 teaspoons tamari or soy sauce
Wilted kale, sautéed mushrooms, and/
   or crisped and crumbled bacon, for
   topping (optional)

**NOTE:** Since the porridge by itself is generally pretty bland, I like to treat it almost like grits and add lots (and lots) of cheese, and for a deeper, more savory saltiness, a splash of tamari or soy sauce. As for topping them, it practically goes without saying that there will be an egg involved, although what kind of egg is really up to you. Poached, fried, and soft-boiled are my favorites. From there, all bets are off. I love finishing it with a sprinkle of toasted buckwheat to bring back some crunch into the mix, but this is also the perfect place for some sautéed mushrooms, wilted kale, roasted sweet potatoes or squash, or even some crisped and crumbled bacon.

Savory porridge might feel a little trendy, but in most of the world, the idea of eating something hearty, soupy, and savory for breakfast is old news. It's the equivalent of being hugged from the inside, the perfect thing on a very cold morning (or when you have your wisdom teeth removed, which is when I first started making this).

The base is simple: just cook some grains with water or broth until you think you can't cook them anymore, and then cook them some more until they've fallen apart, breaking free of their former self into a creamy porridge. The best grains to use are the ones that soften considerably as they cook without turning to total mush, which is why I like a combination of barley (for texture) and millet (for creaminess).

**1** To make the porridge, bring the broth and 3 cups water to a simmer in a medium pot. Add the barley and millet, and season with salt and pepper. Bring the grains to a boil, then reduce the heat to medium-low. Simmer the grains, stirring every now and then, until they are impossibly tender and creamy and have absorbed nearly all the liquid in the pot, 35 to 45 minutes (it should look pretty much like oatmeal). Season again with salt and pepper (especially if you've used only water; the grains will need a bit more help in the flavor department).

**2** Toast the buckwheat in a small skillet over medium heat until it's toasty and starting to pop, 3 to 4 minutes.

**3** For the poached eggs, bring a medium pot of water to a simmer and add the vinegar.

**4** Crack 1 egg into a small dish or bowl and gently drop the egg into the water. The vinegar should help the white hold together here, but if you need even more assistance, use the handle of a spoon or spatula to gently swirl the water in a clockwise motion to create a bit of a vortex motion, encouraging the white to envelop the yolk rather than float away into the abyss.

**5** Once the egg white has just firmed up but the yolk is still runny, remove the egg with a slotted spoon and place it on a paper-towel-lined plate. Repeat with the remaining eggs. (For a fried-egg variation, see page 116; for soft-boiled, page 134.)

**6** Stir the Parmesan into the porridge and divide it evenly among four bowls. Top each with a poached egg, scallions, and ½ teaspoon of tamari. Add wilted kale, sautéed mushrooms, or crumbled bacon, if using. Sprinkle with the buckwheat and shave more Parmesan over.

# Crispy Kimchi and Cheddar Omelette

Serves 4

2 large eggs
Kosher salt and freshly ground black
  pepper
1 tablespoon unsalted butter
2 tablespoons shredded white or
  yellow Cheddar cheese
¼ cup cabbage kimchi, squeezed
  mostly dry, coarsely chopped

**NOTE:** I prefer my omelettes with two eggs rather than three, which means they'll have an almost crepe-like thinness, but if you like a bit more heft, or are especially hungry, you can certainly use three. I use a carbon-steel skillet to make my omelettes, but nonstick or even a well-seasoned cast-iron skillet will work as well.

I first had the pleasure of experiencing Cheddar and kimchi at Milk Bar, where I worked for a spell. One of my coworkers, Helen Jo, would sometimes make little Cheddar and kimchi quesadillas for family meal, especially if we were extra busy that day; they need only three ingredients, each of which we always had on hand anyway. I'll admit that at first I was skeptical. My brain just could not imagine a world in which spicy, fermented kimchi would go well with sharp, creamy Cheddar cheese, but let me say that since then, I have seen that world, and that world is wonderful.

Sometimes quesadillas are a little too much first thing in the morning, so I adapted them into little omelettes. But this is not a fancy, delicate, barely cooked French omelette; this is an improper omelette, an omelette gone rogue. Here the eggs are cooked over a higher flame than usual, so the outside browns while the interior stays delightfully runny. Shredded Cheddar cheese gets sprinkled on as soon as the eggs hit the skillet, and it melts and crisps up along with the eggs, giving you those cheesy, lacy bits and pieces.

**1** Using a fork, beat the eggs in a small bowl until there are no visible bits of white or yolk (you're just trying to get an even mixture, not incorporate a ton of air) and season them with salt and pepper.

**2** Heat the butter in a medium skillet, preferably carbon steel, nonstick, or well-seasoned cast iron, over medium-high heat. Once the butter is melted and foamy, add the eggs, swirling the pan to make sure they are forming an even layer. Immediately sprinkle the eggs with the cheese, followed by the kimchi. Let the eggs cook until the underside is browned and slightly puffed but the top is still rather runny, 2 to 3 minutes.

**3** Using a spatula (preferably silicone if using a nonstick pan), lift the edge of the eggs all around the skillet to release them and, starting at one end, fold the omelette onto itself. You can either roll it like a classic omelette or, if that's just not an option this morning, simply fold it into a half-moon.

# Baked Eggs with Crushed Chickpeas, Chorizo, and Bread Crumbs

*Serves 4*

2 tablespoons olive oil, plus more for drizzling

6 ounces dried chorizo, thinly sliced

1 small yellow onion, finely chopped

½ teaspoon ground cumin

Kosher salt and freshly ground black pepper

2 medium tomatoes, chopped

1 (15-ounce) can chickpeas, drained and rinsed

4 large eggs

¾ cup Spicy, Herby Bread Crumbs (page 25)

¼ cup coarsely chopped fresh parsley or cilantro

¾ cup labne, full-fat Greek yogurt, or sour cream, for serving (optional)

Of all the savory breakfasts in this chapter, this one is definitely the heartiest and most time consuming. Even so, it's still a basic one-skillet deal. It's also the one dish I am most likely to eat for lunch or dinner, with or without eggs, because I find chickpeas simmered with dried chorizo and fresh tomatoes to be one of life's greatest pleasures.

Baked eggs can be tricky to get right, mostly because you're asking a lot of the egg, for the white to be totally cooked before the yolk turns hard and opaque, all with a serious lack of supervision as it goes into the oven. I find baking eggs in just tomato sauce, à la shakshuka, to be even more difficult since the white tends to sink into the sauce, never to be heard from again, so it's hard to tell if they've cooked through. At least here, propped up on little mountains of chickpeas and chorizo, the whites stand a chance of getting visibly cooked, taking a lot of the guesswork out of things.

**1** Place an oven rack in the top third of the oven and preheat to 400°F.

**2** Heat the olive oil in a large skillet over medium heat. Add the chorizo, onion, and cumin and season with salt and pepper. Cook, stirring every so often, until the chorizo has rendered some of that fiery orange fat and the onions are softened and beginning to brown, 5 to 8 minutes.

**3** Add the tomatoes and season with salt and pepper. Cook until the tomatoes have totally softened and released their juices, 5 to 8 minutes.

**4** Add the chickpeas and season with salt and pepper. Stir to coat the chickpeas in everything, using the back of a wooden spoon or spatula to crush them lightly (you don't want to mash them, just break them up a bit). Add ¼ cup water and let everything simmer together, further crushing those chickpeas if they need it, until the liquid has reduced by half and all the flavors are mingling, 5 to 8 minutes.

**5** Using the back of a spoon or spatula, make four little evenly spaced nests in the skillet of chickpeas. Crack the eggs into the chickpeas and season with salt and pepper. Place the skillet on the top rack in the oven and bake until the whites of the eggs are just set and the egg yolks are still runny, 5 to 7 minutes.

**6** Remove from the oven and sprinkle with the bread crumbs and parsley. Serve with labne, if you like.

# Smashed Cucumbers and Scallions over Garlicky Yogurt

*Serves 4*

2 cups full-fat or 2 percent Greek
   yogurt
1 garlic clove, finely grated
2 tablespoons fresh lemon or lime juice
Kosher salt and freshly ground black
   pepper
2 Persian or 1 English cucumber, cut
   into 2-inch pieces
4 scallions, thinly sliced
Decidedly Not-Sweet Granola
   (page 143)
Crushed red pepper flakes (optional)
Olive oil
Flaky sea salt

Cucumbers and yogurt have been friends for a long time, and it just so happens that I like them as much for breakfast as I do on my falafel. Think of this as yogurt and berries for the savory set, for days when eggs seem like too much and a bowl of cereal seems like maybe not enough. I love the craggy texture and juiciness of the smashed cucumbers, but because that isn't always something you'll want to do on a Wednesday morning before work, you can absolutely just slice them.

**1** Mix the yogurt, garlic, and 1 tablespoon of the lemon juice together in a medium bowl. Season with kosher salt and black pepper.

**2** Place the cucumbers, the remaining 1 tablespoon lemon juice, and half the scallions in a large ziplock bag and season with kosher salt and black pepper. Using a rolling pin, the bottom of a skillet, or anything heavy you feel comfortable lifting, smash the cucumbers until they're just starting to fall apart.

**3** Divide the yogurt mixture evenly among four bowls and scatter with the smashed cucumbers, granola, the remaining scallions, and red pepper flakes (if using), and drizzle with olive oil. Finish with flaky sea salt and serve.

# Morning-After Breakfast Salad

Sometimes the best way to demonstrate a decent level of self-care is not to give in to the idea that every time you stay out too late, you somehow deserve a giant burrito stuffed with hash browns (I say this as a person who, on occasion, stays out too late). It's good to remind yourself that, yes, it is actually a good idea to start your day with a giant bowl of tender, leafy greens and lots of protein, especially if you've had a wild amount of wine the night before. I promise your body will thank you for this crisp, green reset.

The breakfast salad of your dreams can contain as much or as little of the ingredients below as you like, but here are some suggestions to get you started.

**FIRST, THE GREENS:** This is the first meal of the day, so start with some nice tender leaves from lettuces like red leaf, baby romaine, Bibb, or butter. If the leaves are larger, tear them into bite-sized pieces. You'll want about 2 cups of lettuce per person.

Herbs! Lots of herbs, about a cup of them. The soft, punchy ones, like tarragon, chives, and cilantro, are great, but I would also happily eat a bowl of mostly parsley.

Next comes protein. For this you can crisp up some bacon or sausage you have lying around, but leftovers also are excellent here. Think bacony pork tenderloin from page 244, turmeric-poached chicken from the broth on page 217, or the perfect steak from your date night in on page 216.

And, of course, the eggs. For the runny yolk and firm egg white, I find soft-boiled to be the way to go here (page 134), but fried (page 116) or poached (page 108) also work. Basically, you're just looking for a runny yolk to kind of dress everything up, and however you want to get there will be delicious.

This salad needs little more than a drizzle of some good olive oil and a squeeze of lemon or a splash of apple cider vinegar, but you can also keep piling on the goods if you like, adding any leftover or lonely vegetables hiding in your fridge. Boiled or steamed potatoes, stewed beans, roasted broccoli or squash— the possibilities are endless.

Buttered toast is optional, but I find it useful when shoveling the salad into my mouth.

# Eggs and Kale Fried in Chicken Fat

*Serves 2*

4 tablespoons chicken fat (either left over from page 229 or purchased schmaltz; see Note)

½ bunch Tuscan (lacinato) kale, thick stems removed, torn into 2-inch pieces

Kosher salt and freshly ground black pepper

4 large eggs (try to use high-quality, free-range ones here)

Flaky sea salt

½ cup yogurt (optional)

2 pieces of toast, English muffins, or other breakfast carb of choice, for serving

Hot sauce, such as Tapatío or Cholula, for serving

**NOTE:** Of course this recipe works with olive oil (even leftover olive oil from the vegetables on page 38) or bacon fat, too.

Eggs fried in chicken fat was an accident, really. I had tons of leftover rich, golden fat from the Crispy Chicken Legs with Rosemary, Tiny Potatoes, and Sour Cream (page 229) and was basically using it every chance I had, because it was so damn good—deeply savory with a hint of garlic, kind of salty, and more delicious than anything that could come from an olive. I thought roasting vegetables in it was the best I could do, until I woke up one morning craving crispy eggs. I proceeded with my usual fried egg routine, except instead of the regular ol' olive oil, I reached for that schmaltz. I rewarded my genius idea with a million mental high-fives. So obvious, so simple, so almost wrong. So delicious.

The kale is here because it's my favorite thing to eat with eggs, and it tastes impossibly good sizzled and lightly crisped up in the chicken fat. The hot sauce is here because I like everything spicy, even first thing in the morning. You can make these eggs without either, but I recommend both.

**1** Heat 1 tablespoon of the chicken fat in a large skillet over medium-high heat. Add the kale and season with kosher salt and pepper. Toss it a few times in the fat and cook until the kale has started to sizzle and crisp at the edges, about 4 minutes. Transfer the kale to a plate or bowl and set aside.

**2** Add the remaining 3 tablespoons fat to the skillet. Once the fat is hot and shimmering, crack the eggs into the skillet and season with kosher salt and pepper. Let them fry away until the edges are golden brown, the white is puffed and bubbly, and the yolk is still bright orangey yellow and runny as hell; this should take about 3 minutes. Resist the urge to move the eggs but rotate the skillet, if needed, for even crisping.

**3** Spoon the yogurt (if using) on the bottom of two plates. Season with salt and pepper. Top with the kale.

**4** Using a spatula, remove the eggs and place them atop the kale and sprinkle with flaky sea salt. Serve with toast and plenty of hot sauce.

# Avocados with Everything

*Serves 1*

1 lemon or lime, halved
1 avocado, halved
**Everything Seed Mixture (page 20)**
**Toast, crackers, or other bready**
    **crunchy vehicle of your choosing**
    **(very optional)**

This isn't so much a recipe as it is a lifestyle choice, because I honestly cannot understand the phenomenon that is Avocado Toast. Yes, this is not a popular opinion; there is a reason I am burying this deep in the Savory Breakfast chapter.

It's not that I think Avocado Toast as a concept is bad, it's just that more often than not, it's never that good. We all know the story: no matter where you live, there's a café or restaurant serving avocado that's been smashed to an unrecognizable paste (if you're lucky, it's still green) sogging out the (undertoasted) bread it sits on, lacking salt, acid, or probably both.

This might be okay if avocados weren't such a special ingredient. Alone, they are stunning in color and shape, rich and fatty with a vaguely nutty, vegetal flavor. They don't need the toast. In fact, toast, I'd argue, needs them. But I'd rather have toast on its own, perfect in its crunchy simplicity, just like I'd rather eat an avocado by itself, dressed with nothing but lemon juice and lots of crunchy salt. There are, of course, exceptions to this rule; hot sauce, lime juice, and red pepper flakes all have a time and place on an avocado. And now, crunchy, salty Everything Mix (as in, the seedy mix that appears in the condiment section of this book).

Like the name indicates, it's got everything—caraway seeds, sesame seeds, dried onion, salt, and as many poppy seeds as needed to make sure at least one gets stuck in your teeth. It's an obvious choice to top springy, doughy bagels, but sprinkled over a creamy, perfectly ripe halved avocado, it's a revelation.

Avocados really don't need anything, except maybe Everything.

**1** Squeeze half a lemon over each avocado half and sprinkle with the Everything mix.

**2** Toast not needed, but I won't stop you.

# A Good Batch

Matzo brei is not quite what I'd call a household food item, unless that household belongs to the Romans. Yes, we take that eggy, buttery, carbohydrate bomb extremely seriously, and nobody more seriously than my dad, Dan. A good or bad "batch," as my sister, brother, stepmom, and I came to call the matzo brei du jour, would set the tone for the rest of the day. Was it dry? Did it have enough salt? Were the onions caramelized enough? (I know what you're thinking, and yes, of course we take ours savory, never sweet.)

Look, I didn't envy him, four pairs of extremely judgy eyes and mouths weighing in, voicing opinions he never asked for. Luckily for Dad, the feedback was almost always positive, as evidenced by clean plates and an empty skillet. It became our ritual, alongside bagels and lox or maybe just on its own; it was never served for company (unless Grandpa was visiting—it was his favorite), only for us five.

When I moved to New York, it became the one thing I craved the most (that, and a Trader Joe's that sold wine). Since I was a professional and developed recipes for a living, I figured I would just make it myself. A box of matzo was certainly cheaper than a plane ticket; plus, how hard could it be? Well, turns out, pretty hard. Was I not using enough butter? Didn't Dad always soak the boards first? What did he soak them

in? I honestly couldn't remember. I guess that was because I never really paid attention, or maybe I was just sleeping in. Every time I came home for a visit, Dad would make his famous matzo brei. I'd hover relentlessly (and annoyingly), partly so I could ensure those onions were seasoned enough, and partly so I could learn how to make it myself.

Here's what, after all those years of not paying attention, I finally learned: It's easier to soak the boards in warm water (sure, some people do it in milk, but I think there's enough butter involved that I don't need the extra creaminess), and if you don't do it long enough, the batch will always be dry; soak them too long, and they fall apart. I learned that sometimes my dad forgets to season his onions, but that he always uses the perfect amount of cracked black pepper, which is almost as important. I learned that instead of frying it hot and fast, making perfect matzo brei is a lot like making perfect scrambled eggs, and that you can't rush something cooked low and slow. I learned that a beat-up old nonstick skillet and a wooden spoon are the best tools you can use, and that matzo brei is the world's best hangover cure. I also learned that no matter how many times you make it, and no matter how professional you are, it will never taste as good as when someone else makes it for you.

# Matzo Brei

*Serves 4*

4 tablespoons (½ stick) unsalted butter
1 medium yellow onion, thinly sliced
Kosher salt and freshly ground black
  pepper
4 salted matzo boards (unsalted will
  work, too, just be sure to
  compensate by adding salt when
  making it)
6 large eggs
Sour cream and applesauce, for serving

The key to good matzo brei lies in two things: very seasoned, very caramelized onions; and properly soaked matzo boards. Not enough soaking and it'll be dry; too much, and it'll feel bland and waterlogged. It may take you a few tries to see what I mean. It is, after all, an art.

**1** Melt the butter in a large skillet over medium heat. Add the onion and season with salt and pepper. Cook, stirring occasionally, until the onions have caramelized and softened completely, about 15 minutes; don't rush this part! Low-and-slow caramelized onions are key to its deliciousness. Remove from the heat and set aside while you deal with the matzo.

**2** Soak the matzo in a large bowl of warm water for a few seconds to soften and just soak through (leave them in there too long and they'll fall apart). You'll know they're properly soaked when they are soft and no longer snap like a cracker. Drain the matzo in a colander.

**3** Beat the eggs in a large bowl and season with salt and pepper. Add the soaked matzo and, using your hands or a spatula, stir to coat so that all the matzo is evenly coated with the egg mixture. Let this sit for 2 to 3 minutes.

**4** Return the skillet to medium-low heat and add the matzo mixture to the caramelized onions; season again with salt and pepper. Cook, scraping the bottom of the skillet occasionally, almost like you're making a soft scramble. Cook until the eggs are just set, then remove the skillet from the heat (they will continue to cook off the heat).

**5** Transfer the matzo brei to a large bowl (or serve straight from the skillet) and serve with plenty of sour cream and applesauce.

# GRAINS AND THINGS

# *Grains and things* is my catchall term for whole grains (like farro, spelt, and oats) and other things made with grains (pasta), as well as lentils, beans, and chickpeas.

Where once a lot of these ingredients lived only among the pages of your well-worn *Moosewood Cookbook* and the co-op bulk bins, grains have gone full-blown mainstream, popping up in restaurant menus, magazine articles, and trendy fast casual restaurants that deal in expensive salads. The rising popularity of these "it girl" ingredients means that now more than ever, there are new and exciting varieties to play with, and different, wonderful ways to cook them. Keeping these grains and things on hand, either precooked or canned, allows them to be true team players—rescuing countless meals, always ready to spring into action and make any breakfast, lunch, or dinner that much more satisfying.

While I do, of course, love the occasional healthyish grain bowl or herby grain salad, I really enjoy doubling down on their heartiness, bolstering them with thick-cut bacon, spicy sausage, or garlicky lamb. Whether I'm reaching for chewy short grains, like spelt or wheat berries, or long, starchy noodles, I tend to treat them similarly, which is to say I enjoy a high ratio of grain to other stuff. This means that in every bite of spelt with sausage and kale (page 130), there are equal parts spelt, sausage, and kale, and with each pasta dish, whether it's squid with lemon (page 156) or anchovies and tomato (page 153), there's no noodle left behind.

# Crispy Chickpeas and Lamb
# with Greens and Garlicky Yogurt

*Serves 4*

## GARLICKY YOGURT
1 cup full-fat or 2% Greek yogurt
1 garlic clove, finely grated
1 tablespoon fresh lemon juice
Kosher salt and freshly ground black
    pepper

## CHICKPEAS AND LAMB
1 large or 2 small bunches Swiss chard,
    mustard greens, or kale
6 tablespoons olive oil
12 ounces ground lamb
3 garlic cloves, finely chopped
1 teaspoon cumin seed
Kosher salt and freshly ground black
    pepper
1 (15-ounce) can chickpeas, drained
    and rinsed
1 teaspoon crushed red pepper flakes
Fresh tomatoes, quartered, or Olive
    Oil–Roasted Tomatoes (page 38),
    for serving

**NOTE:** I've tried to cheat the amount of olive oil here, always astonished that I'd need that much to get the chickpeas to be truly delicious, but it's true. With too little oil, they'll burn before they crisp and become soggy rather than crunchy.

**DO AHEAD:** Garlicky yogurt can be made 5 days ahead and refrigerated; just know the garlic flavor will intensify.

When I was little, I would eat chickpeas out of the can, unrinsed and unseasoned. In college, when a salad bar was my main source of sustenance, my "salad" was generally just a bowl of chickpeas covered in Italian dressing. (Ew, right? But let's be honest, I probably still would eat that.) Now I eat them cooked in lots of olive oil with thinly sliced cloves of garlic until they're golden brown and crispy. Often, I just toss them with greens and top them with a fried egg, but when I want ground meat, I'll turn the chickpeas into a legitimate dinner with crispy spiced lamb and garlicky yogurt.

**1 MAKE THE YOGURT SAUCE:** Combine the yogurt, garlic, and lemon juice in a small bowl. Season with salt and black pepper and set aside.

**2 MAKE THE CHICKPEAS AND LAMB:** Separate the leaves and stems from your greens, then thinly slice the stems and tear the leaves into 2-inch-ish pieces and set aside.

**3** Heat 2 tablespoons of the olive oil in a large skillet over medium-high heat. Add the lamb, garlic, and cumin, and season with salt and black pepper.

**4** Using a wooden spoon or spatula, break up the lamb as it cooks until it's browned and crispy, 8 to 10 minutes (the lamb will not be rare here; that's more than okay because it will be crispy, and in times like these, crispy is better than rare). Using a slotted spoon, transfer the lamb to a bowl, leaving the drippings behind.

**5** Combine the remaining 4 tablespoons olive oil, the chickpeas, and red pepper flakes in the skillet with the lamby drippings and season with salt and black pepper. Cook, shaking the skillet occasionally, until the chickpeas are very well browned and starting to crisp up, 8 to 10 minutes. Return the lamb to the skillet and toss with the other ingredients, letting everything mingle together. Remove from heat and transfer to a large serving bowl, leaving anything in the skillet behind (you're not done with that skillet).

**6** Add the chopped stems to the skillet and season with salt and black pepper. Cook a minute or two, just to soften slightly; they should stay pretty crunchy and fresh. Add the leaves and toss to coat until just wilted, 30 seconds or so. Season with salt and black pepper, if needed.

**7** To assemble a very lovely dinner bowl, smear yogurt sauce onto the bottoms of four bowls and top with the chickpea and lamb mixture, sautéed greens, and tomatoes.

# Split Pea Salad

*Serves 4*

¾ cup dried green (or split) peas
Kosher salt
1½ cups shelled fresh (or frozen and thawed) peas
½ pound slab or thick-cut bacon, cut into ½-inch pieces
¾ pound small new potatoes, golf ball size or smaller, quartered
Freshly ground black pepper
1 tablespoon white wine vinegar, plus more as needed
2 tablespoons whole-grain mustard
¼ cup fresh chives, coarsely chopped

**NOTE:** If you can't find split peas, other legumes or grains like lentils, spelt, or barley also work here.

**DO AHEAD:** The salad can be made 1 day ahead and refrigerated.

Anyone who's ever driven up or down California's 101 Freeway near San Luis Obispo knows about the restaurant Pea Soup Andersen's. When I lived in Santa Cruz right after high school, I'd eat there on my way to or from Los Angeles, always ordering the split pea soup, because how could you not? Nothing there looks especially good, especially not the split pea soup, but hot damn if it isn't tasty. This recipe has nothing to do with that place, other than it's an obvious homage to split pea soup—one of the most delicious and ugly foods out there.

**1** Cook the dried peas in a large pot of salted boiling water until they're tender but not yet split, 30 to 35 minutes. Drain and place in a large bowl along with the fresh peas.

**2** Cook the bacon in a large skillet over medium heat until it is crispy and most of the fat has rendered out, 8 to 10 minutes. Using a slotted spoon, transfer the bacon (leaving the fat in the skillet) to the bowl with the peas.

**3** Add the potatoes to the same skillet and season with salt and pepper. Cook, stirring occasionally, until the potatoes are completely tender and golden brown on all sides, 10 to 15 minutes. Remove from the heat and add the vinegar and mustard, tossing the potatoes to coat and getting any of those awesome bacony potato bits into the mix.

**4** Scrape everything from the skillet into the bowl with the peas and add the chives. Season with salt and pepper, and toss to combine, adding more vinegar if you like your peas on the tangy side (I do).

# Spelt with Crispy Sausage, Flowering Broccoli, and Green Garlic

*Serves 4*

1½ cups spelt or farro

Kosher salt

3 tablespoons olive oil

½ pound spicy Italian sausage
(about 2 links), casings removed

6 stalks green garlic or 3 regular
garlic cloves, thinly sliced

Freshly ground black pepper

1 bunch broccoli rabe or 2 bunches
Tuscan kale, preferably the
flowering kind, if you can find it,
tough stems removed, leaves torn
into 1- to 2-inch pieces

¼ cup finely grated pecorino cheese,
plus more as needed

**DO AHEAD:** Spelt can be cooked
5 days ahead and refrigerated.

Spelt, farro, and most other whole grains are best fried in lots of fat, which I think of as a compromise between what my brain knows I want and what my body knows it needs.

The result is a grain that is chewy on the inside, lightly crunchy on the outside, and insanely delicious.

This dish of whole grains, dark leafy greens, crispy sausage, and salty pecorino is the kind of thing that isn't quite a main course and not quite a side dish, although I would happily eat it as either. If you're able, seek out the flowering varieties of broccoli rabe or kale that will pop up in early spring, although you can find them well into fall on occasion. The flowers on both are bright yellow, slightly spicy, and take this dish from kind of rustic to kind of posh.

**1** Cook the spelt in a large pot of salted boiling water until very tender, 45 to 50 minutes (more like 30 to 35 for farro), tasting along the way for doneness; grains really do vary quite a bit from package to package. Drain and set aside.

**2** Heat the oil in a large skillet over medium heat. Add the sausage, breaking it up into bite-sized pieces. Cook, stirring occasionally, until browned and crisp, 5 to 8 minutes. Add the green garlic and cook a minute or two, just to take the garlicky edge off (if you're using regular garlic, cook a minute or two longer).

**3** Turn the heat up to medium-high, add the cooked spelt, and season with salt and pepper. Cook, tossing occasionally, until the spelt starts to crisp up but is still chewy inside, 5 to 8 minutes. Test a grain or two; keep cooking if it needs it.

**4** Add the broccoli rabe in batches, stirring to coat it in the sausage fat and mix with the spelt, letting it wilt between additions. Season with salt and pepper, and add the pecorino and stir to evenly distribute. Divide among bowls and top with more pecorino, as needed.

# Spiced Black Lentil Salad with Oil-Packed Tuna, Radishes, and Purple Potatoes

*Serves 4*

**2 large eggs**
**¼ pound fresh green beans, ends trimmed**
**Kosher salt**
**¼ pound small purple or yellow potatoes**
**1 tablespoon fresh lemon juice**
**Freshly ground black pepper**
**Spiced Lentils with Spring Onions (page 133), plus any additional spice oil**
**6 to 8 ounces oil-packed tuna**
**4 radishes, preferably a mix of watermelon and regular, chopped or sliced**
**½ cup fresh dill, cilantro, tarragon, and/or parsley, tender stems and leaves**
**2 lemons, halved**

This is a sort of fridge-clean-out salad that always ends up looking fancier than it ought to. If I've got leftover green beans, I blanch them. Potatoes about to turn green? I steam 'em. That way, I'm moments away from an almost intentional niçoise salad. Yes, the spiced lentils here make this a truly special version, but if you have any cooked lentils and some good canned tuna on hand, this works with just about anything else you might have lying around: shaved raw fennel or broccoli, roasted carrots or sweet potatoes from the night before—you name it.

When it comes to buying the tuna, go ahead and splurge on the nice jarred or canned stuff. Just make sure it's packed in olive oil, not spring water, because, yes, there is a huge difference (the stuff packed in oil tends to be richer and more luxurious, whereas the tuna packed in water can come across as dry or watery—or worse, dry *and* watery).

**1** Prepare a medium bowl of ice water.

**2** Bring a small pot of water to a boil. Gently lower in the eggs and boil gently for 6 minutes. Transfer the eggs to the bowl of ice water and let cool completely.

**3** Blanch the green beans in a medium pot of salted boiling water until bright green and just tender, about 4 minutes.

**4** Bring 2 inches of water to a simmer in a medium pot. Place a steamer basket inside and steam the potatoes until totally tender, 10 to 15 minutes. Remove from the heat and let them cool slightly before halving or quartering them, depending on their size.

**5** Toss the potatoes, green beans, and lemon juice together in a medium bowl and season with salt and pepper.

**6** Spoon the spiced lentils into a large bowl and top with the green beans and potatoes, tuna, radishes, and herbs. Gently peel the eggs and cut them in half lengthwise, then nestle them in there. Squeeze lemon juice over the top and serve any extra spiced oil alongside.

# Sour Cream Flatbread

*Makes 4 to 6 flatbreads*

2 ¼ teaspoons active dry yeast
(from one ¼-ounce envelope)
**Pinch of sugar**
**4 cups all-purpose flour, plus more**
**for rolling**
⅓ **cup sour cream**
**2 tablespoons (¼ stick) unsalted butter,**
**melted**
**1 tablespoon kosher salt**
**Olive or vegetable oil, for cooking,**
**grilling, or baking**

**NOTE:** For those of you who are inclined to breeze past this recipe because you "don't bake," let me say that this recipe is for you. Yes, you! If we are being honest, I'm not even sure this totally qualifies as baking. I developed this dough—mostly a dump-and-stir type of thing—to be forgiving, foolproof, and versatile, so you can make it for any situation (grilling party, pizza party, regular ol' dinner party) in nearly any place there is high, direct heat (grill, oven, or skillet).

Making your own flatbread doesn't need to be an insane experience. This is not the *Tartine Bread* cookbook (although if you don't own it, you should, because it's incredible), and while, yes, making it is a bit of a time commitment, with all the dough rising and whatnot, you should think of this as a casual thing, not a total project. There's no kneading involved (just mixing), and the only tools you need are a bowl, a spoon, and your hands.

This means that if you want to make little skillet flatbreads for your turmeric-roasted lamb shoulder (page 235), you can. Or if you just want to bake up some larger pieces for topping with salty ricotta and oil-roasted mushrooms (page 38) as a pre-dinner snack, you can do that, too. Or you can decide to throw a grilled pizza party and use this dough as the crust. With a solid flatbread dough in your back pocket, you really can have it all.

**1** In a large bowl, dissolve the yeast in 1½ cups warm (warm—not hot!) water with the sugar. Using a wooden spoon, stir in the flour until no large dry spots remain. Cover the bowl with plastic wrap and let it sit about 10 minutes. It won't look much different here, you're just letting the flour hydrate.

**2** Add the sour cream, butter, and salt to the dough, and mix until all the sour cream is well blended—use your hands if you have to. You're not kneading but just making sure everything is well mixed.

**3** Cover the bowl again with plastic wrap and let it sit for 2 hours; this will relax the gluten and further hydrate the flour, making the dough easier to work with. Punch down the dough and cover. Let it rise another 2 hours in a warm, draft-free place (alternatively, instead of letting it rise at room temperature, you can refrigerate it and let it rise very slowly over 24 hours).

**4** When it comes time to roll the dough, place it on a lightly floured work surface and divide it into 4 to 6 equal-size pieces, depending on how large you want your flatbreads. If it's been refrigerated, proceed as usual; the only difference is that it'll be a bit stiffer, which actually makes it easier to work with. Oh, and when I say "lightly floured," I mean it! You just want to prevent sticking, not add more flour to the dough, which can dry it out.

**5** Working with one piece at a time, roll out the dough. Using your hands, pick up the dough and lightly stretch it over the backs of your hands, like in the movies where people spin pizza. JK—you don't have to do that, but you do want to make sure that this dough

*recipe continues*

is as thin as possible without creating too many holes, and actually picking up the dough and stretching it is the best way to do that.

## COOK ON THE STOVETOP

Cooking the dough in a cast-iron skillet will give you a soft, fluffy naan texture without the extreme puffiness of pita. Once the dough hits the hot oil, it immediately starts to bubble, getting those blackened Dalmatian-y spots. Be sure to monitor the heat levels and adjust accordingly. The more flatbreads you cook, the hotter the skillet will be, so you might need to turn down the heat as you go.

**1** Heat a large, preferably cast-iron, skillet over medium-high heat. Drizzle a bit of oil (olive or vegetable) into the skillet and lay a piece of dough flat into it. Let it cook until the dough starts to puff and bubble up in spots. Check periodically to see that it's browning and lightly charring on the underside like it's supposed to, 3 to 4 minutes; if not, turn the heat up slightly. After a few minutes, flip the dough and let it cook on the other side (no need to add more oil) until baked through, another 2 to 3 minutes.

**2** Repeat with remaining dough, adding oil as needed.

## COOK ON THE GRILL

This is the kind of thing you can use as the base for outdoor pizzas, or to serve with anything you might be grilling. Because the heat is distributed differently on the grill than in a skillet and there's not as much oil, grilling the dough won't get you anything quite as puffy as it does in the skillet, but it still has an impressive rise. Freed from the confines of the skillet, you can make these a little larger and in any weird oblong shape you please.

**1** Brush a bit of oil on a grill and heat to medium-high. Place the dough directly on the oiled grates, flipping it once it's well charred on one side, 3 to 4 minutes. Cook on the other side until it, too, is lightly charred, another 3 minutes.

**2** Repeat with the remaining dough.

## COOK IN THE OVEN

This will yield a bready, crackery-type flatbread that's an impressive golden brown. The crunchy texture makes it ideal for topping with things like ricotta and roasted mushrooms, and eating like toast.

**1** Preheat the oven to 500°F. Drizzle a baking sheet with lots of olive oil and place 2 or 3 pieces of dough on it, drizzling the tops with more olive oil.

**2** Bake until the flatbreads are puffed and golden brown and crisped, 8 to 10 minutes.

**3** Repeat with the remaining dough.

# Olive Oil–Fried Lentils with Cherry Tomatoes and a Chile-Fried Egg

*Serves 4*

1 ¼ cups black beluga, Puy, green, or
   brown lentils
Kosher salt
¼ small red onion, thinly sliced
1 teaspoon Asian fish sauce
2 tablespoons fresh lime juice
Freshly ground black pepper
¼ cup plus 2 tablespoons olive oil
4 garlic cloves, thinly sliced
1 shallot, very thinly sliced
1 pint cherry or Sun Gold tomatoes,
   stems removed, halved
2 cups tender parsley or cilantro leaves
   and stems, coarsely chopped
4 large eggs
½ teaspoon crushed red pepper flakes
½ cup roasted, salted peanuts, chopped
1 lime, quartered, for serving

**NOTE:** When it comes to this specific treatment, I'm partial to black beluga or Puy lentils, which are a very cute, small shape. Other types, especially orange or yellow, tend to fall apart, and while, yes, they are a lovely color, I wouldn't recommend them here.

**DO AHEAD:** Lentils can be cooked 5 days ahead and refrigerated.

Just like boiled potatoes, cooked lentils are something I keep on hand at all times, because they always seem to be the answer. Soup? Right this way. Grain salad? Come on in! Or you could make these olive oil–fried lentils, which is by far my favorite way to eat them. Essentially a vegetarian variation of the spelt on page 130 and the chickpeas on page 126, the idea is that you should be crisping up all your grains and legumes in lots of olive oil, and lentils are no exception.

These guys also get treated to some sweet little bursts of tomatoes; tons of herbs; crunchy, salty peanuts; and, of course, a crispy fried egg. And sure, while sometimes I feel that throwing a fried egg onto just any ol' thing is a bit of a crutch, it really does serve a purpose here: the frizzled, frilly whites add even more texture and the runny yolk sauces everything up. And there's the added bonus of a quick chile-infused oil to drizzle over the whole thing.

**1** Cook the lentils in a pot of salted water until they're cooked through but still al dente, 15 to 20 minutes (cooking time will vary depending on the type of lentils). Drain and set aside.

**2** Combine the onion, fish sauce, and lime juice in a small bowl; season with salt and black pepper and set aside.

**3** Heat ¼ cup of the oil in a large skillet over medium-high heat. Add the garlic and shallot and season with salt and black pepper. Cook until the garlic is lightly toasted and the shallots are translucent and starting to brown, about 3 minutes.

**4** Add the tomatoes and season them with salt and black pepper. Cook, shaking the skillet occasionally, until the tomatoes have begun to pop and let out some of their juices, about 4 minutes. Add the lentils and season with salt and black pepper. Cook, shaking the skillet every minute or two, until the lentils have started to look a bit dry and crisp at the edges, 8 to 10 minutes. Remove from the heat and add the herbs and red onion mixture, along with any juices in the bowl, tossing to coat. Divide the lentils evenly among four bowls and wipe out the skillet.

**5** Heat the remaining 2 tablespoons olive oil and fry your eggs till they get those crispy edges (see page 116 if you don't know what I'm talking about), and then add the red pepper flakes, swirling the skillet so they sizzle in the oil. Top each bowl of lentils with a fried egg, drizzling them with the chile oil from the skillet. Sprinkle the peanuts on top and serve with lime wedges for squeezing.

# Four-Bean Salad with Green Romesco

*Serves 4 to 6*

½ **pound green beans, trimmed and cut into 2-inch pieces**
1 **lemon, seeds removed, thinly sliced**
**Kosher salt and freshly ground black pepper**
1 **cup Green Romesco (page 21)**
¼ **cup olive oil**
1 **(15-ounce) can black-eyed peas, drained and rinsed**
1 **(15-ounce) can cannellini beans, drained and rinsed**
1 **(15-ounce) can butter beans, drained and rinsed**
1 **cup tender parsley leaves and stems, coarsely chopped**
½ **cup fresh dill leaves, coarsely chopped**

**DO AHEAD:** Bean salad can be made 3 days ahead and refrigerated.

From Memorial Day to Labor Day, bean salads in various forms are in my constant rotation. They are the ultimate do-ahead thing to bring to a barbecue or rooftop party; I've even packed them into ziplock bags and taken them to the beach. They get better the longer they sit, they don't mind being held at room temperature (or even a little warmer than that, should they get left in the sun), and they can be thrown together in less than ten minutes. Because canned beans are so hearty, they need a really assertive dressing to get the point across. Think very salty, very tangy, very spicy, or very herby.

To avoid this becoming a total starch bomb, the inclusion of the fresh beans is very important. Come summertime, you've got a lot of options: skinny haricots verts, fat Romano beans, or classic, stemmy green beans—and all work here. Lightly bruising them with salt and lemon helps them not only soften but also release some of their natural juiciness, which contributes to the dressing of the other beans. When it comes to the canned beans, feel free to mix and match the types, using whatever you have on hand; just make sure you've got four different types of beans all around; otherwise, it's just a regular ol' three-bean salad.

1  Place the green beans in a large ziplock bag along with the lemon slices and season with salt and pepper.

2  Using a rolling pin or heavy skillet, smash the beans until they're bruised and nearly falling apart (this is very cathartic).

3  Transfer the beans and lemon to a large bowl along with any juices.

4  Add the Romesco, olive oil, and all the canned beans. Toss to coat, seasoning with more salt and pepper. Add the parsley and dill and toss to coat again.

# Kinda-Sweet Granola
# with Coconut and Turmeric

*Makes about 6 cups*

3 cups rolled oats

3 large egg whites

2 cups unsweetened coconut flakes
　　or shredded coconut

1 cup chopped pistachios, almonds,
　　walnuts, or pecans

½ cup millet, quinoa, or white sesame
　　seeds

½ cup maple syrup, honey, or agave

⅓ cup coconut oil or olive oil

1½ teaspoons ground turmeric

1 teaspoon ground cinnamon

1 teaspoon kosher salt

**DO AHEAD:** Granola can be made
1 week ahead and stored in an airtight
container at room temperature.

I want my granola to be lightly (very lightly) sweetened, vaguely spiced, and really, really crunchy. This one is, thanks to things like coconut flakes, millet, and some egg whites, which are there to keep things crisp and light.

This recipe is super flexible. Think of it as a general guideline for texture and flavor when making granola, which is why there are so many options offered. The point is that granola should be a good balance of oats (about half) and then a mix of other wonderful, crunchy, flavorful things like nuts, seeds, and uncooked grains. If dried fruit is your thing, add some chopped dried cherries, dates, or apricots at the end for a chewier texture.

**1** Preheat the oven to 325°F. Line a rimmed baking sheet with parchment paper.

**2** Combine the oats, egg whites, coconut flakes, pistachios, millet, maple syrup, coconut oil, turmeric, cinnamon, and salt in a medium bowl, and toss to mix until everything is evenly coated.

**3** Spread the mixture onto the prepared baking sheet and bake, stirring every 15 minutes or so, until everything is golden brown and crisped, 50 to 60 minutes.

**4** Let cool completely and break any large clumps into smaller pieces before storing in glass jars or ziplock bags.

# Decidedly Not-Sweet Granola

*Makes about 5 cups*

1½ cups rolled oats

1 cup raw sunflower seeds

1 cup raw pumpkin seeds

1 cup buckwheat groats

½ cup flaxseeds

½ cup black or white sesame seeds

¼ cup nigella seed (if unavailable, use
   more black or white sesame seeds)

3 large egg whites

⅓ cup olive oil, peanut oil, or
   grapeseed oil

¼ cup maple syrup

¼ cup caraway or fennel seed

2 tablespoons Aleppo pepper
   (optional)

2 tablespoons soy sauce

2 teaspoons kosher salt

Freshly ground black pepper

**DO AHEAD:** Granola can be made
1 week ahead and stored in an airtight
container at room temperature.

Aside from eating this for breakfast over yogurt with cucumbers (page 112), this granola is really great to use like croutons in salads as well as for plain old out-of-hand snacking. I don't want to push this recipe too hard, because it'll seem like I have some sort of savory granola agenda, but just know that it's one of the few things in this book that is in my pantry at all times.

Like the sweet version on the facing page, this one gets its crunch from egg whites, and the ingredients are rather flexible. I like to pack as much variety into this as humanly possible, always adding a new seed or grain when I have them on hand, and you should feel free to do the same. The soy sauce here not only adds some good old-fashioned saltiness, but its residual sugars also help everything caramelize and stick together, which is nice since this contains way less sweetener than a regular granola.

**1** Preheat the oven to 325°F. Line a rimmed baking sheet with parchment paper.

**2** Combine the oats, sunflower seeds, pumpkin seeds, buckwheat, flaxseeds, sesame seeds, nigella seed, egg whites, oil, maple syrup, caraway seed, Aleppo pepper (if using), soy sauce, and salt in a medium bowl and toss to mix until everything is evenly coated. Season with plenty of black pepper.

**3** Spread the mixture onto the prepared baking sheet and bake, stirring every 15 minutes or so, until everything is golden brown and toasty, 45 to 55 minutes. Let cool completely and break any large clumps into smaller pieces before storing in glass jars or ziplock bags.

**Buckwheat**

I find buckwheat groats (aka kasha) to be far more enjoyable simply toasted rather than cooked. Nutty and roasty, with a kind of airy, crunchy texture that reminds me of those half-popped popcorn kernels, they're really quite a revelation. Thrown into a batch of sweet or savory granola (opposite and above, respectively) or used to finish an otherwise minimally textured pasta (like the one with brown-buttered mushrooms on page 148), buckwheat groats offer incomparable crunch with quiet flavor, earning them a place on my "crunchy things I like to put on stuff" shelf, right alongside coarse bread crumbs, toasted nuts, and seeds. Fair warning: they are impossible not to snack on, so when toasting for future use, make extra.

# Dried Beans

There are lots of opinions on whether you need to soak beans before cooking, or what secret ingredients (*cough,* baking soda, *cough*) you can add to speed up the cooking process. In response, I will say this: I have soaked, I have not soaked. I have added secret ingredients, and I have also not. I've simmered, I've accidentally boiled, I've pressure cooked, I've slow cooked.

Regardless of the things I do to them, when I simmer dried beans in liquid, the beans always get cooked. Soaking them beforehand does help them cook more evenly (and maybe *a touch* faster), and because it's generally no big deal, I do it. But I've also forgotten, and if I'm using high-quality dried beans, they still manage to turn out pretty great.

There seems to be only one circumstance where dried beans will not cook, and that is when they are old. But why would anyone have old beans? Well, you could be buying them from a store with little turnover, so they sit on the shelf forever. Or you could be like me and have a bean-hoarding problem.

Some people bring back magnets or shot glasses as souvenirs from trips they take. I like to bring back dried beans. I treasure them so much that I can't bring myself to actually cook them, so they sit in a cute jar on my shelf. When people ask, "What are those beans?" I say, "Oh, those are

from a market in Italy," or "I got them at this cute shop in Bolinas," which makes me feel well traveled, even if I only went once, seven years ago.

When it gets cold out (also known as "bean-cooking season") and the weather is too gross for me to leave the house, the beans on the shelf stare at me. "Now is the time you will cook us!" they say. And because I have nothing else in the house, I think, "Yes! It is!" I soak, I simmer, I whisper to them lovingly. And they don't cook. I add more water, I simmer on the lowest possible setting, I cover them with a lid, I whisper some more. And nothing. No softness, no signs of tender, creamy insides. Anyone who's waited for a subway train, bus, or other form of public transportation knows the feeling: you stare down the tunnel or street and think "Is that a light? I think it's coming!" and it turns out to be another car or just a light in the tunnel. I periodically check the pot, grabbing one bean with a spoon and convincing myself that maybe it is softening. So I keep simmering. And nothing ever happens, so about seven hours later, I end up tossing the whole thing and eating a bowl of pasta.

The moral of the story: Always use the freshest dried beans you can get your hands on, because old beans, no matter how well traveled, will never cook.

# Special Beans in Tomato Broth with Slab Bacon

*Serves 4*

1 pound dried beans, preferably an heirloom variety, such as cranberry, scarlet runner, gigante, or corona (see Note)
¼ cup olive oil
8 ounces slab bacon, sliced 1 inch thick
1 pound tomatoes, halved crosswise
1 head of garlic, halved crosswise
2 large shallots or 1 large yellow onion, halved
6 anchovy fillets
4 sprigs fresh thyme, rosemary, marjoram, and/or oregano
1 hunk of Parmesan rind (optional—if you've got one)

**NOTE:** Presoaked beans can also be drained and frozen in a ziplock bag.

**NOTE:** Making your own beans from dried will give you life-changing baked beans, or the start of what could be an amazing soup (the liquid they simmer in turns into a fantastic broth), or simply use them as you would use canned beans in salads (page 139) or simmered in some spicy garlicky oil to spoon over grilled squid and ripe tomatoes (page 183).

**DO AHEAD:** Beans will keep for 1 week, covered and refrigerated in their own liquid.

I am not the kind of person who will tell you that you should only be making bean dishes from dried beans.

And yet. There is something remarkably special about going the extra mile to seek out some cool, dried heirloom bean you've never heard of before, giving it a good soak, and simmering it with a fat hunk of bacon and other earthly delights. Cooking with dried means you get to control the texture and flavor them from the inside out. Are you an herby, al dente–bean kind of person, or do you prefer them spicy and on the softer side? If you don't cook your own, how will you ever know?

Dried beans also make great contraband when traveling from places like Italy and Mexico, but you didn't hear it from me.

**1** Place the beans in a large pot or bowl and cover with 2 inches of cold water. Let sit at least overnight or up to 2 days (see Note).

**2** When you're ready to cook these glorious legumes, drain them completely of their soaking water (or defrost your frozen beans) and set them aside.

**3** Heat the olive oil in a large pot over medium heat and add the bacon. Cook, turning occasionally, until you've got a nice bit of fat in the pot, 5 to 8 minutes. If the bacon is browning too quickly, turn down the heat; you want to render the fat before the bacon totally browns.

**4** Add the tomatoes, garlic, and shallots, cut-side down, and cook, undisturbed, until they've started to brown (the bacon will have started to brown a bit too, which is okay), about 10 minutes. Add the anchovies, soaked beans, thyme, Parmesan rind (if using), and 8 cups water.

**5** Bring to a simmer and reduce the heat to medium-low. Cook gently (no need to cover), never letting the water come to a full boil, for about 2 hours, adding water, if needed, to keep the beans submerged.

**6** Check the beans, and once they're tender to your liking (some people like them really, really soft; if so, keep cooking), remove them from the heat and let them cool completely in their cooking liquid.

# Clam Pasta
# with Chorizo and Walnuts

*Serves 4*

Kosher salt
½ cup raw walnuts
1 cup fresh flat-leaf parsley leaves,
    chopped
6 garlic cloves, finely chopped
1 lemon
Freshly ground black pepper
12 ounces linguine, fettuccine, or
    spaghetti
2 tablespoons olive oil
2 links fresh chorizo or spicy Italian
    sausage (6 to 8 ounces)
1½ pounds littleneck clams or cockles,
    scrubbed and rinsed

**DO AHEAD:** Walnut gremolata can be made 1 day ahead and refrigerated. Let it come to room temperature before using.

When I crave pasta, most of the time I'm specifically craving clam pasta. The briny liquid, the clams all tangled in strands of linguine like some sort of seaweed situation—it just gets me every time. Even at the most suspect red-sauce Italian restaurant, I'll always order the *linguine alle vongole,* because like pizza, even at its worst, linguine with clams is still pretty great. This version, made with a bit of meaty, spicy chorizo, is just straight-up great.

While it would be hard to go wrong here with this combination of ingredients, the secret to the success of this dish is sauciness. You'll get there, in part, thanks to the briny liquid produced by the clams, but mostly by finishing the pasta in the pasta water, so make sure you hold on to that.

**1** Preheat the oven to 350°F. Bring a large pot of salted water to a boil.

**2** Toast the walnuts on a rimmed baking sheet until they're golden brown and fragrant, about 10 minutes; set aside to cool. Once cool, finely chop and place them in a small bowl with the parsley and a pinch of the chopped raw garlic. Zest the lemon and add it to the bowl; quarter the lemon and reserve it for later. Season with salt and pepper and set aside.

**3** Cook the pasta in the boiling water to al dente according to the package instructions; you want some bite left so it can finish cooking in the skillet.

**4** Meanwhile, heat the olive oil in a large skillet or heavy-bottomed pot over medium heat. Add the chorizo and cook until it's browned and just cooked through, about 5 minutes. Add the rest of the garlic and season with salt and pepper. Cook, stirring every so often, until the garlic just begins to turn golden brown, about 2 minutes. Add the clams and cover the skillet, shaking it occasionally to encourage even cooking. Check after 3 minutes; all the clams should be starting to open. If they are not, give them another minute.

**5** Drain the pasta, reserving about 2 cups of the cooking water (I actually just remove the pasta with tongs, leaving the water behind).

**6** Add the pasta and 1 cup of the cooking water to the skillet and toss to combine everything. Cook over medium-high heat, tossing and shaking the skillet pretty intensely, until a rich, thick, glossy sauce forms (there is starch in that pasta water, which is helping to thicken the sauce), about 5 minutes. Season with salt and pepper. Sprinkle the walnut mixture over the pasta and serve with the lemon wedges alongside for squeezing.

# Whole-Wheat Pasta with Brown-Buttered Mushrooms, Buckwheat, and Egg Yolk

Serves 4

Kosher salt

⅓ cup buckwheat groats

1 pound whole-wheat pasta (noodles or short shapes both work here)

6 tablespoons (¾ stick) unsalted butter

2 tablespoons olive oil

4 garlic cloves, thinly sliced

2 pounds of your favorite mushroom varieties (such as chanterelle, maitake, oyster, trumpet, morel, shiitake, or lobster), cut or torn into bite-sized pieces

Freshly ground black pepper

½ small shallot, finely chopped

2 ounces Parmesan or pecorino cheese, for grating or shaving

4 large egg yolks from very fresh eggs

This recipe is a prime example of how I think pasta should be eaten. Basically equal parts pasta to whatever's in it—especially when it comes to vegetables, and especially when it comes to mushrooms—plus something crunchy sprinkled over the top (here, toasted buckwheat) and a saucy something (here, raw egg yolks).

Speaking of mushrooms, do you know how many mushroom varieties there are? About four million. Even if that's not true (it's not), I feel like I'm always discovering a new type that makes me glad it's socially acceptable to eat fungus. My favorites are the meatier yet more delicately flavored varieties like oyster, maitake, and king trumpet. They contain less water, which not only means less shrinkage, but, more important, higher crisping potential. That said, this recipe works with all types of mushrooms, from the common button to the royal chanterelle, so use what you can find.

**1** Set a large pot of salted water to a boil.

**2** Toast the buckwheat in a large dry skillet over medium-high heat, shaking the skillet occasionally, until all the grains look toasted and smell really fragrant and nutty, about 4 minutes. Transfer to a small bowl and set aside (save the skillet).

**3** Cook the pasta in the boiling water to al dente according to the package instructions. Drain the pasta (no need to reserve any pasta water here).

**4** Melt the butter in that large skillet over medium-high heat until it's foamy and starting to brown, about 3 minutes. Add the olive oil, garlic, and mushrooms. Toss to coat in the browned butter and season with salt and pepper. Cook, tossing occasionally (or using a wooden spoon to stir), until the mushrooms are properly browned and starting to crisp, 12 to 18 minutes. Depending on the type of mushrooms, this can take a while; for example, frilly maitakes and meaty oyster mushrooms will brown faster than chanterelles or lobster mushrooms, which tend to contain more water.

**5** Add the drained pasta and shallots and toss to coat. Cook another minute or two, just to get everything knowing each other in the skillet. Season with salt and pepper, and divide among four plates or bowls. Top with Parmesan and the toasted buckwheat. Plop an egg yolk down into the center of each plate, breaking it to create a sauce.

# WEDNESDAY PASTA NIGHT

**T**he first thing you learn how to cook is rarely the first thing you learn how to cook well. Case in point: Technically, tomato sauce was the first thing I learned how to cook, yet it took me nearly fifteen years to make what I would consider a really good tomato sauce. When you're trying to replicate something that's important to you, the stakes are admittedly higher: Mom's trout, Dad's matzo brei, and Stephanie Mayerson's tomato sauce.

Stephanie Mayerson is the mom of my best friend, Kate. Kate and I met and became inseparable on the first day of kindergarten, so I've known Steph just as long. I spent so much time at the Mayersons' house growing up, basically I had a standing reservation at their dinner table every Wednesday. That's when my mom would spend the evening volunteering at an animal sanctuary (which is another story, better suited for my memoir that I'll never write).

Typically a salmon-and-brown-rice kind of family, they did the pasta thing only once a week, always on Wednesdays. In the beginning, it was a coincidence, likely chosen because it was easy to make, especially with an extra mouth to feed. Stephanie would apologize, "Didn't we have pasta last week? I am SO sorry!" Then, over time, she embraced it, I came to expect it, and Pasta Wednesday was born. We weren't super creative on the branding of our new ritual, but it stuck, and for several years to come, there was hardly ever a Wednesday without pasta.

Because Kate and I went to different high schools, the weekly dinners became less regular as we got older, and I started to miss the taste of that tangy and perfectly garlicky tomato sauce. At home, my mom was such a great cook that it never occurred to me to, you know, cook anything myself. But the absence of my weekly pasta was starting to get to me.

So I decided I'd make it myself, and this was really the first time I had the desire to cook something. By myself. From scratch.

Since my culinary experience was limited to removing sausage casings for my mom's stuffed mushrooms or trimming the leaves of artichokes, I had no idea what I was doing. Of course, that didn't stop me from abandoning all obligations to schoolwork so that I could dedicate myself to getting this sauce right. It was VERY important, obviously.

The pasta was the easy part: dried spaghetti. Nailed it! Then came the sauce, which was slightly more challenging. Steph made hers from canned stewed tomatoes, caramelized red onions, chopped garlic, fresh basil, and, of course, lots of olive oil. My mom would pick up the ingredients and she bought me a basil plant at the nursery so I could have fresh leaves (not knowing the difference, I wanted "the purple one," which was Thai basil and definitely not what you'd use in an Italian pasta dish, but whatever).

For a spell, I was making this sauce once or twice a week. Sometimes not even with the intention of eating—I was cooking it just so I could get it right. Well, edible (delicious, even) results were produced, but I was never able to quite dial it in. Eventually, my interests crawled beyond Stephanie's sauce and I became fixated with perfecting other things in the kitchen, like biscuits (page 00) and re-creating the Newman's Own dressings (never dialed that one in, either). But that didn't stop me from making tomato sauce: My own version, which had yellow onions, whole peeled tomatoes, and lots of crushed red pepper flakes, was good, but different.

While I was testing the recipes for this book, I became obsessed with the oil-roasted tomatoes on page 38. I ate them with fried eggs, with crispy chickpeas and lamb (page 126), chopped in grain salads, and just as a side to roasted chickens. For whatever reason, it never occurred to me to use them for pasta until one night I had a surplus of oil-roasted tomatoes and a craving for something extremely carby. I slapped the sauce together with such casualness that I think I nearly dropped the bowl on the floor when it tasted, unmistakably, just like Pasta Wednesday.

The trick, I realized, was in two places: Number one, the slow-roasted tomatoes. Obviously these things are magical, but combined with the leftover garlicky olive oil and caramelized, golden bits that I scraped into the skillet, I somehow replicated the exact flavor of the tomatoes used in Stephanie's sauce (the stewed kind, not the whole, canned kind). Number two: the red onion. I didn't have any yellow onion, so I used red, something I'd never ever do. Why? I honestly don't know, it just always felt wrong. But it was right. So very, very right. The flavor it took on as it cooked in the skillet, all the onion-y bite fading into a caramelly sweetness that other alliums just can't seem to mimic.

This just goes to show how I literally never listen (I'm sure she told me to use red onion and even the brand of tomatoes to use), but eventually, I figured it out. Sure, it took me nearly half my life to figure out how to make this sauce, but I can say that it was worth it since it was the sauce that inspired me to cook in the first place. I've since added some anchovies, because I truly believe they make everything (especially tomato sauce) better, and kept the crushed red pepper flakes (because I like everything a little spicy), but the recipe on page 153 is as close as I've ever come to Stephanie Mayerson's original, which means now I can have Pasta Wednesday literally any day of the week.

# Roasted Tomato
# and Anchovy Bucatini

*Serves 4*

**Kosher salt**
**¼ cup olive oil, plus more for drizzling**
**½ small red onion, very thinly sliced**
**Crushed red pepper flakes**
**4 anchovy fillets**
**2 tablespoons tomato paste**
**1 recipe Olive Oil–Roasted Tomatoes**
      **(page 38) or 1 (28-ounce) can**
      **whole peeled tomatoes, crushed**
**12 ounces bucatini or spaghetti**
**Lots of grated Parmesan cheese**

**DO AHEAD:** Tomato sauce can be made 5 days ahead and refrigerated or 1 month ahead and frozen.

I put this recipe in here because, while yes, this simple combination of anchovies melted into slow-roasted tomatoes with barely caramelized red onion is truly revelatory, it's the dish that inspired a teenaged me to start cooking in the first place (thanks, Stephanie Mayerson!), and I'm overly sentimental.

While you could use canned tomatoes here, the real joy comes from using tomatoes slow roasted in olive oil. As they roast, their sugars come out and caramelize, water evaporates, and flavors concentrate, making a superlative tomato sauce. When I'm blessed with an abundance of tomatoes in the summer, I like to make this sauce and freeze it so that I can eat this pasta in the coldest months, when I want it the most.

**1** Bring a large pot of salted water to a boil.

**2** Meanwhile, heat the olive oil in a large skillet or heavy-bottomed pan over medium heat. Add the onion and season with salt and a pinch of red pepper flakes. Cook, stirring occasionally, until the onion is totally cooked through but not browned, 10 to 15 minutes. Add the anchovies and stir until they've melted into the pan, about 30 seconds. Add the tomato paste and cook until it turns a brick-red color and sticks a bit to the bottom of the pan, about 90 seconds.

**3** Add the tomatoes, scraping up any bits on the bottom of the skillet. Season with salt and reduce the heat to medium-low. Cook, swirling the skillet occasionally, until the sauce thickens and it tastes so good you can hardly stand it. Add more salt and red pepper flakes if you want. Keep warm and set aside.

**4** Meanwhile, cook the pasta in the boiling water. Drain, reserving 1 cup of the pasta cooking water.

**5** Add the pasta along with ½ cup of the pasta cooking water to the skillet and toss to coat. Cook, tossing occasionally, until the pasta is really well coated, the sauce sticking to each individual noodle in a way that can only be described as perfect.

**6** Remove the skillet from the heat and transfer the pasta to a large bowl, or divide it among four smaller bowls. Top with lots of Parmesan cheese.

# The Best Baked Beans

*Serves 6*

¼ cup plus 2 tablespoons olive oil
4 ounces slab bacon, sliced into
  ½-inch pieces
1 medium yellow onion or 3 leeks,
  white and light green parts,
  thinly sliced
Kosher salt and freshly ground pepper
4 garlic cloves, finely chopped
1 tablespoon fresh thyme, marjoram or
  oregano leaves, coarsely chopped
¼ cup dry white wine
4 cups cooked beans (from Special
  Beans in Tomato Broth, page 145)
  or 3 (15-ounce) cans cannellini,
  navy, or butter beans, drained and
  rinsed
1 cup bean cooking liquid (or vegetable
  or chicken broth)
½ cup finely grated Parmesan cheese
2 cups Fresh Bread Crumbs (page 24)

Disclaimer: These are not Boston Baked Beans. They are not sweet, and there is no ketchup. They are deeply savory, bacony, and cheesy, and have a delightfully crunchy topping. Maybe it's because I'm from California, but I think they are better than anything you can find in the Northeast. If you like things on the spicy side, feel free to add some crushed chiles to the beans or even the bread crumbs.

**1** Preheat the oven to 400°F.

**2** Heat ¼ cup olive oil in a large skillet over medium heat. Add the bacon and cook until it's starting to brown and lots of the fat has rendered out, 5 to 8 minutes. Add the onion and season with salt and pepper. Cook, stirring occasionally, until the onion is softened and deeply caramelized, 15 to 20 minutes. Add the garlic and thyme and cook a minute or two, just to soften and take the edge off. Add the wine and scrape up any bits on the bottom of the skillet. Cook until the wine has reduced by about half. Add the beans, their cooking liquid, and the Parmesan. Season with salt and lots of pepper. Transfer everything to a 2-quart baking dish.

**3** Mix the bread crumbs with the remaining 2 tablespoons oil and season with salt and pepper. Scatter over the beans and bake until the beans are bubbling and the bread crumbs are golden, 30 to 35 minutes. Let cool slightly before eating.

# Spicy, Garlicky White Beans

*Serves 4*

¼ cup olive oil or chicken fat
6 garlic cloves, thinly sliced
1 teaspoon crushed red pepper flakes
½ teaspoon fennel seed, crushed
   (optional)
1 (15-ounce) can cannellini, navy, or
   gigante beans, drained and rinsed
Kosher salt and freshly ground black
   pepper

**DO AHEAD:** Beans can be made 5 days ahead and refrigerated. Rewarm slowly before eating.

Yes, cooking dried beans from dried is great and all (especially simmered with slab bacon and tomatoes) but sometimes I just don't get it together in time to make that happen, and I don't believe I should be punished for that. The good news is that canned beans are cheap and widely available–Goya does a great job, and I hope they are around for many years, creating superlative canned bean products for all my weeknight needs. They also happen to be an excellent blank canvas for imparting other more interesting, bolder flavors like toasted chile and garlic. Slow cooking them in some super-flavorful fat (like this garlicky olive oil or the leftover chicken fat from page 229) is a quick way to breathe some much needed excitement into an otherwise pretty boring food.

**1**  Heat the olive oil, garlic, red pepper flakes, fennel seed (if using), and beans in a medium pot over medium heat. Season with salt and black pepper, and cook, stirring occasionally (being careful not to break up any of the beans), until everything begins to sizzle and smell fragrant, about 5 minutes.

**2**  Reduce the heat to medium-low and continue to cook until the garlic is browned and the skin on the beans begins to fry slightly, 15 to 20 minutes. Remove from the heat and let them hang out until you're ready to eat.

# Pasta with Crispy Squid, Lemon, and Chile

*Serves 4*

12 ounces pasta, such as a noodle like spaghetti or linguine, or a short shape like campanelle or spaccatelli

Kosher salt

6 tablespoons olive oil

¾ pound cleaned squid bodies and tentacles, bodies sliced into ¼-inch rings, tentacles halved

Freshly ground black pepper

4 garlic cloves, thinly sliced

1 lemon, thinly sliced and seeds removed

1 red Fresno chile or jalapeño pepper, thinly sliced into rings, seeds removed, if you like

1½ cups fresh dil, cilantro, basil, and/or mint leaves

**NOTE:** When you're buying squid, there is no shame in purchasing the frozen kind; most of the stuff you find at the grocery store is previously frozen and then thawed anyway. Just make sure you get a nice mix of tentacles and bodies to vary the textures. For more information on this most delicious sea creature, check out page 183.

This is sort of an all-star pasta dish for me. It's got all the hits: crispy squid, caramelized lemons, and lots of fresh chile. The key here is to give the squid the space and time it needs to brown properly. This means working in batches, being patient, and letting it do its thing in the skillet. You'll notice that despite being patted dry beforehand, squid has quite a bit of liquid in it, which tends to come out while cooking. This is okay, and while it looks like maybe your squid is simmering rather than sautéing, the liquid will evaporate and the squid will brown, and there will be dark, crispy bits on the bottom of the skillet. Those bits are what you came here for. When scraped up with a bit of pasta water, simmering along with those fresh chiles and caramelized lemon slices, they are what make this whole thing so damn delicious, creating a sauce to coat every piece of pasta, inspiring you to shout, "Squid! I finally get it!"

**1** Cook the pasta in a large pot of salted boiling water until al dente (time will vary depending on pasta type, so consult the box). Drain, reserving 1 cup of the pasta water; set aside.

**2** Meanwhile, heat 2 tablespoons of the olive oil in a large skillet over medium-high heat. Add half the squid and season with salt and pepper. Cook, stirring only a few times, until the squid is golden brown and crisped up around the edges, about 5 minutes. Transfer to a plate or bowl and set aside. Repeat with another 2 tablespoons of the olive oil and the remaining squid (no need to wipe the skillet between batches).

**3** Heat the remaining 2 tablespoons olive oil and add the garlic and lemon slices; season with salt and pepper. Cook, stirring pretty frequently, until the garlic is golden and the lemons start to caramelize around the edges, about 4 minutes. Return the squid to the skillet along with the chile pepper and stir to coat. Add the pasta, along with ½ cup of the reserved pasta water. Toss everything together, using a wooden spoon or spatula to scrape up all the browned bits on the bottom of the skillet (this is where the good stuff is).

**4** Season with salt and pepper, and cook over medium heat, tossing occasionally, until a sauce has formed (you might need to add a bit more pasta water to do this), 2 to 3 minutes. Scatter the herbs over the top right before serving.

# Baked Pasta with Artichokes, Greens, and Too Much Cheese

*Serves 6 to 8*

12 sheets lasagna noodles, fresh or dried, or 12 ounces pasta

Kosher salt

4 tablespoons olive oil, plus more for drizzling

1 large yellow onion, thinly sliced

Freshly ground black pepper

1 bunch spinach (about 10 ounces), stems removed, leaves chopped (about 3 cups)

1 bunch kale (about 8 ounces), stems removed, leaves chopped (about 4 cups)

6 garlic cloves, finely chopped

1 (14-ounce) jar marinated artichoke hearts, drained and chopped

2 cups fresh full-fat ricotta cheese

½ cup heavy cream

2 cups finely grated Parmesan or pecorino cheese (about 4 ounces), plus more as needed

8 ounces good mozzarella cheese, shredded

**DO AHEAD:** The pasta can be assembled and baked 1 day ahead, then refrigerated. Cover with foil and reheat in a 350°F oven until warmed through, 30 to 40 minutes.

I'll come right out and say that I'm really not into béchamel. Cooked flour with milk is just not my thing. Plus, to be honest, it's really annoying to make (all that whisking, the splattering—no thanks!). So instead of calling this a lasagne, which traditionally is made with béchamel, I'm calling it a baked pasta. Use lasagna noodles, use campanelle, use elbows, use any pasta you like. I won't judge.

This dish will only be as good as the cheese you use. Cheap ricotta just isn't going to cut it here, so seek out the kind that is fresh and most definitely full-fat. As for the artichoke hearts, using the marinated variety, in all their tangy glory, will make the whole dish seem a little more well seasoned, but non-marinated artichokes will also do, because with all that cheese, it's hard to go wrong. Oh, and yes: This *is* spinach artichoke dip in pasta form. You're welcome.

**1** Preheat the oven to 400°F.

**2** Working in batches, cook the sheets of pasta in a large pot of salted boiling water (if you crowd the pot, they will most definitely stick together), just to al dente, 5 to 8 minutes, depending on the brand and type of pasta; if you're using fresh pasta, it'll be more like 30 to 60 seconds, just enough to soften.

**3** Once it's ready, transfer each sheet, one by one, to a paper-towel-lined baking sheet. Don't let the pasta sheets touch or they'll stick together and your blood pressure will rise trying to get them apart (a truly impossible task). Drizzle a small amount of olive oil onto each sheet of pasta before separating each layer with paper towels. Set aside while you prepare the filling.

**4** Heat 2 tablespoons of the olive oil in a large skillet over medium heat. Add the onion and season with salt and pepper. Cook, stirring occasionally, until the onion is totally softened and deeply caramelized, 15 to 20 minutes.

**5** Working in batches, add handfuls of greens to the skillet, seasoning with salt and pepper and letting them wilt down before adding the next handful (when the skillet becomes too crowded even after wilting, transfer cooked greens to a bowl and continue wilting raw greens in the skillet). Once your last batch of greens has finished cooking, add the garlic and any cooked greens you set aside and toss to coat. Add the artichoke hearts and mix well; set aside.

*recipe continues*

**6**  Mix the ricotta, cream, and Parmesan together in a medium bowl; season with salt and pepper.

**7**  Drizzle olive oil into the bottom of a 9 × 13-inch or 3-quart baking dish. Place a layer of cooked pasta on the bottom and top with one-third of the ricotta mixture. Top with one-third of the greens and artichokes, and top that with one-third of the mozzarella. Repeat until you have a layer of pasta on the top. Drizzle with olive oil and sprinkle more Parmesan over the top.

**8**  Cover with foil and bake until everything is warmed through and the cheese has started to melt, 15 to 20 minutes. Remove the foil and raise the oven temperature to 500°F. Bake until the top is browned and the filling is bubbling along the edges, 8 to 10 minutes longer. Let cool slightly before slicing and eating.

**Fancy Pasta**

All whole-wheat pastas are not created equal, and if you're going to use it, it's worth seeking out some really good, high-quality stuff. Easier to find now more than ever, even the most popular brands are going the way of Bob's Red Mill and revisiting all those ancient grains to turn into pasta—think emmer wheat, rye, spelt, and einkorn wheat.

One of my favorite suppliers, New York–based Sfoglini, has an extensive selection of whole-wheat, spelt, and rye pastas that come in many different shapes, *plus* you can order them online. What a world!

# Cold Garlicky Pasta
# with Capers and Salsa Verde

*Serves 2*

1 tablespoon olive oil

4 garlic cloves, finely chopped

Kosher salt and freshly ground black pepper

2 tablespoons brined capers, drained and chopped

2 cups chopped greens, such as kale, spinach, or Swiss chard

3 cups leftover cooked pasta

1½ cups Another Salsa Verde (page 21)

1 lemon, halved

Flaky sea salt

I find cold pasta to be tragically underrated and pasta salad to be tragically uninteresting, which is how this dish came to be. Because it drives me crazy to have a half-opened box of pasta, especially long noodles—the top never stays closed, which means long, thin strands of dried pasta end up all over my kitchen floor, and it's a real nightmare—I'll just cook the whole box and use only what I need for that night. This means, more often than not, I'm left with at least a few cups of naked, plain cooked pasta lurking in my refrigerator.

Some people might find this leftover pasta annoying ("Why not just use tape to close the box of pasta?" you're asking), but not I. I take joy in this, knowing that, tomorrow or the next day, there will be COLD PASTA! Cold pasta for me to adorn however I please with whatever leftover roasted vegetables I have stashed, sauce I have frozen, greens I need to cook before they're past their prime, or—better yet—salsa verde I almost certainly have on hand.

Sure, you could definitely use freshly cooked pasta, or even reheat the cold pasta in a skillet or pot of hot water to great results, but you know what they say: "Leftover pasta is a dish best served cold."

**1** Heat the olive oil in a small skillet or pot over medium heat. Add the garlic and season with kosher salt and pepper. Cook, stirring, until it's just beginning to brown (but do not let it get too brown), about 2 minutes. Add the capers and toss to coat, letting them sizzle and pop slightly. Add the greens and season with kosher salt and pepper. Toss to coat, cooking just to wilt, then remove the skillet from the heat.

**2** Place the pasta in a large bowl and pour the garlic and greens over it, followed by the salsa verde, and toss to coat everything evenly, slightly warming and softening the previously chilled pasta.

**3** Squeeze lemon juice over the pasta and top with flaky sea salt.

# Cold Soba with Cucumbers, Watercress, and Sesame

*Serves 4*

Kosher salt
¼ cup white sesame seeds
1 pound soba noodles
¼ cup soy sauce, plus more as needed
2 tablespoons toasted sesame oil, plus
    more as needed
2 tablespoons unseasoned rice vinegar
1 tablespoon yuzu kosho
2 cups watercress
4 scallions, thinly sliced
2 Persian cucumbers, thinly sliced
    lengthwise
½ cup tender cilantro leaves and stems
1 lime, halved

Soba noodles are one of the few noodles that are actually better cold than hot, in my opinion. They don't have that gummy, starchy thing happening, and they stay soft and wonderful even after a sleepover in your fridge. I eat this salty, refreshing dish most often on hot summer days, when the thought of consuming anything warmer than the ambient temperature is literally out of the question.

Yuzu kosho is one of those specialty ingredients that you'll likely have to order on the Internet, but it's worth the Google search, trust me. A Japanese paste made from fermented chiles, yuzu (a citrus fruit, a more fragrant version of both lemon and lime), and salt, it's got a really unique yet vaguely familiar fermented, spicy, bright citrus flavor that makes it taste good with nearly anything (especially vinaigrettes and slaws). Thicker than hot sauce and not as spicy as sambal, a little goes a long way, which may explain why it always comes in such a teeny jar.

**1** Bring a large pot of salted water to a boil.

**2** Toast the sesame seeds in a small skillet over medium-high heat, tossing frequently, until the seeds are evenly golden brown and smell roasted, about 4 minutes. Transfer the sesame seeds to a small bowl and set aside.

**3** Cook the soba noodles in the boiling water until just done, about 5 minutes (soba cooks much faster than regular pasta, so keep an eye on it). Drain the soba and rinse it under cold water to chill completely.

**4** Meanwhile, combine the soy sauce, sesame oil, vinegar, and yuzu kosho in a small bowl. Finely chop half the watercress and add it to the soy sauce mixture, along with half the scallions.

**5** Toss the soba with the dressing and season with more soy sauce or sesame oil, if you like. Divide the soba among four bowls and top with the cucumbers, cilantro, sesame seeds, and the remaining watercress and scallions.

**6** Squeeze lime juice on top before eating.

FISH

# If my years in the editorial world taught me anything, it's that for many people, fish—for whatever reason—is a hard sell.

And I get that. When I was a kid, my dad would chase me around the house with trout heads worn like finger puppets, so I had a hard time with fish, too. But if you can sear a chicken breast or pop a baking sheet into the oven, you, too, can cook fish. And in the unlikelihood you can't, there are about a million other ways to prepare fish in a fast, delicious, inexpensive way that will make you wonder why you haven't been doing it more often.

There is something sort of magical about cooking seafood at home (especially on a weeknight) that seems simultaneously virtuous and fancy. Whipping up a perfectly crispy piece of salmon with green romesco (page 175) or a skillet of buttery shrimp with lots of herbs is the kind of thing you can feel good about eating and proud of yourself for making. The other beautiful part about exploring the world of seafood is that it truly does have range. From assertively flavored and meaty (sardines!) to briny and chewy (clams!) to delicate and tender (trout!), there's something for everyone.

In contrast to meat and vegetables (which can be a little more forgiving), where you live greatly determines the availability and quality of seafood you'll find. While these recipes call for various specific types of fish, nearly all of them include pescatarian alternatives that will work in their stead. That is to say, should you have your heart set on Scallops with Corn, Hazelnuts, and Brown Butter Chermoula (page 187), but the scallops you find look less than excellent, maybe call an audible and use shrimp instead. These recipes are flexible and meant to be cooked with whatever kind of seafood you can get your hands on.

# Shrimp in the Shells with Lots of Garlic and Probably Too Much Butter

*Serves 4*

½ cup (1 stick) unsalted butter

2 tablespoons olive oil

8 garlic cloves, thinly sliced

Kosher salt and freshly ground black pepper

1 tablespoon tomato paste

4 chiles de árbol, crushed, or
    1 teaspoon crushed red pepper flakes

1½ pounds medium head-on shrimp

1 cup chopped fresh cilantro, parsley, or basil

1 lemon, halved

Toast, for serving (optional)

**NOTE:** You can, of course, use regular medium shrimp here, although you'll only need about 1¼ pounds.

When I was growing up, my mom had a thing called the "One Bite Rule." With anything, no matter how weird or gross I thought it was, I had to have one bite. This is how I was forced into eating *uni* before the age of twelve, but I am the better for it.

So here comes a One Bite Rule recipe where I am suggesting you buy something that is (*a*) expensive and (*b*) scary for some. But hear me out: head-on shrimp in the shell are one of life's greatest pleasures. This dish is really best eaten with your hands, and the only way to describe it gets pretty graphic. If eating the shell is not your speed—it is 100 percent my speed—you gotta rip the shells off to separate the head from the body of the shrimp, and suck the juices out of the head end to get the full experience. And what a delicious experience it is. Come on. It's the One Bite Rule!

**1** Heat the butter and oil in a large skillet over medium-high heat. Once the butter starts to melt, add the garlic and season with salt and black pepper. Cook until it starts to sizzle and soften, about 3 minutes. Add tomato paste and chiles, stirring until the tomato paste begins to caramelize, about 2 minutes. Add the shrimp and 2 tablespoons water, and season with salt and black pepper, tossing to coat them in the butter-and-garlic mixture. Cook until they're bright pink and just cooked through, about 5 minutes (less if the shrimp are smaller or headless).

**2** Remove from the heat, add the herbs, and squeeze lemon over everything.

**3** Pick a shrimp out of the skillet and peel the shell away. Remove the head (you are gonna suck on the head, right?) and drag the shrimp through that garlicky butter, squeezing a little more lemon over. This is perfect with nearly burnt toast (if desired), a cold beer, or just on its own.

# Littleneck Clams with Green Garlic Butter and Leftover Wine

*Serves 4*

2 cups fresh parsley leaves (from about 1 bunch), chopped

6 tablespoons (¾ stick) unsalted butter

6 stalks green garlic, thinly sliced, or 3 regular garlic cloves, finely grated

Kosher salt and freshly ground black pepper

1 tablespoon olive oil

¼ cup dry, acidic white wine, such as Sauvignon Blanc or Pinot Blanc

3½ pounds small littleneck clams, steamers, or mussels, scrubbed and rinsed

1 (15-ounce) can white beans, such as cannellini, drained and rinsed (optional)

1 lemon, quartered, for serving

Crusty bread, for serving

**NOTE:** When choosing your clams, the smaller, the better here. The larger, chewier ones are great for things like chowder or pasta when they are pulled out and chopped, but to slurp one from the shell, you want them to be petite and tender. Littlenecks are a great choice (again, pick the smallest ones you can find, even if that means hand-picking them at the grocery store or fishmonger), but extra-small cockles would also be fun.

**DO AHEAD:** Green garlic butter can be made 1 week ahead and refrigerated.

Leftover wine is a foreign concept to most people (myself included), but in the rare event that you're left with wine that you didn't drink and it's maybe spent a day too many in the fridge, there is no better use for it than steaming clams in it. Should this never happen to you and you still wish to make this recipe, you can certainly open a fresh bottle, but then you gotta drink it.

This pretty basic parsley butter is the most complicated part of the whole recipe, and it can either be made by smashing the ingredients all together in a bowl or by using a food processor; the food processor will give you a really bright, vibrant green color (and you won't have to chop as much), but that's really the only difference. It's good with nearly every type of steamed, roasted, grilled, or boiled seafood, but mingled with that briny, pleasantly metallic clam juice and some acidic white wine, it is truly spectacular.

I would gladly sit down to a bowl of just clams for dinner, dipping hunks of almost too-crusty bread into the leftover juices, but you can also add a can of rinsed white beans to the broth at the bottom, letting them simmer for a few minutes in the juices and parsley butter before serving them alongside the clams.

**1** Combine the parsley, butter, and 2 stalks of the green garlic (or 1 garlic clove) in a food processor. Pulse until the parsley is finely chopped and well incorporated into the butter. Alternatively, finely chop the parsley and garlic and smash into the butter using a fork. Season aggressively with salt and pepper; set aside.

**2** Heat the oil in a large pot over medium heat. Add the remaining green garlic and cook, stirring occasionally, until it turns bright green (or just before it browns, if using regular garlic) and has softened, about 3 minutes. Add the wine and cook a minute or two, just to take the edge off. Add the clams and cover. Cook, shaking the pot every now and then, until the clams start to open, 5 to 10 minutes, depending on the size of your clams and your pot.

**3** Remove the pot from the heat and add the parsley butter, shaking to make sure the butter melts and gets into each clam. Transfer the clams to a large serving bowl or divide among four bowls.

**4** If using, add the beans to the pot with the clam juice and butter. Season with salt and pepper and let simmer over medium-high heat for a minute or two, just to warm through.

**5** Pour the beans (if using), melted butter, and clam juice from the pot over the clams and serve with lemon wedges for squeezing and bread for sopping up the juices.

# Grilled Branzino with Lemons All of the Ways

*Serves 4*

2 tablespoons canola oil, plus more for the (optional) grill

1 preserved lemon, homemade (page 27) or store-bought, finely chopped

1 garlic clove, finely grated

⅓ cup olive oil

1 tablespoon white wine vinegar

Kosher salt and freshly ground black pepper

3 lemons

2 (1¼-pound) branzinos, gutted and scaled

**DO AHEAD:** Lemon relish can be made 5 days ahead and refrigerated.

I find grilled, lightly charred whole fish to be so delicious on its own that coming up with a recipe for things to serve it with always seems like a disservice—with the exception of citrus, specifically beautiful, sunny, perfect lemons. And sure, three types of lemon might be a bit of overkill, but not here. They all have a role, each one providing lemon in a different and important way. The raw lemon slices season and perfume the fish from the inside; the juices of the caramelized, grilled lemons have a slightly sweet, smoky flavor that bathes the fish post-grill, and the salty, garlicky preserved lemon relish delivers punchiness in all the right salty, garlicky places.

Good news: If you don't have a grill, or the weather doesn't permit, the fish can also be roasted in the oven, served with the relish, and enjoyed all the same.

**1** Heat a well-oiled grill to medium-high heat or preheat the oven to 450°F.

**2** Combine the preserved lemon, garlic, olive oil, and vinegar in a small bowl. Season with salt and pepper and set aside.

**3** Thinly slice 1 lemon and divide the slices between the 2 fish, inserting the slices where the fish is open from cleaning (typically from the head to the middle of the belly), seasoning with salt and pepper in there while you're at it. You can tie the fish closed with butcher's twine if you like, but the lemon slices should stay put. Rub the outside of the fish with the canola oil and season with salt and pepper.

*recipe continues*

## FOR GRILLING

**1** Once the grill is as hot as it's going to get, place the fish on the grill with the backbone facing you (as opposed to the open side)— it's easier to flip it from this side. And now don't touch it for 8 to 10 minutes. After 8 minutes, you can try to flip the fish to see if the skin is charred, puffed, and crispy (it should be). If the fish is ready to be flipped, it will release easily; if it doesn't, give it a few more minutes.

**2** Once the fish is ready to be flipped, take a large, wide spatula (a fish spatula works really well here, but so does a large grilling spatula) and place it under the fish, just like you're flipping a pancake. From there, flip it so that the open side is now facing you. Continue to grill until the other side is also charred and crispy and the fish is cooked through, another 8 to 10 minutes.

**3** Meanwhile, halve the remaining 2 lemons crosswise and throw them on the grill, cut-side down, until they're charred and starting to caramelize, about 5 minutes.

**4** Serve the fish with the preserved lemon relish and roasted lemons alongside.

## FOR ROASTING

**1** Place the prepared fish on a wire rack set inside a rimmed baking sheet (or on a foil-lined rimmed baking sheet). Halve the remaining 2 lemons and put them on the rack, cut-side down. Roast, without turning, until the fish is cooked through and the skin is starting to brown, 15 to 20 minutes. (The oven provides more even heat than the grill, so there's no need to flip them.)

**2** Serve the fish with the preserved lemon relish and roasted lemons alongside.

# Crispy-Skinned Salmon with Spicy Radishes and Green Romesco

*Serves 4*

4 large radishes, preferably watermelon, thinly sliced

1 small shallot, thinly sliced into rings

1 tablespoon white wine vinegar or fresh lemon juice

½ teaspoon crushed red pepper flakes

Kosher salt and freshly ground black pepper

1 tablespoon vegetable oil

4 (4- to 6-ounce) skin-on salmon fillets

1 cup Green Romesco (page 21)

Flaky sea salt

¼ cup fresh parsley, tender leaves and stems

1 lemon, quartered

You'll notice this dish is more about technique than ingredients, but I wanted to include it because I think it's important that everyone knows how to properly sear a piece of fish, specifically salmon. The skin has almost as much fat in it as chicken skin and, when seared properly, can get just as crispy.

This wildly versatile salt-and-pepper recipe works alongside nearly everything in the Vegetables chapter, over any cooked grain of choice, and with most of the condiments starting on page 19, but the Green Romesco in all its herby, nutty, garlicky glory really stands up to the salmon, which is maybe one of the more flavorful fish out there. The texture, additional heat, and lovely color of the spicy radishes bring a lot to the table here, but this will also work with thinly sliced fennel, carrots, cucumbers, kohlrabi, or turnips in their place.

All that said, there's not much that a perfectly seared, crispy piece of salmon won't go with, so if you don't feel like all the bells and whistles tonight, know that this will work with nearly any basic cooked grain or most things in the Vegetables chapter, especially the spring peas and radishes (page 37), blistered green beans (page 34), or simple steamed artichokes (page 56).

**1** Combine the radishes, shallot, vinegar, and red pepper flakes in a small bowl, season with kosher salt and black pepper, and set aside.

**2** Heat the vegetable oil in a large skillet over medium-high heat. Season the salmon on both sides with kosher salt and black pepper.

**3** One at a time, gently lower in the fillets, skin-side down, away from you (to avoid splattering hot oil on yourself) and, using a spatula (preferably a fish spatula), immediately press down to make sure the skin makes contact with the skillet (this is how you get that crispy skin!).

**4** Cook, pressing down occasionally, until the skin is super crispy and the salmon is nearly cooked through and turns opaque on top, 4 to 6 minutes. Pressing the fish with the spatula to hold it in place, tilt the skillet and drain the fat into a bowl or empty can. Gently flip the salmon to just barely cook the other side, 30 to 60 seconds.

**5** Spoon Green Romesco onto the bottom of each plate and top with the salmon (spooning the sauce over the top of the salmon would de-crisp the skin). Sprinkle the salmon with flaky salt and scatter the radishes and parsley around. Serve with lemon wedges for squeezing.

# Whole Roasted Snapper with Harissa and Sun Gold Tomatoes

*Serves 4*

2 tablespoons harissa

2 garlic cloves, finely grated

3 tablespoons olive oil

1 (1½-pound) snapper or 2 smaller sea bream, porgies, or branzinos, scaled and gutted

Kosher salt and freshly ground black pepper

2 pints yellow (Sun Gold) or red cherry tomatoes

1 orange, lime, or lemon, halved, for squeezing

Flaky sea salt

**NOTE:** If you wish to make this with fillets, choose the largest, meatiest ones you can find and decrease the cooking time to 10 to 15 minutes.

Whole fish is not always an obvious choice for lots of people, and I get that. There are fins involved, sometimes a whole head (with *eyes*), and all those bones. But just like cooking a steak or chicken breast on the bone, fish also benefits from leaving it au naturel. The fat from the skin and the bones keeps it from drying out, and—best of all—you don't have to do anything besides pop it into an oven. When picking up your new friend, be sure that the fishmonger has cleaned the fish for you, meaning it's been gutted and scaled (I like leaving the heads on, but that's up to you). This will almost always be the case, but better safe than sorry, so double-check.

The garlicky harissa mixture here not only seasons the snapper but also the supersweet Sun Gold tomatoes that burst alongside the fish as it roasts, creating a kind of spicy tomato sauce to serve with it. This is good as is, or serve with a bowl of couscous, quinoa, or even some herby pasta next to a pile of some lightly dressed lemony greens.

**1** Preheat the oven to 500°F.

**2** Combine the harissa, garlic, and olive oil in a small bowl. Season the fish with kosher salt and pepper, including inside the cavity. Rub some of the harissa mixture on both sides and the inside of the fish.

**3** Place the fish on a rimmed baking sheet. Toss the tomatoes with the remaining harissa mixture and scatter them around the fish. Place in the oven and roast until the fish is cooked through and the tomatoes all burst and are starting to caramelize, 15 to 20 minutes.

**4** Remove the fish from the oven and let it rest about 5 minutes. Using a spoon, separate the fillets from the spine, and place the fillets on a separate serving platter. Lift the spine out (the head and tail should come with it) and save it for stock or give it to a cartoon cat.

**5** Place the first fillet on top of the second one and top with the tomatoes. Squeeze the orange over everything and sprinkle with flaky sea salt.

# Spring Seafood Stew with Peas, New Potatoes, and Tarragon

*Serves 4 to 6*

¼ cup fresh parsley leaves, finely chopped

2 tablespoons fresh tarragon leaves, finely chopped

1 lemon

2 tablespoons olive oil

2 tablespoons (¼ cup) unsalted butter

2 leeks (white and light green parts only), thinly sliced

4 stalks green garlic, thinly sliced (if you can't find it, use 2 large garlic cloves, thinly sliced)

4 celery stalks or 1 fennel bulb, chopped

1½ pounds teeny, tiny new potatoes (about the size of a quarter), halved, or other waxy potato, like fingerling or Yukon Gold, quartered

Kosher salt and freshly ground black pepper

½ cup dry white wine

2 fresh bay leaves (optional)

2 cups fish stock or 1 cup clam juice plus 1 cup water

2 cups fresh or frozen peas

8 ounces smoked trout, flaked into large bite-sized pieces

1½ pounds small littleneck clams or cockles, scrubbed

1 pound cod, halibut, or rockfish fillets, cut into 2-inch pieces

1 cup crème fraîche

Crusty bread, torn or sliced, warmed or not, for serving

Since I didn't grow up on the East Coast, I really have no claim to fish chowder, but I do know I love the stuff. So here's a lighter, very springy version of fish chowder, which I'm calling a stew, because after thinking long and hard, I'm not sure there's a difference.

When buying cod, make sure to ask for the center piece. You don't want a tail end, which will be too thin and fall apart almost instantly once dropped into the pot.

**1**  Combine the parsley and tarragon in a small bowl. Zest the lemon into the bowl with the herbs and set aside. Cut the lemon into wedges and set aside.

**2**  Heat the olive oil and butter in a large (at least 5-quart) heavy-bottomed pot over medium heat. Add the leeks, green garlic, celery, and potatoes. Season with salt and pepper, and cook, stirring occasionally, until all the vegetables are softened, about 10 minutes. Add the white wine and cook until it's reduced by about half, about 3 minutes. Add the bay leaves (if using), stock, and 4 cups water, and season with salt and pepper.

**3**  Bring the whole pot to a simmer and cook until the potatoes are nearly falling apart and the liquid has thickened nicely (thanks, potatoes!), 35 to 45 minutes. Check for seasoning before you add any of the seafood. The liquid should be pretty flavorful on its own here, but remember not to add too much salt yet; the clams will add lots of brininess after they open.

**4**  Add the peas, smoked trout, and clams, and cover the pot. Cook until the clams have just opened, 10 to 15 minutes. Timing will depend on the size of the clams, and when they are submerged in liquid, they tend to take a bit longer to open than if you were steaming them.

**5**  Season the fish with salt and pepper, and gently lay the pieces in the pot (the fish should be just submerged). Cover and cook until the fish is opaque and just cooked through, 8 to 10 minutes.

**6**  Divide the stew among bowls (try not to break up the fish too much) and top with crème fraîche and the herb mixture. Serve with the lemon wedges and crusty bread.

# Quick Weeknight Fish Stew with Olives

*Serves 4*

3 tablespoons olive oil, plus more for
   drizzling
1 large or 2 medium shallots, thinly
   sliced
4 garlic cloves, thinly sliced
Kosher salt and freshly ground black
   pepper
2 chiles de árbol, crumbled, or
   ½ teaspoon crushed red pepper
   flakes
2 sprigs fresh thyme or 2 fresh bay
   leaves (optional)
⅓ cup dry white wine
1 pound medium tomatoes, quartered,
   or 1 (14.5-ounce) can whole peeled
   tomatoes, drained
½ pound medium shrimp, peeled and
   deveined
¾ pound skinless flounder, tilapia,
   halibut, cod, or rockfish fillets, cut
   into 4-inch pieces
1 pound mussels, scrubbed and rinsed
⅓ cup coarsely chopped oil-cured black
   olives
1 cup fresh parsley, dill, cilantro, or
   tarragon, tender leaves and stems,
   coarsely chopped

**DO AHEAD:** The base for the stew can
be made 5 days ahead and
refrigerated. When ready to add the
seafood, bring to a simmer and
proceed.

This recipe is admittedly a little basic, but sometimes, basic
is good. Basic is comfortable. Basic is a garlicky, white winey,
tomatoey broth that will take care of your expensive seafood,
cook it gently, and make everything taste so delicious that you
won't even be mad that fish costs so much. Basic is weeknight
friendly.

   The important lesson here is that a good base will give you the
flexibility you need to riff. Add some dried chorizo to the olive
oil to start or a tablespoon of harissa at the end for something
spicier. Use clams if you don't like shrimp, scallops if you are
feeling fancy. If you stick with basic, the possibilities are endless.

**1**  Heat the olive oil in a large, heavy-bottomed pot or large, deep
skillet over medium-high heat. Add the shallot and 3 garlic cloves,
and season with salt and black pepper. Cook, stirring occasionally,
until the shallots are browned and the garlic is toasted, about
4 minutes.

**2**  Add the chiles, thyme (if using), and wine, and let simmer until
reduced by about half, about 4 minutes.

**3**  Crush the tomatoes with your hands and add them to the pot
along with any juices. Add 4 cups water and season with salt and
black pepper.

**4**  Simmer everything together, seasoning it along the way, until the
broth has thickened slightly and all the flavors have come together,
15 to 20 minutes.

**5**  Season the shrimp and fish with salt and black pepper. Add the
mussels to the pot and cover. Once the mussels have started to
open, after about 5 minutes, carefully add the shrimp to the pot,
followed by the fish. Cover the pot and cook until the shrimp are
bright pink, the fish is opaque white, and everything is cooked
through, 6 to 8 minutes. Add the olives and remove from the heat.

**6**  Meanwhile, finely chop the remaining garlic clove, add it to the
chopped herbs, and season with salt and black pepper.

**7**  Serve the stew with a drizzle of olive oil and the herbs sprinkled
over, alongside obscenely garlicky bread, a good salad, and lots and
lots of wine.

# Grilled Squid with Spicy, Garlicky White Beans and Vinegared Tomatoes

*Serves 4*

¾ **pound cleaned squid bodies and tentacles**
**2 tablespoons canola oil**
**Kosher salt and freshly ground black pepper**
¾ **pound heirloom tomatoes, in as many shades and colors as you like, sliced about ½ inch thick**
**2 tablespoons red wine vinegar**
**Spicy, Garlicky White Beans (page 155)**
**Olive oil, for drizzling**

**NOTE:** If you're not grilling, cook the squid in a large skillet over high heat, working in batches and turning the pieces often, until they're golden brown, 6 to 8 minutes per batch.

Come late summer, most things I'm cooking or grilling get thrown onto a pile of salty, vinegary, ripe tomatoes, which creates a sauce that pools on the bottom and is good enough to drink (I know, because I drink it). It's basically "tomato as plate," and a very good way to eat things. Nothing benefits more from this technique than grilled, charred squid mixed with some garlicky, oily white beans. When I eat this dish, something about the light breeziness of it all makes me feel like I might be on the Amalfi coast, where I have never been.

**1** Toss the squid in a large bowl with the canola oil and season with salt and pepper. Heat a grill to high. Place the squid on the grill, taking care to lay the pieces so that they won't fall through the grates (that's why you grill whole, slice later). Grill the squid, turning the pieces occasionally, until it's lightly charred all over (by this time it will definitely be cooked through), about 5 minutes.

**2** Transfer the squid to a cutting board. Once the squid is cool enough to handle, slice the tubes into ½-inch rings. Leave the tentacles whole or slice them in half lengthwise for more bite-sized pieces.

**3** Arrange the sliced tomatoes on a large platter and pour the vinegar over them. Season with salt and pepper. Scatter the beans and squid over the tomatoes and drizzle with olive oil.

---

**How to Squid**

I keep thinking squid is going to catch on at any moment, because why wouldn't it? Squid, aka calamari, is delicious and should be cooked at home. Yes, it loses some of its sex appeal to talk about how affordable and sustainable it is, how well it freezes and defrosts, and how quick-cooking it is, but all those things are worth noting.

When buying squid, most of what you'll find at a fish market or grocery store has already been cleaned, meaning all the bits have been removed from the inside. If the squid isn't cleaned, they'll do it for you—just ask for a mix of "bodies and tentacles," which means you'll get equal parts long, white tube-like bodies and wild-looking purple tentacles. It not only looks good, but because the tentacles are slightly meatier than the bodies, which tend to be chewier (in a good way), there's lots of variety in texture, which will make any dish better.

You may notice that more often than not, each squid has a very long, rogue tentacle. I don't know why it's there (whatever you do, do NOT Google "long tentacle on squid"). If it bothers you, cut it off, or just leave it, because it's definitely edible. As for the rest of the squid, if you're grilling it, keep the pieces whole to avoid anything falling through the grates, then slice after cooking. If sautéing, cut the bodies into rings about ½ inch thick and cut the tentacles in half—this will get you the most evenly cooked squid with the crispiest bits.

# Black Bass with Salty, Spicy Celery

*Serves 4*

4 (4- to 6-ounce) skin-on black bass fillets (fluke, flounder, tilapia, and snapper work here, too)

Kosher salt and freshly ground black pepper

3 tablespoons lime pickle, finely chopped (see Note)

2 limes, 1 thinly sliced and the other quartered

½ bunch fresh cilantro

4 tablespoons olive oil

2 celery stalks, halved crosswise

2 scallions, thinly sliced

1 tablespoon unseasoned rice vinegar

**NOTE:** Lime pickle is a spiced Indian condiment made from, yes, limes. The limes aren't pickled, per se; rather they are salted and left to ferment with other seeds and spices like coriander, fenugreek, and turmeric. It's salty, tangy, and wildly, insanely flavorful, and a little bit goes a long way. You can find it at specialty grocery stores and, of course, on the Internet.

Steaming is an ideal method to cook fish for those who are really afraid that it will dry out or stick to a skillet. There is zero danger of either of those things happening if you steam fish, especially if you do so inside foil or parchment, because all that moisture (and flavor) stays inside. Keep in mind, however, that this method is not for every type of fish— you should choose one that is mild in flavor, firm, and relatively thin. Black bass checks all those boxes, making it an ideal candidate for a trip inside a cute little foil packet.

This super-light fish dish is great on its own or over a bowl of crunchy lettuces, but if you just gotta have some starch, this would be great served over rice or rice noodles.

**1**  Preheat the oven to 400°F.

**2**  Season the fish with salt and pepper. Cut four pieces of foil about 8 x 10 inches.

**3**  Place a fish fillet, skin-side down, in the center of each foil square. Top each with a scant 1 teaspoon lime pickle, a few slices of lime, and some cilantro sprigs. Drizzle each with 1 tablespoon oil. Bundle up the package by joining the two long edges of the foil and gathering the sides. You don't want to press on the fish; it's more as if you're creating a tent for it.

**4**  Place the packets on a rimmed baking sheet and bake until the fish is cooked through, 8 to 10 minutes.

**5**  Meanwhile, peel the celery into long, thin ribbons using a vegetable peeler. In a small bowl, toss the celery with the scallions, vinegar, and the remaining lime pickle, and season with salt and pepper. Serve the fish in its cute little packet with celery salad and lime wedges alongside.

# Scallops with Corn, Hazelnuts, and Brown Butter Chermoula

*Serves 4*

1¼ pounds sea scallops, muscle
    removed
Kosher salt and freshly ground black
    pepper
2 tablespoons canola oil
2 tablespoons (¼ stick) unsalted butter
2 garlic cloves, finely chopped
2 teaspoons coriander seed or
    ½ teaspoon ground
1 teaspoon cumin seed or ½ teaspoon
    ground
1 teaspoon hot or smoked paprika
½ teaspoon crushed red pepper flakes
2 cups corn (from about 3 ears; frozen
    will work in a pinch)
½ cup coarsely chopped fresh cilantro
¼ cup chopped toasted hazelnuts
    (see page 50)

**NOTE:** This dish also works with medium shrimp—head on or off.

I'll admit that I find seared scallops to be sort of 1997, but they are also undeniably delicious and maybe even my favorite seafood, tragically unhip as they may be. You know what else I find uncool? Sautéed corn. So I guess you could say that this is one of the lamest dishes in the book, but you know what? It's so delicious I don't care. Maybe like mom jeans, both will come back into style by the time this book comes out.

**1** Season the scallops with salt and black pepper. Heat the canola oil in a large skillet over medium-high heat. Add the scallops, pressing slightly when adding them to ensure they make good contact with the skillet. Cook until they're deeply golden brown on one side, about 5 minutes. Using a spatula, flip each scallop over and continue to cook until browned on that side as well, another 5 minutes.

**2** Transfer the scallops to a large plate or baking sheet.

**3** Melt the butter in the skillet, letting it foam up and get all browned and wonderful. Add the garlic, coriander, cumin, paprika, and red pepper flakes, using a wooden spoon or spatula to scrape up any bits left over from the scallops into the mix (those bits are what dreams are made of ). Cook the spices until toasted and fragrant, a minute or so.

**4** Add the corn, season with salt and black pepper, and toss to coat. Cook until the corn is bright yellow and evenly coated in all that spice business. Remove the pan from the heat and stir in the cilantro.

**5** Serve the scallops with the corn mixture, sprinkling the toasted hazelnuts on top.

# Oil-Roasted Sardines with Mayonnaise, Pickled Onions, and Lots of Parsley

*Serves 6 to 8*

1 ¼ pounds whole head-on sardines,
    gutted and cleaned
Kosher salt and freshly ground black
    pepper
2 heads of garlic, halved crosswise
½ bunch fresh thyme
¾ cup olive oil
½ small red onion, thinly sliced
2 tablespoons fresh lime juice
1 cup fresh flat-leaf parsley leaves
Mayonnaise for People Who Hate
    Mayonnaise (page 26)
Thick slabs of toast, if you like

**DO AHEAD:** These sardines are actually great at room temperature or even cold. Store them covered in oil, and refrigerated for up to 2 days.

There are people who are into sardines and people who are decidedly not into sardines, and I'm friends with both types of people. I happen to be the former, and if you think you're the latter, I'd still recommend you try this at least once (One Bite Rule, *hello!*).

Roasting these small fishes at a high temperature in olive oil is almost like deep-frying them without actually deep-frying them. Their usual fishiness is replaced with salty, garlicky flavors, and once you've dipped them in the best aioli ever and topped them with citrusy pickled onions, you won't even recognize yourself, because you, too, will have turned into a sardine lover.

**1** Preheat the oven to 425°F.

**2** Place the sardines (heads and all!) in a 2-quart baking dish (they should fit pretty snugly, but if they're too snug, pick a larger baking dish or even a skillet) and season them with salt and pepper. Add the garlic and thyme, and drizzle the olive oil over the top.

**3** Roast the sardines until their skins start to crisp up and they're totally cooked through, 15 to 20 minutes (you'll notice them start to really sizzle away—it is an extremely satisfying sound).

**4** Remove them from the oven and let them cool slightly.

**5** Meanwhile, combine the onion with the lime juice in a small bowl, season with salt and pepper, and let sit, tossing occasionally to evenly coat everything. Add the parsley and toss to coat.

**6** Serve the sardines whole with spoonfuls of mayonnaise and the pickled onion situation. Thick toast is optional but recommended.

# Mom's Trout
# with Herby Bread Crumbs

*Serves 4*

4 tablespoons (½ stick) unsalted butter, melted

1 garlic clove, finely grated

1 tablespoon chopped fresh thyme

2 tablespoons chopped fresh parsley

1 cup Fresh Bread Crumbs (page 24)

Kosher salt and freshly ground black pepper

2 whole trout (about 8 ounces each; see Note), butterflied (head on or off, your call)

1 lemon, cut into wedges, for serving

**NOTE:** Most trout is sold already butterflied, which means it's still whole (head on or off), just gutted, leaving you with two fillets that are still attached; you'll want to ask for two of these. If they are not attached, they are simply called fillets and you should buy four.

When I was growing up, my mom made trout with bread crumbs at least once a week. It was her signature dish, if you will (*chef kisses fingertips*). She used Progresso Italian bread crumbs, real butter, and lots of garlic salt. The crunchy, buttery bread crumbs and tender, mild fish definitely reminded me of a fish stick, which, in retrospect, makes me think I was being tricked into eating head-on trout. Regardless, I guess I fell for it, since I still crave this dish on the regular.

I've slightly adapted her original recipe, preferring the coarser texture of fresh bread crumbs and the punch from real garlic, but it's still one of the first and most important things I learned how to cook. Thanks, Mom.

**1** Preheat the oven to 450°F. Line a baking sheet with foil.

**2** Combine the butter, garlic, thyme, and parsley in a small bowl. Pour the butter mixture over the bread crumbs and, using your hands, combine them, making sure they are really well mixed. Season with salt and pepper.

**3** Season the trout on both sides with salt and pepper and place them, skin-side down, on a foil-lined baking sheet. Scatter the bread crumbs over the fish and bake until the crumbs are bubbling and browned and the fish is cooked through, 8 to 10 minutes.

**4** Serve with lemon squeezed on top and probably some rice pilaf or steamed asparagus, just like Mom used to do.

# Slow Salmon
# with Citrus and Herb Salad

*Serves 4 to 6*

1 (1½-pound) piece of skinless salmon (skinless halibut or cod work well here, too)

Kosher salt and freshly ground black pepper

2 lemons, Meyer or regular, thinly sliced

1 blood orange, mandarin, or regular orange, thinly sliced

6 sprigs fresh thyme, rosemary, oregano, or marjoram (optional)

1½ cups olive oil

2 cups fresh herbs, such as parsley, cilantro, dill, and tarragon

1 tablespoon fresh lemon juice

Flaky sea salt

**NOTE:** As I mentioned, other ingredients can be added to the baking dish to cook alongside. Try thinly sliced fennel or chiles or sprigs of herbs like rosemary and thyme.

Confession: I can't find a better way to cook salmon. I've tried, but this is truly the best. Slowly roasting an already fatty fish in even more luxurious fat (here, olive oil) makes it nearly impossible to overcook; plus, you can flavor that oil with whatever you fancy: spices, herbs, citrus, chiles, which will flavor the fish, which is why you're here.

The first time I made a version of this dish was for *Bon Appétit* magazine a few years back, and people still tell me it's their most favorite salmon in the land. This salmon isn't meant to one-up that salmon (which also had slices of fennel and fresh chiles), but to introduce it to those who haven't yet met its magic. It's also to remind those who maybe have had that dish that this very simple method is by far the most delicious, easy, and customizable way to cook *any* large piece of fish (it's hard to beat a perfect fillet of wild salmon, but other fish like cod or halibut also work), so feel free to explore your options.

Oh, and if you're wondering, why yes, this *is* the ideal dinner party trick, sitting perfectly in the center of the Venn diagram where "looks impressive" and "not a ton of work" overlap. You can even double the size of the fillet to feed a real crowd, where you will be praised endlessly by at least ten people for how silky and rich your now famous salmon is.

Should you have any salmon left over, store it in the remaining oil, which will help keep it from drying out. It makes for ideal salmon niçoise, rice bowl, bagel topping, and more, so even though I say this serves four to six, feel free to make it just for one.

**1** Preheat the oven to 300°F.

**2** Season the salmon with kosher salt and pepper on both sides and place it in a large baking dish (a rimmed baking sheet will also work in a pinch, although the salmon will not quite be submerged) with the sliced lemons, oranges, and herb sprigs, if using.

**3** Drizzle the olive oil over everything and place the baking dish in the oven. Cook the salmon until it is just turning opaque around the edges and is nearly cooked through, 20 to 25 minutes.

**4** Toss the herbs with the lemon juice and flaky sea salt, and serve with your perfect salmon.

# Soy-Brined Halibut with Mustard Greens, Sesame, and Lime

*Serves 4*

¼ cup plus 1 tablespoon soy sauce or
    tamari
2 tablespoons rice vinegar
4 (4- to 6-ounce) halibut fillets
2 tablespoons raw sesame seeds
2 tablespoons toasted sesame oil
6 cups mustard greens (from about
    1 bunch), torn into 2-inch pieces
2 tablespoons fresh lime juice
4 scallions, thinly sliced
Lemon or lime, quartered, for serving

**NOTE:** This will work with other firm white skinless fish such as fluke or flounder; just cut the cooking time in half if the fillets are thin.

While it's not quite the same thing as brining a turkey or chicken, brining thick, meaty fish like halibut is an excellent way to impart flavor and sort of season it from the inside out. You can do this with highly salted water (makes sense, given where fish come from in the first place), but I love the dark, caramel color and flavor of this tangy soy brine. Because both the brine and the liquid used to gently simmer the halibut are both so well seasoned already, don't worry about adding any additional salt.

**1** Combine the ¼ cup of soy sauce, the vinegar, and 1 cup water in a large ziplock bag. Add the halibut and refrigerate, flipping once, for 1 to 2 hours.

**2** Toast the sesame seeds in a large skillet over medium-high heat, tossing frequently until the seeds are evenly golden brown and smelling toasted, about 4 minutes. Transfer the sesame seeds to a small bowl and set aside, reserving the skillet.

**3** Bring the sesame oil, remaining 1 tablespoon soy sauce, and 1 cup water to a simmer over medium heat in that same large skillet. Remove the halibut from its brine and place in the skillet. Cover and gently simmer (make sure the liquid never comes to a boil) until it's just cooked through, 5 to 7 minutes. Scatter the mustard greens around the fish and cook, covered, just until the mustard greens turn bright green and wilt, about 2 minutes.

**4** Transfer the fish and greens to a large serving platter, leaving the soy brine behind. Add the lime juice to the skillet with the brine, swirling to combine, then spoon over the greens and fish. Sprinkle with the scallions and sesame seeds and serve with lemon or lime for squeezing. This is good with rice, of course, but also with crispy smashed potatoes (page 73).

# Dad's Scotch Gravlax

*Serves 8*

⅓ cup kosher salt

¼ cup chopped fresh dill

2 tablespoons light brown sugar

2 tablespoons fresh grapefruit or
lemon zest

1 tablespoon Aleppo pepper or freshly
ground black pepper

1 pound skin-on salmon fillet

1 tablespoon extremely smoky Scotch
whiskey, such as Laphroaig

**NOTE:** I've made a few tweaks to his
original recipe, using Aleppo pepper
for even more smokiness and
grapefruit instead of lemon, because I
love the floral notes and slightly adult
bitterness it brings; and because I like
things to taste more salty than sweet, I
cut back on some of the brown sugar.

How you serve this will ultimately
come down to personal preference.
Are you a Wasa cracker or bagel kind
of person? Cream cheese or labne?
Red onion or scallion? Lots to decide.

**DO AHEAD:** Gravlax can be kept for
up to 1 week, refrigerated. Just make
sure you wrap it super tightly before
storing, changing out the plastic wrap
between uses to keep moisture out.

I know everything about good pastrami and lox and bagels from
my dad. Growing up in New Jersey, he had access to all the good
stuff in New York, but when he moved to LA, he found that while
pastrami wasn't a problem (Langer's is better than anything you
can find in NYC *or* Montreal), there was no good lox.

After years of store-bought subpar smoked salmon always
sliced too thick, my dad decided he was going to make his own.
My dad dabbles in cooking (mainly taco nights and grilling in
the summer), but Ina Garten he is not. So when I heard he was
actually, like, making gravlax, I definitely raised an eyebrow or two.
But . . . it was good (really!). It was complex and insanely flavorful,
somewhere between smoked salmon and herby gravlax. He told
me it was because he had used a smoky Scotch (Laphroaig,
always) as the rinse, rather than the traditional vodka. He was
smug, I was impressed, and the salmon was delicious.

**1** Combine the salt, dill, brown sugar, grapefruit zest, and
Aleppo pepper in a small bowl, rubbing with your hands to blend
everything really well. The mixture should feel almost like wet sand.

**2** Place the salmon on a cutting board and pour the Scotch on top,
rubbing it all over; discard any that runs off. (Lots of rubbing in this
recipe—get ready.) Rub the salt mixture over the salmon, packing
it on pretty well, like you're building a sand castle. Wrap the whole
piece of salmon in plastic wrap a few times so it's well sealed.

**3** Using a fork, poke a few holes in the skin side of the salmon, just
to pierce the plastic, not necessarily the salmon. Place the salmon,
skin-side down, on a wire rack set inside a rimmed baking sheet.
Place a large plate or another baking sheet on top of the salmon,
and then put a few heavy cans or a large cast-iron skillet on top. The
idea here is that you are pressing the cure into the salmon, and as
that happens, some water will leach out (the holes you poked let out
any excess moisture).

**4** Place this in the refrigerator and let it sit for 3 to 5 days. Dad likes
his a little more cured; I like mine a little fresher. Check it at 3 days
and give it a taste; feel free to keep curing.

**5** You can rub the cure off before slicing and serving, but I like to
leave it on, because I'm into all that additional herby saltiness.

**6** Whatever you're serving it with (or on), slice your gravlax as thinly
as possible. To do this, use a very sharp knife (preferably a slicing
knife, but if you don't own one, reach for the thinnest blade you
have). Cut on a strong bias to create wider, thin sheets of salmon.

# Swordfish-Like Steak with Crispy Capers

*Serves 4*

2 (8-ounce) swordfish steaks, preferably center cut

Kosher salt and freshly ground black pepper

1 tablespoon canola oil

2 tablespoons (¼ stick) unsalted butter

2 garlic cloves, smashed

2 anchovy fillets

2 tablespoons capers, drained

4 sprigs fresh marjoram, oregano, or rosemary

Swordfish is one of the few types of fish that is meaty enough to sear fearlessly, without skin, in a skillet. No sticking, no tearing—just golden brown crust, almost like steak (almost). So why not treat it like one? I am very into the way the capers crisp up in the browning butter here, but you can swap them for 2 tablespoons crushed olives or a few lemon slices if capers aren't your favorite.

**1** Season the swordfish with salt and pepper. Heat the oil in a large skillet over medium-high heat. Sear the swordfish until golden brown on both sides, about 4 minutes per side. Add the butter, garlic, anchovies, and capers. Once the butter has melted and begun to brown, tilt the skillet toward you (carefully) and spoon any pooling melted butter over the swordfish a few times.

**2** Remove the skillet from the heat and add the herbs (stand back a second, because the butter will splatter a bit), swirling to coat them in the browned butter, continuing to spoon everything over the swordfish for another minute or two.

**3** Serve the swordfish with the butter and herbs spooned on top.

# I consider myself more omnivorous than carnivorous, eating meat only once in a while, like holidays or when I've had a bad day and need a pepperoni pizza.

Maybe it's residual frugalness from my early twenties, when I ate rice for every meal, but eating meat for a simple weeknight meal somehow still feels quite decadent, indulgent even. That's why when I do decide to cook meat, even on the most casual evening, I tend to go all out: thick rib eyes cooked to the rarest side of medium-rare, fatty chicken legs with ridiculously crispy skin, or fancy lamb chops with meat left on the bones for nibbling, all cheering, "It's Thursday, and you deserve it!"

In this chapter you'll find some larger format, low-and-slow recipes for entertaining friends as well as hot-and-fast weeknight-friendly recipes for when you're entertaining yourself, along with a few things in between. While there are some instances where salt and pepper are the only two additional ingredients you need to make a great piece of meat, adding simple flourishes like paprika and garlic (page 227), fennel and herbs (page 241), or anchovy butter (page 246) into the mix amplifies the deliciousness without adding any complications, which is always the goal, isn't it?

Many of the recipes here can be mixed and matched. What you do for one cut of meat can be cross-pollinated with another: use the paprika rub for the chicken (page 227) on pork tenderloin; serve a roast chicken with buttered radish toasts meant for steak (page 216); prepare lamb chops instead of chicken thighs with those crushed olives and sumac (page 206). The idea is that each recipe will give you one takeaway to apply to all your other protein cookery. Whether it's using rendered chicken fat to cook your side of vegetables (page 229), or the bits left over in your skillet from the crispy pork to dip your tortillas in (page 208), there's always an aha moment to be had.

# Skillet Chicken with Crushed Olives and Sumac

*Serves 4*

½ small red onion, thinly sliced

2 tablespoons fresh lemon juice

Kosher salt and freshly ground black pepper

1½ pounds bone-in, skin-on chicken thighs (4 to 6, depending on size) or bone-in, skin-on chicken breasts (2 or 3, depending on size)

2 tablespoons olive oil

1 cup pitted Castelvetrano olives, crushed

1½ teaspoons ground sumac

1 cup fresh herbs, such as parsley, mint, or dill

This is a pretty hot take, but I think bone-in, skin-on chicken might be the most delicious type of meat you can eat. The skin gets crispier than any bacon you could fry, and the fat left rendered in the skillet is worth the price of admission alone (once you have those briny olives coated in the stuff, you'll see why).

This recipe can be infinitely adapted. Once you sear the thighs, feel free to add thinly sliced vegetables (such as fennel, turnips, or carrots), torn dark leafy greens, a rinsed and drained can of beans, or precooked grains into the skillet, coating them in that liquid gold and serving them alongside your new favorite way to eat chicken.

**1** Toss the onion with the lemon juice and season with salt and pepper; set aside.

**2** Season the chicken with salt and pepper. Heat the oil in a large skillet over medium-high heat. Add the chicken, skin-side down, and cook until the skin is golden brown and crispy, 8 to 10 minutes. Flip the chicken and continue to cook it until the bottom is golden brown and the chicken is cooked through, 5 to 8 minutes more.

**3** Transfer the chicken to a large plate or cutting board. Add the olives, sumac, and ½ cup water to the skillet, stirring to scrape up those browned bits on the bottom.

**4** Return the chicken to the skillet, skin-side up so it stays crispy, and cook over medium heat until the liquid has almost totally evaporated, about 4 minutes; remove from the heat. Add the red onion (plus any liquid) and toss to coat with the olives and the other bits. Transfer the chicken and olives to a large serving platter; scatter the herbs over the top before serving.

# Fennel-Rubbed Pork Chops for Two

Serves 2

1 tablespoon fennel seed

1 tablespoon light brown sugar

2 teaspoons kosher salt, plus more as needed

½ teaspoon freshly ground black pepper

1 (1½-inch-thick) bone-in pork chop (about 1¼ pounds)

1 tablespoon canola oil

1 fennel bulb, sliced lengthwise ¼ inch thick

½ cup fresh herbs, such as parsley, cilantro, dill, and/or tarragon, tender leaves and stems, coarsely chopped

1 tablespoon finely grated lemon zest

**DO AHEAD:** The fennel seed mixture can be made 2 weeks ahead and stored at room temperature. It is also great on chicken.

These are thick, fancy, Saturday-night chops, not thin, pedestrian Tuesday-night chops (only in spirit—you can definitely make them on a Tuesday). The type of pork (for example, Berkshire) will vary regionally, but the thickness here, at least 1½ inches, is nonnegotiable. Larger chops, whether pork or steak, are fattier and richer in flavor than thinner chops and are also nearly impossible to overcook. Even while searing them for what feels like forever, watching the outside develop a too-good-to-be-true deeply golden brown crust, the inside miraculously remains that perfect shade of pink and juicy as hell.

You're not likely to find pork chops like this unless you go to the butcher (or butcher counter) and ask for them, but I have been surprised before. I know, it's an extra step—the butcher! What a hassle. But trust me, it's worth it and what makes these chops so dang special. I suggest going and getting a few and then freezing them for next time.

**1** Toast the fennel seed in a small skillet over medium heat, swirling the skillet, until the seed starts to smell fragrant and turn a light golden brown, about 2 minutes. Remove from the heat and grind in a spice grinder, pound with a mortar and pestle, or finely chop with a knife.

**2** Combine the fennel seed with the brown sugar, salt, and pepper, and rub the mixture all over the pork chop. Cover and let it sit at least 30 minutes at room temperature or up to 24 hours in the refrigerator.

**3** Heat the canola oil in a large skillet over medium-high heat. Sear the pork chop until it's super browned and caramelized on one side, 5 to 8 minutes. Flip the pork chop and add the sliced fennel to the skillet. Cook, stirring the fennel every so often, until it is tender and golden brown, but try not to disturb the pork chop. Cook until the deepest part of the pork chop registers 145°F on an instant-read thermometer, another 8 to 10 minutes (if you don't have a thermometer, you can cut off an end piece and check for proper pinkness). Transfer the meat to a cutting board and let it rest a few minutes.

**4** Meanwhile, combine the herbs and lemon zest in a small bowl, and season with salt.

**5** Serve the sliced pork alongside the fennel and garlic with the herb mixture sprinkled on top.

# MEETING "THE ONE"

Just after I moved to New York, I went on a date to what would later become my favorite East Village restaurant, Prune. There in that small, almost too brightly lit room, we had martinis with extra olives, and radishes with butter, and we split a whole fish made with fennel and *sel gris*. The tables were uncomfortably close together, and between the other diners and whatever album was being played from start to finish at too loud a volume, I found myself falling in love—with Prune, not my date.

I knew about the chef, Gabrielle Hamilton, but only peripherally (her memoir, which I'd later obsess over, had not yet come out), but after eating in her restaurant, I felt the way many people feel after watching Jennifer Lawrence trip on the red carpet—that if we met, we'd *definitely* be best friends. Everything they served spoke to me, as if someone had tapped into my brain and pulled out the exact menu I'd write if I had a charming New York restaurant of my own. The kitchen and front of house were comprised 100 percent of women, which I found equally fantastic, all of them with a severely confident, zero-fucks-given attitude. I could also relate to this.

Prune became my spot for romantic dates, for friend dates, and for dates with myself, always starting with a martini and radishes with butter and salt. If my date was game, there'd also be the bone marrow, because that's something I'd never cook for myself but really, really love eating, all soft and custardy, spread onto thick crunchy toast and topped with lots of parsley, anchovy, and capers. I'm not quite an organized-enough person to have true rituals, but coming to Prune and having this meal is as close as I've come to that.

I had the pleasure of meeting Gabrielle a few years ago, when, at a *Bon Appétit* dinner, she told me that she was "a fan" of my work. After looking around me to make sure she wasn't talking to someone else, I nearly passed out. Of course, after this I fantasized about our future friendship, what it would be like to have her over for dinner. We'd drink cold rosé and even colder martinis, talking about food and travel and cooking and life and relationships, and take turns guessing how Triscuits are made, because, of course, we both think they are the perfect cracker.

I'd make us a big bone-in rib eye to share, because we are women who love to eat meat for special occasions (and if the beginning of a fantasy friendship isn't a special occasion, I don't know what is!), and then as a subtle wink to say, "See how much we are alike? I, too, love radishes with butter and lots of capers and parsley and anchovies," there would be thick toast slathered with good butter, topped with thinly sliced radishes, capers, parsley, and anchovy. A modestly festive plate of food that summarizes my feelings about my favorite things at Prune and generally how I love to eat. It would be the equivalent of sharing my truest self with her, fast-tracking our path to becoming *best* friends.

I've still never cooked for Gabrielle Hamilton, and after reading this, she might never want me to, but I hope she knows the offer still stands.

# Perfect Steak
# with Buttered Radish Toast

*Serves 2*

1 (1¼- to 1½-pound) rib-eye steak, preferably bone-in, 1¼- to 1½-inches thick
Kosher salt and freshly ground black pepper
1 tablespoon canola oil
4 tablespoons (½ stick) unsalted butter, at room temperature
4 sprigs fresh thyme
4 garlic cloves, crushed
2 (1-inch-thick) slices crusty bread, such as ciabatta, sourdough, or country loaf
¼ cup fresh parsley, chopped
2 anchovy fillets, finely chopped (optional)
2 tablespoons capers, drained and chopped
4 radishes, preferably watermelon, thinly sliced
Flaky sea salt

**NOTE:** Depending on what kind of kitchen you're working in, you might want to disable your smoke detector before searing this one (just don't forget to put it back together). Because it's such a large, thick piece of meat that you're searing in a good deal of fat, it'll take quite a while to get it properly browned, during which even more fat will render, producing a *lot* of smoke. I learned that the hard way—about a million times.

I really think that a thick, bone-in rib eye is the most perfect steak you can cook. It's got the best fat-to-meat ratio (a good fat cap on one side with plenty of, but never too much, marbling on the inside), a texture that's firmer than tenderloin and juicier than a strip, and that giant bone (!). Well, a few nibbles on that giant bone and you'll see that it alone is literally worth the price of admission (which can, admittedly, be kind of steep).

**1** Season the steak with kosher salt and pepper. Let it sit at room temperature for about an hour before cooking, or feel free to season it up to a day in advance (just cover and refrigerate it).

**2** Heat the oil in a large skillet, preferably cast iron (you knew I was going to say that, right?), over high heat. Let this skillet get really, really, really hot, until the oil starts smoking a bit.

**3** Add the steak (carefully, because that oil is going to splatter a bit) and let it cook on one side until it is deeply, insanely, gorgeously browned, forming a crust of golden deliciousness. This will take 6 to 8 minutes, and you're not allowed to fuss with it, so get comfortable.

**4** Flip the steak and cook on the other side until it reaches that same browned promised land, another 6 to 8 minutes. Remove the skillet from the heat and add 2 tablespoons of the butter, along with the thyme and garlic. Tilt the skillet and, using a large spoon, spoon the butter over the steak repeatedly, for 1 to 2 minutes. Transfer the steak to a cutting board, leaving the drippings in the skillet, and let it rest for about 10 minutes.

**5** Meanwhile, toast your bread (in a toaster, in an oven, in a toaster oven). Combine the parsley, anchovy, and capers. Spread the remaining 2 tablespoons butter onto the toast and top with some sliced radishes and the parsley mixture.

**6** Once the steak has rested, slice it against the grain, about ¾ inch thick (this is my preference; if you like it thicker or thinner, go for it). Serve it on the cutting board or on a large plate with everything from the skillet poured over it. Sprinkle with flaky sea salt and serve with the buttered radish toast and a fancy red wine.

**7** A pretty good (dare I say mandatory) move here is to take any remaining radishes and dip them into the meat juices from the pan. This is called "a radish snack" and just might be the best part. You won't be sorry.

# Golden Chicken Broth with Turmeric and Garlic

*Makes 10 cups*

1 tablespoon canola, vegetable, or
    coconut oil
1 large yellow onion, unpeeled, halved
2 heads of garlic, halved crosswise
2 (2-inch) pieces fresh turmeric, peeled
    and halved lengthwise,
    or 1 teaspoon ground
1 (4-inch) piece ginger, peeled and
    halved lengthwise
4 celery stalks, chopped
1 large fennel bulb, chopped
2 fresh or dried bay leaves (optional)
2 whole star anise or 3 whole cloves
1 (3½- to 4-pound) chicken or 3½ to
    4 pounds chicken carcasses,
    backbones, and/or wings
Kosher salt and freshly ground black
    pepper

**NOTE:** While this vibrant yellow, lightly anise-flavored stock is great used immediately and consumed as is, or frozen for later in ziplock bags as Martha Stewart would tell you to do, it's also exceptional turned into a soup (like the one with celery and mushrooms on page 219), which is like a cleanse, but for people who eat.

**DO AHEAD:** Broth can be made 5 days ahead and refrigerated and/or up to 1 month frozen.

I am one of those annoying people who stores chicken carcasses and fennel bulb scraps in their fridge so I can make stock on some random Sunday afternoon. I do it for two reasons: Number one, because store-bought chicken broth is just not great. Generally flavorless and exceptionally expensive, it's a challenging ingredient to get behind. Number two, stock is one thing you can cook that requires almost zero skill and will let you feel like you accomplished something after you make it.

So, yes, I make my own chicken broth. I make it to cook with, but more often than not, I'm making it so I can drink it when I'm feeling less than 100 percent or when I just need a break from stuffing my face 24/7. I tried to do a cleanse once, and let's just say that around 7:30 p.m., I was no longer doing a cleanse.

While it doesn't do much in the way of flavor, I always leave the onion skin on when making broths, stocks, or soups for the deep golden, almost burnt sienna color it lends. Here it assists the turmeric in making this one look like bottled sunshine.

**1** Heat the oil in a large, heavy-bottomed pot over medium-high heat. Add the onion, garlic, fresh turmeric (if using ground, you'll add it later), and ginger, all cut-side down. Cook, without stirring, until everything starts to lightly char and smell good, about 4 minutes. Add the celery, fennel, bay leaves (if using), and star anise, and stir to coat (add the ground turmeric now also). Cook, stirring everything around, until the vegetables start to soften and take on a touch of color, about 4 minutes. Add the chicken and 12 cups water. Bring to a simmer and reduce the heat to medium-low.

**2** Simmer the stock, uncovered, until the chicken is just cooked through but still has some life left in it (you don't want to dry it out), about 30 minutes. Remove the chicken and let it cool enough to handle (if using chicken parts, skip this step and keep simmering), keeping the stock at a simmer while the chicken cools.

**3** Pick the meat from the cooled bird, separating it from the fat, bones, and cartilage, and set the meat aside. Place all the fat, bone, and cartilage into the pot and keep simmering for another 2 to 2½ hours, seasoning as you go with salt and pepper.

**4** Once the stock has reduced by about a third and is as delicious as can be, strain everything. From here, you can drink it, freeze it for later, or start building a soup (like the one on page 219). Add the chicken you picked to that cold soba (page 162), Little Gem salad (page 80), or lentils with cherry tomatoes (page 139), or simply add it to the broth when you're ready to eat.

# Chicken Soup with Toasted Garlic, Mushrooms, and Celery

Serves 4

2 tablespoons unrefined coconut or vegetable oil

8 garlic cloves, thinly sliced

Kosher salt and freshly ground black pepper

2 large shallots, thinly sliced crosswise into rings

1 pound mushrooms, such as maitake, oyster, shiitake, or cremini, quartered

8 cups Golden Chicken Broth (page 217) or store-bought low-sodium chicken broth

4 celery stalks, thinly sliced on the diagonal, plus ½ cup celery leaves

2 to 3 cups cooked chicken meat

1 teaspoon Asian fish sauce, plus more as needed (optional)

1 lime, quartered

½ cup fresh cilantro, tender stems and leaves

Crunchy Chili Oil (page 20), yuzu kosho, or other hot sauce of your choice

Celery just does not get the respect it deserves. It has an incredibly versatile texture (ridiculously crunchy and refreshing when raw, soft and impossibly tender when cooked!) and lends a clean, green, leafy flavor to nearly everything it touches, especially chicken soup. Once the lightly fried shallots and mushrooms simmer along with all that celery in the golden chicken broth, you'll see what I mean.

This recipe was born from the Golden Chicken Broth with Turmeric and Garlic, but it's flexible by design. It can most definitely be made with store-bought chicken broth (low sodium, please!), chicken from any bird (meaning the one from the broth, a whole rotisserie bird from the store, or any leftovers you might have), and any mushrooms and vegetables you like—I prefer the combo of meaty maitakes with crisp celery, but thinly sliced carrots or fennel and torn kale leaves would all work here, too.

**1** Heat the oil in a large pot over medium heat. Add the garlic, and season with salt and pepper. Cook, stirring occasionally, until the garlic is lightly fried and turning golden brown, 2 to 3 minutes. Using a slotted spoon, remove the garlic and drain on a plate lined with a paper towel. Season with salt and set aside.

**2** Add the shallots to the same pot and season with salt and pepper. Cook, stirring occasionally, until the shallots are lighty fried and turning golden brown but are not yet crisp, 3 to 4 minutes.

**3** Add the mushrooms, seasoning them with salt and pepper. Cook, stirring occasionally, until they're beginning to brown and are totally softened, about 4 minutes. Add the broth and season with salt and pepper. Bring to a simmer and cook, uncovered, for 30 to 40 minutes, until the flavors get to know each other and the broth tastes a little shalloty and a little mushroomy, seasoning with additional salt and pepper as needed.

**4** Once the broth is as good as can be, add the sliced celery and chicken. Cook until the celery is just tender and the chicken is warmed through, 3 to 4 minutes. Season with the fish sauce, if using, and lots of fresh lime juice. Stir in the celery leaves, cilantro, and a generous spoonful of chili oil before topping with the toasted garlic and serving.

**5** This is good on its own, but I have also eaten it over rice or rice noodles to great delight.

# Vinegar-Braised Chicken with Farro and Watercress

*Serves 4*

1 (3½- to 4-pound) chicken, cut up into
    pieces, or 2 bone-in breasts and
    2 bone-in legs
Kosher salt and freshly ground black
    pepper
1 tablespoon canola oil
1 head of garlic, halved crosswise
1 cup farro or spelt
½ cup white distilled vinegar or white
    wine vinegar
1 tablespoon yuzu kosho (optional)
4 cups watercress, thick stems removed

**NOTE:** Please do not sell this chicken
on the street unless you have a permit
to do so.

**DO AHEAD:** Chicken can be cooked
2 days ahead and refrigerated.
Rewarm over low heat with the lid on,
adding a bit of water to the pot to
prevent the chicken from drying out.

During the summer of extreme recipe testing for this book, a friend of mine came to visit his brother and newborn nephew in New York. They lived in my neighborhood, and I wanted to send them something as congratulations. During this specific time, my kitchen was producing food at an alarming rate. Roasts and stews, cakes and pies—I had basically turned into the hottest restaurant in Brooklyn that nobody had ever heard of.

For whatever reason, I chose to send my friend off with some chicken so he could bring it to his family. Not a remarkable chicken, either. It's maybe one of the simplest dishes in the whole book: a one-pot meal made from a few humble ingredients, two of which are salt and pepper. I plopped it into a ziplock bag (I ran out of Tupperware) and made him promise he would transfer it back to a pot, a plate, a bowl—literally *anything* to conceal the fact that I had just gifted his family a chicken in a ziplock bag to welcome their newborn into the world.

I want to think he tried to explain the situation ("She ran out of Tupperware!"), but even still, I couldn't help feel a little mortified. He eventually confessed the chicken never made it onto a plate, but if it was any consolation, his mom said, "This chicken-in-a-bag is so good, she should sell it on the street."

**1** Season the chicken with salt and pepper. Heat the oil in a large Dutch oven over medium heat. Sear the chicken (working in batches, if needed), skin-side down, until golden brown on both sides, 10 to 12 minutes per side. Transfer the chicken to a plate or cutting board.

**2** Add the garlic and farro to the pot, stirring to coat them in the rendered chicken fat. Season with salt and pepper and cook until the garlic and farro begin to smell toasty, 5 to 8 minutes. Add the vinegar, yuzu kosho (if using), and 4 cups water, scraping up any bits on the bottom of the pan, and bring to a simmer.

**3** Return the chicken to the pot, skin-side up, and cover. Reduce the heat to medium-low and gently simmer until the chicken is practically falling off the bone and the farro is totally cooked through—it should be tender but not mushy—about 90 minutes.

**4** Stir in the watercress before serving.

# Seared Short Ribs with Quick Kimchi and Sesame Salt

*Serves 4*

2 pounds bone-in English-cut short ribs

Kosher salt and freshly ground black pepper

2 tablespoons light brown sugar

1 tablespoon canola oil

¼ cup toasted sesame oil

1 teaspoon flaky sea salt, plus more as needed

3 cups cooked rice, for serving

Quick Kimchi (page 70) or store-bought kimchi, for serving

1 head of crunchy lettuce, such as romaine, butter, or Little Gem, leaves separated, for serving

2 Persian or 1 hothouse cucumber, thinly sliced, for serving

2 cups tender cilantro and/or mint leaves and stems, for serving

This might be the ultimate lazy recipe. Short ribs, generally reserved for braising, are seared (because their perfect thickness and ridiculous marbling of fat just might make them the best cheap steak you can buy), and kimchi, which is fermented for basically forever, is made in 5 minutes (okay, so it's more slaw than kimchi—that lactic acid tang just can't be replicated, no matter how much salt and vinegar you use). The results are not the same, but that's more than okay, because the results are still great.

While this could certainly be done with any cut of steak or style of short rib, I love the thick, meatiness of bone-in English-style short ribs (the ones where there is one thick piece of meat sitting atop one large bone). Seared for what feels like an eternity, they still come out almost too rare, which is to say, pretty perfect. While I love how rare the short ribs on the bone come out and the way they hold their perfectly rectangular shape, you could use boneless short ribs of course; just make sure they are the thickest ones you can find, not those thinly sliced prepackaged ones.

**1** Season the short ribs generously with kosher salt and pepper and rub the meaty sides all over with the brown sugar (no need to season the bone). If you can swing it, let them sit at room temperature for 30 to 40 minutes to let them get deeply seasoned (if not, that's okay, they'll still be great).

**2** Heat the canola oil in a large skillet over medium-high heat. Sear the short ribs on all three meaty sides until they are very, very browned with a good crust on the outside, 6 to 8 minutes per side. Let them rest about 10 minutes (this would be a good time to make that quick kimchi).

**3** Combine the sesame oil and flaky sea salt in a teeny dish. Set out the rice, kimchi, crunchy lettuce, cucumbers, and herbs on separate plates and bowls.

**4** To serve, remove the bone from the meat using a sharp knife. Thinly slice the meat against the grain (just like a regular steak). Place the sliced meat on a serving platter and sprinkle with more flaky sea salt.

**5** For the perfect bite, place some rice inside a lettuce leaf, drag a slice of meat through the sesame oil, and place it on the rice. Top with some kimchi, cucumbers, and cilantro and eat it like a taco.

# Cumin Lamb Chops with Charred Scallions and Peanuts

*Serves 4*

2 tablespoons cumin seed

2 teaspoons Sichuan peppercorns

1 teaspoon crushed red pepper flakes

1½ teaspoons kosher salt, plus more as needed

1½ pounds rib lamb chops, un-frenched

1 tablespoon vegetable oil

4 scallions, cut into 2-inch pieces

1 tablespoon unseasoned rice vinegar

2 tablespoons chopped roasted, salted peanuts (optional)

Freshly ground black pepper

The spicy cumin salt in this recipe is reason enough to go out in search of the finest lamb chops you can find, but it's truly good on chicken, pork, and beef as well (and potatoes, strangely enough). When buying your chops, you'll likely have a choice between New Zealand chops (which tend to be more petite) and American (probably from Colorado; these are a bit heftier). Both are equally delicious, and you can't go wrong; just make sure, whichever ones you get, they are un-frenched, meaning they still have all the meat and fat on the bone. Choose these not only because they look better but also so you can gnaw on the bones. As inelegant as it might be, that's where all the best stuff is, and you deserve it.

While I'd be perfectly happy with this plate of lamb chops for dinner, serving it alongside some steamed rice or a few pieces of flatbread to sop up all the juices would also be a good idea.

**1** Combine the cumin, Sichuan peppercorns, and red pepper flakes in a spice mill or mortar and pestle, and process or pound to a coarse powder (alternatively, place all the spices in a ziplock bag and crush with a rolling pin or heavy skillet). Add the salt to the spice mixture and mix well. Season the lamb chops with the cumin-salt mixture and set aside.

**2** Heat the oil in a large skillet over medium-high heat. Sear the lamb chops (which should all fit in the skillet) until both sides are deep golden brown but the inside is still a nice pinkish rare, 3 to 4 minutes per side, depending on size. Transfer the chops to a large serving platter and let rest for 5 minutes.

**3** Meanwhile, add the scallions to the skillet and cook, stirring occasionally, until lightly charred and all coated in the Sichuan-y, lamby fat. Add the vinegar and peanuts (if using), season with salt and black pepper, and serve alongside the lamb chops.

# Paprika-Rubbed Sheet-Pan Chicken with Lemon

*Serves 4*

1 (3½- to 4-pound) chicken, spatchcocked (see below)
2 tablespoons fennel seed
1 tablespoon hot paprika
1 tablespoon kosher salt
2 teaspoons smoked paprika
1 teaspoon freshly ground black pepper
2 garlic cloves, finely grated
¼ cup olive oil
2 lemons, quartered

## How to Spatchcock

Should you want to do it yourself, I find the best way to spatchcock a bird is to use heavy-duty kitchen shears and cut out the backbone first. Think of it like arts and crafts, except it's, you know, a chicken. Place the chicken, breast-side down, on a cutting board. Using kitchen shears, start at the butt end of the chicken and snip along one side of the spine, taking care not to cut into the thigh. Repeat on the other side; you should have a chicken backbone in your hands (freeze it in a ziplock bag and save for the next time you're making chicken stock).

Once that's removed, flip the chicken over, breast-side up. Splay the legs out slightly and, using the palms of your hands, firmly press on the breastbone to flatten it. You should hear a slight crack as the breastplate opens up, flattening the chicken and creating a more even surface for cooking.

I use this paprika-fennel-garlic situation to smear onto pork shoulders and pork chops, marinate chicken thighs or breasts, and toss with fried or grilled chicken wings. Basically, it's my go-to seasoning, and it makes everything taste like really great Italian sausage.

You may notice that this bird can take upward of 2½ hours to roast if you're using a 4-pound chicken, but this is not a crispy-skin chicken; this is a melty, tender, sticky, juicy chicken, worth every minute. The low-and-slow treatment ensures that none of the spices or bits of garlic burn, while giving the chicken fat plenty of time to render out slowly and evenly.

If the idea of spatchcocking a chicken puts you in a bad place mentally or emotionally, the information below should help you out, but let it be known that most butchers or meat-counter people will do it for you. Let it also be known that this recipe can be made with a non-spatchcocked chicken; you just might need to give it an extra 30 to 40 minutes in the oven.

1 Preheat the oven to 325°F.

2 Using paper towels, pat the chicken dry. Place the chicken, breast-side up, on a rimmed baking sheet (you can also use a very large 10- to 12-inch ovenproof skillet).

3 Grind the fennel seed in a spice mill or mortar and pestle (alternatively, chop it with a knife or smash it in a ziplock bag with a heavy skillet) and place it in a bowl with the hot paprika, salt, smoked paprika, pepper, garlic, and olive oil, and smear this all over the bird. Skin side, underside, in every nook and cranny possible. Really get in there with that rub. Rub any of the leftover mixture onto the quartered lemons and scatter them around the chicken.

4 Roast the chicken until it is completely tender and cooked through and the lemons are soft and jammy (perfect for squeezing), 2 to 2½ hours. You don't need to do much to it once it's in the oven, but around hour 2, sometimes I'll use a spoon or pastry brush to baste the chicken with all the garlicky business that has dripped off along with the chicken fat.

5 The drippings from this particular chicken are truly magnificent. Fiery orange, deeply savory, and just the most delicious thing on the planet. *Do not waste these drippings.* Instead, drizzle them over the chicken once it's carved, use them to crisp up smashed potatoes (page 73), drag crusty bread through them, or toss with vegetables before a quick roasting to serve alongside the chicken.

# Crispy Chicken Legs with Rosemary, Tiny Potatoes, and Sour Cream

*Serves 4*

**4 chicken legs (the drumstick and thigh should be attached)**
**Kosher salt and freshly ground black pepper**
**12 ounces very small, waxy potatoes (about the size of a quarter or smaller)**
**1 head of garlic, split crosswise**
**4 sprigs fresh rosemary**
**1½ cups olive oil**
**½ cup finely chopped fresh chives**
**½ cup sour cream**

Conventional wisdom suggests that covering something in fat to slow cook it (aka "making a confit") is only worthy of some glorious game bird like duck or goose. But guess what, this isn't 1778, and I think even Thursday-night chicken deserves this kind of treatment. It's pretty much the most hands-off technique that will yield the most showstopping results.

Something to note is that while, yes, the chicken gets crazy, fall-apart tender and the crisped skin rivals even the best fried chicken, something else happens here that makes this worth cooking and justifies the amount of olive oil called for. As the chicken slow cooks, the fat melts into the oil and infuses with garlic and rosemary, leaving you with something so delicious that it's basically worth its weight in gold.

After straining the oil, I keep it in my fridge (it'll keep for about a month) and use it to roast vegetables, crisp up potatoes (page 73), sauté greens, and, maybe in the most genius way possible, use it to fry my morning eggs (page 116).

**1** Preheat the oven to 325°F.

**2** Season the chicken with salt and pepper. Place it in a large baking dish with the potatoes, garlic, and rosemary. Cover the whole thing with olive oil and bake until the chicken is basically falling apart and the garlic is golden brown, 1½ to 2 hours. Remove it from the oven and let cool slightly.

**3** Heat 2 tablespoons of the oil and chicken fat from the baking dish in a large skillet over medium-high heat. Carefully remove 2 chicken legs from the baking dish and place them, skin-side down, in the skillet.

**4** Cook until the skin is browned and crisp, 5 to 8 minutes. Return the chicken to the baking dish, crispy-skin-side up, and repeat with the remaining 2 chicken legs (you can also serve this chicken straight from the baking dish without crisping up the skin, but if you have 5 minutes and a skillet, I highly recommend the added step).

**5** Sprinkle the chives over the sour cream and serve alongside the chicken.

# Slow-Roasted Pork Shoulder with Garlic, Citrus, and Cilantro

*Serves 8*

1 (3½- to 4-pound) boneless, skinless pork shoulder, any twine or netting removed
Kosher salt and freshly ground black pepper
1 tablespoon vegetable oil
1 orange, halved
2 heads of garlic, halved lengthwise
6 sprigs fresh thyme
3 fresh or dried bay leaves
3 chiles de árbol or 1 teaspoon crushed red pepper flakes
2 tablespoons coriander seed
1 cup fresh orange juice (from about 4 oranges)
½ bunch fresh cilantro, thick stems separated from the tender stems and leaves
4 limes, halved

**DO AHEAD:** Pork can be made 2 days ahead and refrigerated. Heat in a 325°F oven until warmed through.

It's well understood that in most any form, a large hunk of pork is predisposed to deliciousness. The sheer size of a standard pork shoulder, in addition to the abundance of marbled fat throughout, makes this particular cut nearly impossible to mess up, which means it's ideal for anyone who's unsure about cooking such a large piece of meat. Unlike a standing rib roast or rack of lamb, you're not aiming for rare, which reduces a lot of the pressure.

Because I don't really love braised, shredded meat, I think this large, flavorful, fatty cut of meat is best slow cooked, then sliced when it's just tender enough. I eat it almost like a prime rib, doused in its own fat and juices. That said, if it were to fall apart into tender, shreddy bits, would that really be the worst thing?

These juices are super citrusy and garlicky, and remind me of my favorite Cuban restaurant growing up (where I'm pretty sure they cooked everything in Sprite).

**1** Preheat the oven to 325°F.

**2** Season the pork with salt and pepper. Heat the oil in a large, heavy-bottomed pot (with a lid) over medium-high heat. Sear the pork, fat-side down, until it's really well browned, 8 to 10 minutes. Turn the pork and brown on the other side, another 8 to 10 minutes. Transfer the pork to a large serving platter or cutting board, and drain the pot of all but 1 tablespoon of the fat (drain it into an empty glass jar or can for easy disposal).

**3** Add the halved orange and garlic to the pot, cut-side down, followed by the thyme, bay leaves, chiles, and coriander. Cook, stirring for a second, to lightly brown the oranges and garlic. Add the orange juice and 2 cups water, stirring to scrape up any bits. Return the pork to the pot (the liquid should come a little less than halfway up the pork—add more water if it doesn't). Cover and transfer it to the oven.

**4** Roast the pork until it is super tender but not quite falling apart (you want to be able to slice it, not shred it), 3 to 4 hours.

**5** Remove the pot from the oven and, using tongs or two large serving utensils, transfer the pork to a cutting board and let it rest a few minutes. Chop the thicker stems of cilantro and add them to the pot with all the pork juices. Juice 2 limes into the pot, throwing the limes themselves in there, too. Slice the pork and return it to the pot with any juices (alternatively, lay the sliced pork on a large serving platter and ladle the juices over it). Top the pork with the remaining tender stems and leaves of cilantro before serving, along with the remaining limes for squeezing over.

# Pork and Red Chile Stew with Tomatillos

*Serves 6 to 8*

6 large New Mexican or guajillo chiles
    (about 2 ounces)
Kosher salt
4 garlic cloves, chopped
½ yellow onion, chopped
Freshly ground black pepper
2½ pounds boneless pork shoulder, cut
    into 2-inch pieces
2 teaspoons ground cumin
1 tablespoon vegetable or canola oil
1 pound tomatillos, quartered (or
    halved, if small)
1 (25-ounce) can hominy, drained and
    rinsed
2 limes, quartered, for serving
4 radishes, thinly sliced, for serving
2 cups shredded cabbage or iceberg
    lettuce, for serving
¼ cup fresh oregano leaves, for serving
Tortilla chips, for serving

The first time I had posole, I was working as a pastry cook at Quince in San Francisco. The head prep guy, Alejandro, would make it every Saturday morning when he came in at seven, knowing that by the time all the cooks came in around noon, it would be ready for them. The spicy, life-giving soup made from bright red dried New Mexican chiles, hunks of fatty pork shoulder, and kernels of just-cooked hominy was, turns out, the only thing that could get us through a thirteen-hour workday that started with a Friday-night hangover.

While this may not be a true posole—it's thicker and more stew-like, there's less hominy, and I've added tomatillos for body and acidity in addition to dried chiles—you can, and should, still garnish it like one, piling your bowl high with shredded cabbage, coins of thinly sliced radish, and tons and tons of fresh lime.

**1** Toast the chiles, which you can do in one of three ways: toast them over a live gas flame (using tongs, hold them over a high flame, almost like you're toasting a marshmallow), in a cast-iron skillet over medium-high heat (toast, shaking the skillet frequently, for about 5 minutes), or in a 375°F oven on a baking sheet (just let them do their thing, 8 to 10 minutes). You want the chiles to be puffed and lightly charred, not burned, and any of these methods will get you there with equal results.

**2** Once the chiles are delightfully toasted, use kitchen shears to remove the stem and cut them into rings. I like the extra heat, so I keep the seeds, but you can discard all or half the seeds for something more mild.

**3** In a medium saucepan, bring 4 cups salted water to a simmer and add the chiles. Remove from the heat and let sit 15 minutes; the chiles should be soft enough that they basically fall apart when rubbed between your fingers.

**4** Using a slotted spoon, transfer the chiles to a blender (save all that chile water!) along with the garlic and onion, and season with salt and black pepper. Add about ½ cup of the chile water and puree until you've got a smooth paste, adding more water as needed to help the blender do its job.

*recipe continues*

**5** Season the pork with cumin, salt, and black pepper. Heat the oil in a large Dutch oven over medium-high heat. Add the pork and cook, turning occasionally, until the meat is well browned all over, 10 to 15 minutes.

**6** Transfer the pork to a large plate or cutting board. Pour the fat from the Dutch oven into a glass jar or can (there will be plenty of fat to go around as the pork cooks; you just want to get rid of the excess so the stew doesn't feel greasy). Return the pot to medium heat and add the chile paste. Cook, stirring occasionally, until the paste is fragrant and starts to caramelize along the bottom of the pot, about 5 minutes (this will take the edge off the raw onions and garlic in the paste).

**7** Add the tomatillos, hominy, remaining chile water, reserved pork (plus any juices that have accumulated), and an additional 4 cups water. Season with salt and black pepper, and bring to a simmer.

**8** Reduce the heat to low and cover. Let it simmer and do its thing for about 1½ hours, peeking in only when you just can't stand how good it smells. Remove the lid partially, just to let some of the steam escape and the liquid evaporate (this will give you a good thick stew texture), and continue to cook until the pork has completely fallen apart with tenderness and the flavors have all come together in sweet, porky harmony, another hour or two.

**9** Season with salt and more black pepper, if needed, before serving with limes, radishes, cabbage, oregano, and tortilla chips.

# Turmeric-Roasted Lamb Shoulder and Carrots with All the Fixings

*Serves 8*

**LAMB**

1 (3½- to 4-pound) boneless lamb shoulder, untied

Kosher salt and freshly ground black pepper

1½ ounces fresh turmeric (from about four 2- to 3-inch pieces), peeled

10 large garlic cloves (from about 1 head)

¼ cup olive oil

1 tablespoon ground cumin

1 tablespoon vegetable oil

2 bunches small carrots (about 1 pound), scrubbed, tops trimmed to 1 inch

**THE FIXINGS (ONE OR ALL OF THESE WOULD BE A WELCOME ADDITION TO THE ROAST, BUT REALLY THERE IS NO PRESSURE)**

8 pieces Sour Cream Flatbread (page 137) or something store-bought, such as pita or lavash

Beet-Pickled Turnips (page 23), sliced raw turnips, or radishes tossed with a splash of vinegar

Another Salsa Verde (page 21)

¼ head of small red cabbage, shredded

Preserved Lemon Labne (page 27) or full-fat Greek yogurt

**NOTE:** This also works with boneless leg of lamb; just make sure it's still in the 3½- to 4-pound range.

It took a long time for me to come around to liking lamb. I had only experienced the meat as braised shanks or ground up in some too-sweet moussaka, and the only word I'd use to describe its aggressive flavor was *gamey*. Not necessarily a compliment.

That was before I discovered the shoulder cut. Here it gets rubbed with earthy turmeric and tons of garlic, cooked medium-rare (not braised to hell), thinly sliced, and served with tons of condiments. And it's amazing. Not "gamey" or "lamby" or even aggressive, just delicious. It's kind of a fancy cut of meat, so I wouldn't recommend you whip this up for a casual Tuesday; that said, this roast does make for supremely delicious, even casual, leftovers.

While the "fixings" here are rather specific, feel empowered to serve this however and with whatever you like. This happens to be my fantasy spread, but if you don't have cabbage or you feel like using just regular pita bread, the lamb will still blow your mind.

**1  PREPARE THE LAMB:** Season the lamb on both sides with 1 tablespoon salt and pepper, and let sit at room temperature while you make the turmeric rub.

**2**  Very finely chop the turmeric and garlic and place them in a small bowl with the olive oil, cumin, and 2 tablespoons salt. Alternatively, place the turmeric, garlic, cumin, and 2 tablespoons salt in a food processor and pulse until you've got a coarse paste. Add the olive oil and pulse to blend (your food processor will be stained for a bit, but who cares). Oh, you could also do this with a mortar and pestle. The options!

**3**  Smear this turmeric mixture all over the lamb and season with pepper, making sure to get inside all the nooks and crannies.

**4**  Roll the lamb, fat-side up (it won't really "roll" so much as it will just sorta close like a book), and, using butcher's twine, tie the lamb every inch or so. Cover with plastic wrap and let the lamb sit for anywhere from 1 to 24 hours in the refrigerator. It will be good after 1 hour, but after 24, it will be magnificent. Plan accordingly.

*recipe continues*

**5** Preheat the oven to 325°F.

**6** Heat the vegetable oil in a large, heavy-bottomed, ovenproof skillet over medium heat. Sear the lamb on all sides until golden brown, 4 to 6 minutes per side, emptying the skillet of some of the fat as needed (don't worry about pouring some out; there is plenty to go around). The goal here is not only to brown the outside but also to render some of that excess fat, so make sure your flame is not too high or else the outside will start to burn before that can happen. Add the carrots to the skillet, toss them in the pan drippings, and season with salt and pepper.

**7** Place the skillet in the oven and roast until the internal temperature at the deepest part of the lamb reaches 145°F, 45 to 55 minutes (this is rare; if that freaks you out and you prefer your lamb on the medium side, cook to 160°F, which'll take closer to 60 to 65 minutes).

**8** Let the lamb rest for 20 to 30 minutes before removing the twine. Use this time to prepare the fixings: warm up the flatbread, cut the pickled turnips into bite-sized pieces, and set out all your small bowls filled with salsa verde, shredded cabbage, and preserved lemon labne.

**9** Once the lamb is ready, slice it about ½ inch thick and serve with all the fixings.

# A Beautiful Brined Bird

Brining poultry is a much-debated, hot-button issue. Does it really do anything? What's the point? Is it better than not brining at all? Lots to unpack here. But yes, I truly do believe in the merits of brining a bird. Whether you're trying to keep it moist (debatable) or not, it undoubtedly improves the chicken on matters of both flavor and tenderness by replacing much of the liquid in the bird with salty, flavorful brine. Is it a must for every weeknight? No. But if you've got the time and the desire, I think it's a worthy addition to your chicken cooking repertoire.

Before you tell me, "There is no way I'm going to *brine* a chicken," I hear you—but listen, this isn't Thanksgiving, and it's not a turkey. There's no ill-fated cooler filled with ice and a brining bag large enough to hold your entire family. Plus, like I said, it's not a turkey, which we all know is an uphill battle to deliciousness. All you need for this is a gallon-sized ziplock bag and some space in your fridge.

While a good old-fashioned water-salt solution will get the job done, some of my favorite things to brine chicken in are the tangy by-products of items I've already got in my fridge: the liquid from preserved lemons; leftover kimchi, sauerkraut, or pickle brine; the whey from fancy feta or other cheeses; and that last bit of buttermilk I just can't bring myself to throw away. Beer works, too.

For the brine, you'll need about 2 cups liquid total per 3 to 4 pounds chicken (this can be either a whole bird or parts). Generally, what I'll do is add whatever leftover liquid I already have, then make up the difference with water and salt. Because the liquid you're starting with can be very salty or not at all, I prefer to season the brine rather than worry about ratios.

The brine should be fairly aggressively flavored and salty if you really want it to penetrate all the way to the bone (you do), so when using things without salt, like beer or buttermilk, be sure to compensate.

Place the chicken in a large ziplock bag and add your liquid of choice. Feel free to add aromatics: crushed garlic, citrus peel, herbs, spices, chiles, and, of course, lots of cracked black pepper.

The amount of time you brine a bird will depend on the size: up to an hour will do the trick if you're brining boneless, skinless thighs, but you'll want a solid 12 to 24 hours for a whole chicken.

When it comes time to cook the chicken, drain the brine (discarding it entirely) and pat the chicken dry. Go forth and roast, sear, fry, or braise.

# Buttermilk-Brined Chicken with Fresh Za'atar

*Serves 4*

4 cups buttermilk or 2 cups sauerkraut or kimchi brine, whey, or pickle juice

1½ tablespoons kosher salt, plus more as needed

4 garlic cloves, crushed

1 shallot or ½ yellow onion, thinly sliced

Freshly ground black pepper

3 pounds bone-in chicken parts or 1¾ pounds boneless, skinless chicken

1 bunch spring onions (or scallions), tops left on, quartered if large

2 tablespoons olive oil

3 tablespoons Fresh Za'atar (page 20)

1 lime or lemon, quartered

I find roasting a buttermilk-brined chicken to be the best way to see for yourself why it's worth the effort. While the brine helps flavor and tenderize the chicken if you're frying, braising or stewing, it's the golden-brown skin and juicy white meat of the oven-roasted breast that'll turn you into a brining believer. Use this basic buttermilk brine recipe as is, or throw in whatever spices or herbs you're feeling at the moment.

**1** Combine the buttermilk, salt, garlic, and shallot together in a large bowl or ziplock bag; if you're using another liquid instead of buttermilk, also add 1 cup water. Season with pepper, add the chicken, and toss to coat. Leave it in the bag, refrigerated, for at least 1 hour and up to 24 hours (boneless, skinless thighs will take closer to 2 hours, but a bone-in breast should get the full 24).

**2** When you're ready to cook the chicken, preheat the oven to 425°F.

**3** Toss the spring onions with the olive oil and season with salt and pepper. Remove the chicken from the brine and pat it dry; discard the brine. Place the chicken on a rimmed baking sheet along with the spring onions and roast until the chicken is golden brown and cooked through, 25 to 35 minutes (closer to 25 minutes for those boneless, skinless thighs; closer to 35 for those bone-in breasts), and the onions are tender and starting to caramelize at the edges (if the onions are left on there a little longer, that's okay).

**4** Serve the chicken with the onions alongside, sprinkling everything with fresh za'atar and squeezing lime or lemon juice over it all.

# Lamb Stew with Fennel, Preserved Lemon, and Crispy Fried Bread

*Serves 6 to 8*

**2½ pounds boneless lamb shoulder or leg, cut into 2-inch pieces**
**Kosher salt and freshly ground black pepper**
**1 tablespoon canola oil**
**6 garlic cloves, chopped**
**4 anchovy fillets (optional)**
**2 large shallots, finely chopped**
**1 large fennel bulb, coarsely chopped**
**1 tablespoon fennel seed**
**1 tablespoon cumin seed**
**2 tablespoons tomato paste**
**½ cup dry white wine**
**1 (28-ounce) can whole peeled tomatoes, crushed**
**2 fresh or dried bay leaves**
**3 tablespoons olive oil, plus more for drizzling**
**½ loaf crusty country bread, torn into 2-inch pieces**
**1 tablespoon Aleppo pepper**
**1 Preserved Lemon, homemade (page 27) or store-bought, thinly sliced**
**2 tablespoons fresh marjoram leaves**

**NOTE:** No matter what kind of stew you're making, the size of the meat cubes you start with is everything. You want large pieces (about 2 inches) so you get more surface area to brown (where all the good stuff like caramelized bits happens).

**DO AHEAD:** Stew can be made 4 days ahead and refrigerated.

The anchovies might seem like a strange move here, but lamb and anchovies are actually best of friends, complementing each other with rich, meaty flavor. Sure, they add salt, but there's also that elusive umami they bring to the table, which makes them the closest thing I have to a secret weapon. Once they're added to the pot, they disappear almost immediately, fading into the background to pleasantly mingle with all the other flavors, sneakily making this one of the best stews you've ever had.

Secret ingredients help, sure, but for a truly magnificent stew, there must be garnishes, and they must be plentiful, offering texture and a direct flavor punch. Dollops of sour cream and sprinkles of herbs are great, but never underestimate the power of salty preserved lemons and spicy, crispy bread.

**1** Season the lamb with salt and black pepper. Heat the canola oil in a large Dutch oven over medium-high heat and add about half the lamb. Cook, stirring every so often, until the lamb is well browned on all sides, 8 to 10 minutes. Transfer the lamb to a bowl or plate while you sear the rest of it.

**2** Once the second batch of lamb is seared, drain off any excess fat.

**3** Return all the lamb to the pot and add the garlic, anchovies, shallots, fennel, fennel seed, and cumin seed. Cook, stirring and scraping up any bits on the bottom, until the fennel has softened and is starting to brown, about 4 minutes. Add the tomato paste and cook, stirring, until it's a dark brick-red color, about 2 minutes. Add the wine and really get in there with the spatula or wooden spoon, scraping up all the bits on the bottom (yes, there are more bits).

**4** Add the tomatoes, bay leaves, and 6 cups water, and season with salt and black pepper. Bring to a simmer and reduce the heat to medium-low. Cook, uncovered, until the lamb is completely tender and falling apart and the stew has thickened nicely (it should definitely coat the back of a spoon), 2 to 2½ hours. Adjust for seasoning along the way (this will yield better results than just waiting till the end).

**5** When ready to serve, heat the olive oil in a large skillet over medium heat. Add the torn bread and stir it around so it soaks up a lot of that olive oil. Season with salt and black pepper, and cook, stirring occasionally (but try not to squish the bread; you want it fluffy), until the bread is golden brown and crispy on all sides, 5 to 8 minutes. Remove from the heat, add the Aleppo pepper, and toss to coat.

**6** Top the stew with the preserved lemon, marjoram, and fried bread.

# Hanger Steak with Dandelion, Arugula, and Grana Padano

*Serves 4*

½ **small red onion, very thinly sliced into rings**
½ **teaspoon Asian fish sauce or 2 anchovy fillets, finely chopped**
⅓ **cup olive oil**
4 **cups arugula**
½ **bunch dandelion greens, mizuna, small mustard greens, or baby kale (about 2 cups)**
**Kosher salt and freshly ground black pepper**
1¼ **pounds hanger steak, cut into two pieces**
1 **tablespoon vegetable oil**
1 **tablespoon fresh lemon juice**
**Flaky sea salt**
1 **ounce Grana Padano or Parmesan cheese, for shaving**
**Lemon wedges, for serving**

I am not and will never be an "I'll just have a salad" kind of person. Salad on the side, yeah. Salad to start, of course. But to think that *just* a salad would be enough to satisfy me on any level—emotional, spiritual, physical—is totally delusional. Believe me, I've tried. It always ends with a feeling of deep emptiness and probably a bag of salt-and-vinegar chips.

But this salad is different. This salad has spicy, bitter, sturdy leaves that won't wilt like some mixed greens out of a plastic clamshell. This salad has a punchy, assertive dressing and properly charred, almost-too-rare steak. This salad will make you forget that salt-and-vinegar chips even exist. This salad will never be "just a salad."

When shopping for the greens here, look for the arugula that is a little wilder, a little larger than the packaged stuff. It typically comes by "the bunch," and while it's a sure bet at your local farmer's market, higher-end grocery stores will likely carry it as well. Bitter dandelion, while not as widely available, is starting to become a bit more "mainstream," which I'm happy to see. If you really can't find it (or simply don't care for it), choose another spicy, sturdy green like mizuna, frilly mustard greens, or even baby kale.

**1** Soak the onions in a bowl of cold water; set aside.

**2** Combine the fish sauce and olive oil in a small bowl. Finely chop ½ cup of the arugula and ½ cup of the dandelion greens, and add them to the bowl; season with kosher salt and pepper.

**3** Season the steak with kosher salt and pepper. Heat the vegetable oil in a large skillet over medium-high heat and sear the steak until it's well browned on both sides and reaches for a solid medium-rare (more rare than medium), 4 to 5 minutes per side. Transfer the steak to a cutting board and let rest about 5 minutes.

**4** Toss the remaining arugula and dandelion greens with the lemon juice and season with kosher salt and pepper. Drain the onions and add them to the bowl with the greens. Arrange on a large serving platter.

**5** Slice the steak against the grain and add it to the salad, pouring any cutting board juices over the top. Spoon the chopped arugula and dandelion mixture over the top of the steak salad and sprinkle with flaky sea salt and pepper. Shave the cheese over everything and serve with lemon wedges for squeezing.

# Bacon-Roasted Pork Tenderloin with Caraway'd Cabbage and Apples

*Serves 4*

1½ pounds pork tenderloin
Kosher salt and freshly ground black
    pepper
5 bacon strips
4 garlic cloves, smashed
1 small or ½ medium head red cabbage,
    cut into eighths
2 medium apples, such as Cortland
    or Honeycrisp, quartered
    (I don't mind the core, but remove
    it if you do)
2 teaspoons caraway seed
2 tablespoons olive oil
1½ tablespoons apple cider vinegar or
    red wine vinegar

**NOTE:** This can be done with a number of vegetables if cabbage is not your thing; fennel, turnips, carrots, or parsnips would all be great.

My enthusiasm for all things cabbage related knows no bounds. As uncool as it is, fermented, shredded, braised, seared, or roasted, cabbage has a crisp, hearty texture and kind of funky flavor that I just cannot get enough of. While wildly versatile, and I shouldn't pick favorites, cabbage when roasted in lots of garlicky pork fat until lightly charred around the edges might be my favorite way to eat it. Don't tell kimchi.

To make sure you've got well-roasted cabbage, caramelized apples, crispy bacon on the outside, and juicy, medium-rare pork on the inside, buy the thickest tenderloin you can find. A thinner piece will likely overcook by the time everything else has had a chance to properly do its thing.

**1** Place an oven rack in the upper third of the oven. Preheat the oven to 450°F.

**2** Season the tenderloin with salt and pepper and wrap it in the bacon, tucking the ends so that they stay put. Place the garlic, cabbage, apples, and caraway seed in a large baking dish or cast-iron skillet and drizzle everything with the olive oil; season with salt and pepper, and toss to combine.

**3** Nestle the pork in the center of the dish and roast it on the top rack until the bacon is crisped and the pork is cooked through but still a nice medium-rare (145°F), 30 to 35 minutes.

**4** Transfer the pork to a cutting board to rest for 5 minutes before slicing. Toss the cabbage mixture with the vinegar and serve alongside the pork.

# Anchovy-Butter Chicken with Chicken Fat Croutons

*Serves 4*

1 (3½- to 4-pound) chicken
Kosher salt and freshly ground black
    pepper
4 tablespoons (½ stick) unsalted butter,
    at room temperature
10 anchovy fillets, finely chopped
2 garlic cloves, finely chopped
1 head of garlic, halved crosswise
½ bunch fresh thyme, marjoram,
    oregano, and/or rosemary
2 small red onions or large shallots,
    unpeeled, and quartered
½ loaf crusty bread, torn into 2-inch
    pieces
½ cup fresh parsley, coarsely chopped

When people ask me what my favorite thing to cook is, often I'll give them the most boring but honest answer possible: roasted chicken. In a personal quest for "the one," I've tried a bird every way possible—simple salt-and-pepper birds, spatchcocked (see page 227) and slow roasted, brined, and trussed—but I always come back to this version: smeared inside and out with a salty, garlicky anchovy butter; roasted at a high temperature for brown skin, then low for juicy breasts; stuffed only with more garlic and maybe some herbs; legs akimbo (I have a strict "no truss, no fuss" policy).

I'm going to be honest with you: this recipe is almost too much. The sticky juices from the roasted chicken, the caramelized bits from anchovy butter, and the croutons that cook in the skillet and crisp in the fat, well . . . I mean, it's really all just too much. Almost. For what other dish would you be tempted to lick a hot skillet?

**1** Preheat the oven to 425°F.

**2** Pat the chicken dry with paper towels and season it with salt and lots of pepper; let it hang out while you make the anchovy butter.

**3** Using a fork, smash the butter, anchovies, and chopped garlic together in a small bowl and season with salt and pepper. Smear the chicken all over and inside every nook and cranny with this butter (like, really get in there). If you're comfortable doing so, I encourage you to smear the butter under the skin, too.

**4** Stuff the chicken cavity with the halved garlic and herbs, and place the bird on a rimmed baking sheet or in a large skillet. Scatter the onions around the chicken and roast until the bird starts to brown, 25 to 35 minutes. Toss the onions around to coat them in whatever amazing fat has dripped off the chicken. Reduce the oven temperature to 350°F and continue to roast until the chicken is cooked through and the onions are gloriously golden, another 25 to 30 minutes.

**5** Transfer the chicken to a cutting board or large serving platter, leaving the juices and onions behind. Increase the oven temperature to 425°F (ugh, I know, annoying—just do it, though) and toss the bread in all the glorious fat and cooking juices on the baking sheet, making sure the pieces are soaking up all the business left behind. Return the baking sheet to the oven to crisp up the bread, 10 to 15 minutes. Serve this alongside the chicken, with the roasted onions and parsley scattered around and on top.

SWEETS

# Desserts and I have a funny relationship, partly because I spent several years obsessing over them as a professional pastry chef, and partly because I've never had a particularly strong sweet tooth.

Despite retiring my "serious baker" apron many moons ago, lots of people still think of me as the Dessert Person, which is both a blessing and a curse; I get away with bringing only pie to potlucks, but then I'm also asked to make wedding cakes (okay, so I offered). As hard as I try to shatter this perception (I roast pork shoulders, too!), it's a legacy that has led me to discover a great joy in my life, which is writing recipes for people who think they "can't bake" or "aren't dessert people." Well, I didn't used to be a dessert person, either.

Desserts don't have to be complicated, and even though I am a fussy person, I am not a fussy baker. I don't go out of my way to use room-temperature eggs (straight from the fridge always works for me), and just as I never bother trussing a chicken, you'd never catch me sifting flour (a good whisking will do the trick). Recipes like Honey-Yogurt Pound Cake (page 277) can be made in one bowl, and when it comes to frosting Everyone's Favorite Celebration Cake (page 281), you can totally use a butter knife if you don't have an offset spatula. Take comfort in knowing that while not every recipe in this chapter is for the beginner, even those who don't own a KitchenAid will still find plenty of things to make.

When it comes to the use of sugar, I find restraint to be a good move, which means some might think that the Lemon Shaker Tart (page 289) is a bit too sour (I respectfully disagree), or that the topping for the Pistachio-Plum Crisp (page 286) should be a bit sweeter (I really don't think it should).

Part of what I enjoy about making desserts is the ability to turn down and control the sweetness, letting the tartness of lemons or buttery nuttiness of toasted pistachios take center stage, sugar taking a backseat. So, to those lacking a sweet tooth, I say these not-too-sweet desserts just might turn you into a dessert person, too.

# Sorbet in Grapefruit Cups

*Serves 8*

2 pints sorbet or sherbet
4 large grapefruits (or any mix of
    citrus, really)
4 kumquats, thinly sliced (optional)
½ cup grapes, halved (optional)
1 cup pomegranate seeds (optional)

**NOTE:** Despite the name of the recipe, you could fill these with just about any frozen, scoopable treat. Ice cream, sorbet, and sherbet are all fair game.

**DO AHEAD:** Cups can be made 1 week ahead, wrapped tightly, and frozen.

When I was little, I had frequent sleepovers at my grandma's house. She fed me lots of macaroni and cheese (Velveeta, not the powdered kind), Peeps that she microwaved to make soft again (this is a good trick, actually), and orange sherbet served in halved oranges. When she was feeling fancy, she'd stud the top with kumquats from her tree, because this was California. I was so wildly impressed with this dessert that it truly rocked my world when I started to hear from other members of the family that "Grandma wasn't a great cook." *Not a great cook?* Hello! Have you even *had* those orange cups?

Anyway, turns out, Grandma really isn't a great cook, but she is a great grandma.

**1** Allow the sorbet to sit at room temperature for 10 to 15 minutes, just to soften slightly (you don't want it melted).

**2** Cut the grapefruits in half and, using a large spoon, go around the inside of the peel and remove the fruit from the white pith, sort of peeling it away—it should come out pretty easily, no need to cut or use a knife. Juice the fruit, eat it whole, or maybe make the fennel and grapefruit salad on page 103.

**3** Peel away any white pith so that all you're left with is pure rind. Fill each half with the sorbet of your choice, mixing, matching, swirling, and combining. Smooth the top with a spoon or butter knife. Freeze until totally solid again, about 30 minutes (or do like Grandma Prue and dot the top of the cups with sliced kumquats, halved grapes, or pomegranate seeds before freezing).

**4** Serve the halves or, using a sharp knife, cut each half into quarters before serving (unless you've got the kumquats, grapes, or pomegranate seeds nestled in there, then you basically eat the sorbet cups like cereal from a bowl).

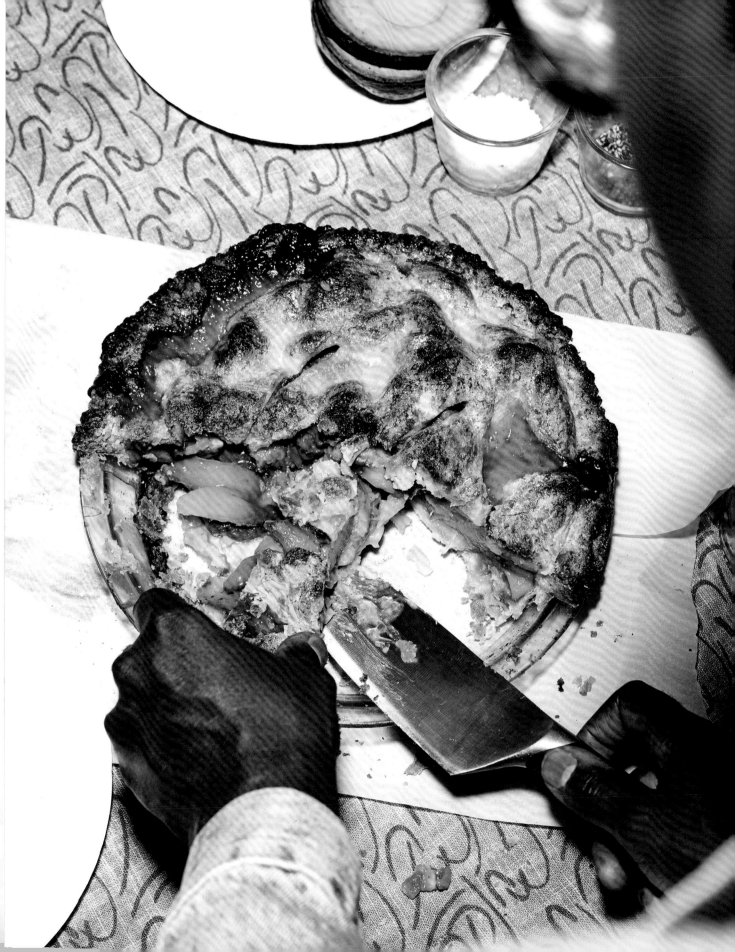

moisture and steam to escape as the pie bakes. This is a necessary step that allows the filling to thicken properly, as well as ensures a flaky, crunchy crust.

**7** Brush the top with the egg wash and sprinkle with the Demerara sugar. Place the pie on a parchment- or foil-lined baking sheet and bake for at least 60 minutes before you even think about checking on it. I'm serious. Pies take a *really* long time to bake, much longer than most people actually keep them in the oven. I sound like a broken record over here, but I feel very passionately about this and need my voice to be heard.

**8** After about an hour, rotate the pie; it'll likely need another 30 to 45 in there. *Yes, I am serious!*

**9** The piecrust should be the color of a perfect croissant all over—dangerously golden, almost to the brink of "Is my pie burned?" (No.) If the edges start to get too dark for your liking before the top is ready, place thin strips of foil over the parts that are getting too far ahead of the game.

**10** Remove the pie from the oven and let it cool completely before eating. To me, that means about 4 hours, but people get really upset when you tell them they should wait that long, so do what you please.

### Three Other Really Great Fillings

**TANGY APPLE PIE**
Swap apples for the peaches, apple cider vinegar for the lime juice, and add a pinch of cinnamon.

**BLUEBERRY LEMON**
Swap blueberries for the peaches, lemon juice for the lime juice.

**SOUR CHERRY–SHERRY**
Swap pitted sour cherries for the peaches, sherry wine for the lime juice.

---

**So You're Going to Bake a Pie**

When it comes to making pies, baking is the most critical step. I've said it before, and I'll say it again here in case you didn't read it elsewhere: there is nothing more tragic in the kitchen than an underbaked pie (or any pastry, for that matter). When butter and flour are baked for the proper time, they do this magical thing—the butter and flour both browning, taking on flavor and character, not to mention crispiness and, in some cases, flakiness. Especially with larger items like pies, you'd literally have to forget about them in the oven before they burn (which I have done—it takes a while), so don't think twice about giving them those extra few minutes.

# Buttered Raspberry Hand Pies

*Makes 8 hand pies*

1 recipe (2 disks) **The Only Piecrust**
    **(page 256)**
**All-purpose flour, for rolling**
**1 large egg**
**2 pints fresh raspberries (about 4 cups)**
**¼ cup granulated sugar**
**1 teaspoon finely chopped fresh thyme,**
    **plus fresh thyme leaves for garnish**
    **(optional)**
**1 teaspoon finely grated lemon, lime,**
    **or orange zest**
**4 tablespoons (½ stick) unsalted butter,**
    **cut into 8 pieces, chilled**
**¼ cup Demerara or granulated sugar**

**NOTE:** As an aside, I entered these into
a pie contest once, and they didn't win
because they didn't conform to the
traditional idea of what a pie should
be (i.e., baked in a pie dish). But don't
worry, I'm over it!

**DO AHEAD:** Pies can be baked 1 day
ahead.

I love a hand pie for a few reasons:
- They have a higher crust-to-filling ratio than a regular pie.
- Because of their size, they don't need to bake for an eternity.
- You can make them even if you don't own a pie dish.
- They are *adorable*.

That said, I pretty much make hand pies exclusively with
raspberries, because a whole regular-sized pie of raspberries
is just *too much* raspberry. In a hand pie, they get enough oven
time so the juices properly thicken just as the crust turns that
perfect golden brown. The ideal pie scenario, really.

**1** Preheat the oven to 375°F. Line two baking sheets with
parchment paper.

**2** Roll the pie dough out on a lightly floured work surface about
⅛ inch, but no thicker than ¼ inch. Transfer the dough to a
parchment-lined baking sheet. Chill for about 10 minutes so it's
easier to work with.

**3** Beat the egg with 1 teaspoon water and set aside (this is your egg
wash, and it will help seal the pies and make them golden brown).

**4** In a small bowl, combine the raspberries, granulated sugar,
thyme (if using), and lemon zest. Gently mix this all together,
breaking up the berries a little (this will happen pretty naturally).

**5** Using a 4½-inch ring cutter (or a close approximation; sometimes
I eyeball it and just use a paring knife with some sort of coffee
mug as my guide), cut out 16 circles. Place 8 circles on the second
parchment-lined baking sheet (so you don't have to move them later).

**6** Divide the raspberry mixture evenly among the 8 circles, piling
up the goods in the center (don't worry if some juices start going
rogue), place one small piece of butter on top of the berries, and
brush the edges of the circle with some of the egg wash.

**7** Place the remaining 8 circles on top of the raspberries, matching
the edges. Pressing with the tines of a fork, seal the pies. Brush the
tops of each pie with egg wash and sprinkle with a few thyme leaves
(if using) and the Demerara sugar. Using a sharp knife, cut one or
two slits in the center of each pie (this allows the steam to escape,
which thickens the filling and prevents a soggy crust).

**8** Place the pies in the oven and bake until the juices start bubbling
out of the top and the crust is deliciously golden brown, the color of
a perfect croissant, 25 to 30 minutes. Let cool before eating.

# Salted Butter and Chocolate Chunk Shortbread, or Why Would I Make Another Chocolate Chip Cookie Ever Again?

*Makes 24 cookies*

1 cup plus 2 tablespoons (2¼ sticks) salted butter (see Note), cut into ½-inch pieces
½ cup granulated sugar
¼ cup light brown sugar
1 teaspoon vanilla extract
2¼ cups all-purpose flour
6 ounces semi- or bittersweet dark chocolate, chopped (but not too fine, you want chunks, not thin shards of chocolate)
1 large egg, beaten
Demerara sugar, for rolling
Flaky sea salt, such as Jacobsen, for sprinkling

**NOTE:** If you find it tragically annoying to buy salted butter just for this recipe, you can use unsalted butter and add ¾ teaspoon kosher salt to the flour.

**DO AHEAD:** The cookie dough can be made ahead and stored, tightly wrapped in plastic, up to 1 week in the refrigerator, or 1 month in the freezer. Cookies can be baked and stored in plastic wrap or an airtight container for 5 days.

I've always found chocolate chip cookies to be deeply flawed (to know this about me explains a lot). Too sweet, too soft, or with too much chocolate, there's a lot of room for improvement, if you ask me. But no one asked me, and rather than do a complete overhaul on the most iconic cookie known to man, I took all my favorite parts and invented something else entirely.

Made with lots of salted butter (it has a slightly different flavor and a deeper saltiness than using just salt—I prefer unsalted butter everywhere else but here), the dough has just enough flour to hold it together and the right amount of light brown sugar to suggest a chocolate chip cookie. The chocolate is cut into chunks to prevent chip congregation, and once the dough is formed into a cylindrical log, the whole thing gets rolled in Demerara sugar for the crispiest-ever edges. Less chocolate chip cookie, more brown sugar shortbread with chocolate chunks—they just might be the cookie you've been looking for.

**1** Line a rimmed baking sheet (two, if you've got 'em) with parchment paper.

**2** Using an electric mixer and a medium bowl or a stand mixer fitted with the paddle attachment, beat the butter, both sugars, and vanilla on medium-high till it's super light and fluffy, 3 to 5 minutes. Using a spatula, scrape down the sides of the bowl and, with the mixer on low, slowly add the flour, followed by the chocolate chunks, and beat just to blend.

**3** Divide the dough in half, placing each half on a large piece of plastic wrap. Fold the plastic over so that it covers the dough to protect your hands from getting all sticky. Using your hands (just like you're playing with clay), form the dough into a log shape; rolling it on the counter will help you smooth it out, but don't worry about getting it totally perfect. You can also do this using parchment paper, if you prefer, but I find using plastic wrap easier when it comes to shaping the log. Each half should form two logs 2 to 2¼ inches in diameter. Chill until totally firm, about 2 hours.

**4** Preheat the oven to 350°F.

**5** Brush the outside of the logs with the beaten egg and roll them in the Demerara sugar (this is for those really delicious crispy edges).

**6** Slice each log into ½-inch-thick rounds, place them on the prepared baking sheet(s) about 1 inch apart (they won't spread much), and sprinkle with flaky salt. Bake until the edges are just beginning to brown, 12 to 15 minutes. Let cool slightly before eating them all.

# LUCKIEST BISCUITS IN AMERICA, OR HOW DID I GET HERE?

**A** **good biscuit recipe is the LBD of the food world.** Everyone's got one, and everyone's is the best. For them. With all the different types of biscuits out there (cream biscuits, laminated biscuits, buttermilk biscuits, lard biscuits, drop biscuits, etc.), biscuit making and eating is an extremely personal experience, and what might do it for one person just might not fulfill the next.

Does the world really need another recipe that will promise the perfect combination of towering height; endless flaky layers; impossibly fluffy interior; buttery, crunchy edges; easy-to-assemble execution; foolproof results; and life-changing deliciousness? I mean, I think it might.

And before you say that a biscuit recipe can't change your life, hear me out. To be clear, this recipe isn't about superlatives. This isn't the "flakiest ever" or the "fluffiest" or even "world's greatest." But they are, perhaps, the luckiest, and I'll tell you why (but also, FYI, they are pretty flaky, fluffy, and great).

When cooking first sparked my interest in a real way, I decided I needed to master the biscuit. Not coming from a family of biscuit makers, or from a place known for excellent biscuits, I wasn't even sure what made a great biscuit, if we are being honest. But I was on a quest for perfection.

My starter recipe came from James Beard, because the Internet was a scary and unreliable place, and I trusted him. Looking at the recipe now, it definitely wouldn't sound the alarm for anything remarkable: there's no buttermilk, and the only place melted butter appeared was brushed on top of the biscuits before they went in the oven. It was a real dump-and-mix situation, with no real folds or kneads, no tang or surprise ingredients. Just flour, salt, sugar, heavy cream, and an ungodly amount of baking powder.

Straight from the oven, they're fluffy little steamy clouds of joy, but after cooling to room temperature, the biscuits hardened to pale little rocks of flour. I will also say that they are, for sure, more of a scone than a biscuit. No disrespect, just calling it like I see it, and what I see is a mediocre biscuit.

After making biscuits with buttermilk in addition to cream (or sometimes instead of) and adding butter, experimenting with different leavenings, I would never consider using only cream ever again. That said, I wouldn't claim I ever really mastered a biscuit I was super happy with until I moved to New York in 2009.

While "general life change and exploration" were the main reasons I picked up and moved across the country, I also saw it as an opportunity for a clean break from the restaurant industry. I was completely burnt out, and anyone who's ever worked in a restaurant knows why (it wasn't just the thirteen-hour days and ridiculous pressure, but I have only so much room here).

When gearing up to move, I knew that while I figured out what this new career of mine would be, I'd have to likely (and ironically) find work in another kitchen. So I took a job at Milk Bar, a fun, quirky, of-the-moment bakery known for wildly creative soft-serve flavors, cookies, and cakes. I justified taking the position because I'd have enjoyable morning hours (like a regular human!) and because it was a bakery, not a restaurant. The fact that it was run by an extremely charismatic and talented woman named Christina Tosi who folded me into her little family of badass pastry chefs didn't hurt.

Because I was at Milk Bar only four days a week and my very small Brooklyn apartment wasn't going to pay for itself, I needed a second gig. Some of my new coworkers recommended I reach out to ex-Milkmaid Sarah Sanneh, who had recently reopened her extremely popular Williamsburg restaurant, Pies 'n' Thighs, known for its fried chicken and exemplary biscuits. She took me in, and it was there that she taught me how to make the best biscuit ever.

Even though we made them side by side, hers consistently turned out better. It wasn't the recipe; it was the touch. Knowing when to add the buttermilk, knowing the exact moment to stop pulsing the butter into the dry ingredients. I had a lot to learn, but luckily she was willing to teach me.

Eventually I was promoted at Milk Bar, so I had to leave my biscuit mentor. But that was not the end of our biscuit-making relationship. A few years later, when I left Milk Bar to again figure out that "career change" I had moved across the country to pursue, she took me back. She didn't have any real positions available. "But we could always use more biscuits. Would you be interested in just making biscuits?" *Would I ever!* So, a few days a week, I'd set up shop in the makeshift kitchen near the office upstairs in the restaurant, listen to NPR, and make biscuits. After two years in a demanding kitchen job, it was exactly the kind of relaxing, meditative work my brain needed.

A few months into my new life as the world's happiest biscuit maker and after putting out feelers for a job in magazines, a friend I'd met through the Milk Bar family introduced me to Hunter Lewis, at the time the food editor for *Bon Appétit*. It was six months after Adam Rapoport had taken over the masthead, and they were looking for some freelancers in the test kitchen.

I showed up for an interview, which turned out to be not unlike a restaurant kitchen trial. They showed me a photo of biscuits and asked, "Can you make a recipe for biscuits that look like this?"

Oh, Jesus Christ. What were the odds that I had just spent two months only mixing, rolling, and baking biscuits, and *that* was what they asked me to make? I was feeling insanely lucky but no less panicked that I had to pull a recipe out of thin air that would magically match the biscuits in the photo. So I took what I knew of biscuits—flaky versus buttery, buttermilk versus cream—and I did it. I made those biscuits, and they were just like the ones in the photo. And I got the job.

So, in my opinion, above being flaky, buttery, and fluffy, these are truly the luckiest biscuits in America.

# Luckiest Biscuits in America

*Makes 8 biscuits*

3 cups all-purpose flour, plus more for
    dusting
1 tablespoon baking powder
2 teaspoons kosher salt
1½ teaspoons sugar
¼ teaspoon baking soda
1 cup (2 sticks) unsalted butter, cut into
    1-inch pieces, chilled
1¼ cups buttermilk, plus more
    for brushing
Flaky sea salt, for sprinkling (optional)

**DO AHEAD:** Biscuit dough can be made 2 weeks ahead, wrapped, frozen. You can bake them from frozen—just add 5 to 8 minutes to the bake time.

Biscuit making is a practice, a recipe you begin to feel rather than follow. Like pie dough, they'll only get better every time you make them, but starting with a great recipe will help. This one does not require a food processor, because I believe flat, shaggy pieces of butter create flakier layers than small, pebble-like bits, and it uses two types of leavening in conjunction with buttermilk for foolproof lift.

**1** Preheat the oven to 425°F. Line a baking sheet with parchment paper.

**2** Whisk the flour, baking powder, kosher salt, sugar, and baking soda in a large bowl. Using your hands, smash the butter into the flour mixture. It should be almost like you're making pie dough (you've made pie dough before, right?), with little bits of butter but no large chunks.

**3** Drizzle the buttermilk all over the dry mixture and, using a wooden spoon or, better yet, your hands, mix everything until it comes together in a sort of ball. Knead the mixture a few times in the bowl, making sure to get any of those dry bits at the bottom up into the mix.

**4** Turn the dough out onto a lightly floured work surface and knead another two or three times.

**5** Pat the dough into a 1½-inch-thick rectangle about 12 inches long and 6 inches wide. Cut it in half lengthwise, then crosswise into 4 pieces (you should get 8 biscuits). Alternatively, you can pat the dough into a 1½-inch-thick disk (or whatever shape) and punch out 2-inch circles.

**6** Place the biscuits on the parchment-lined baking sheet and brush the tops with buttermilk, letting some drip down the sides. Sprinkle the tops with flaky sea salt, if you're feeling fancy.

**7** Bake, rotating once, until the biscuits are deeply, fantastically, wonderfully golden brown on the bottoms and tops, and the sides have puffed up like an accordion, 20 to 25 minutes.

**8** Remove from the oven and let cool slightly before destroying.

# Frozen Blackberries and Labne with Honey

*Serves 8*

Nonstick cooking spray, for the pan
2 pints fresh blackberries, raspberries, or hulled and quartered strawberries (12 ounces)
¾ cup mild-flavored honey, such as alfalfa or wildflower
1 cup heavy cream
1½ cups labne or full-fat Greek yogurt
Small pinch of kosher salt

**DO AHEAD:** This can be made 1 week ahead and frozen; just make sure to wrap it tightly in plastic wrap. Let it soften in the fridge before serving.

In my opinion, homemade ice cream, like homemade ketchup, is rarely worth the effort and never as good as you think it's going to be. I'm of the belief that Baskin-Robbins perfected the game as soon as they made mint chocolate chip, and everyone else can just go home. But you know what is good? This frozen dessert.

Semifreddo-like in nature, this tangy frozen yogurt of sorts has the creaminess of ice cream and, like picking up a pint of Baskin-Robbins, requires no equipment. You can use any fruit here, really, but I love the vibrancy and acidity of fruits like blackberries, raspberries, strawberries, and plums.

**1** Spray a 9 x 4-inch loaf pan with nonstick spray and line it with plastic wrap (the nonstick spray helps the plastic adhere better, making an otherwise impossible task totally doable).

**2** Cook the fruit and ¼ cup of the honey in a small pan over medium-high heat until the berries have started to break down and the liquid has thickened, 8 to 10 minutes (simmering the berries quickly will reduce and thicken the liquid while keeping many of the berries somewhat intact, which is what you want). Remove the pan from the heat and let cool completely, placing it in the fridge if you'd like to speed up the process. Once cooled, the berries should have the texture of a loose, spreadable (not pourable) jam.

**3** In a large bowl, use an electric mixer or your forearms and a whisk—your choice—to whip the cream to medium-stiff peaks. Fold in the labne, the remaining ½ cup honey, and the salt just to blend.

**4** Add the cooled berry mixture and, using a spatula, just barely fold it in (maybe three or four times), leaving large streaks of berry throughout. Pour the mixture into the prepared loaf pan, smoothing the top with a spoon or offset spatula.

**5** Place the loaf pan in the freezer until it's firmed up, about 2 hours. This is best served around the 2- to 3-hour mark, when it's just the perfect texture (not too soft, not too hard). If serving beyond that, let it sit in the fridge for 10 to 15 minutes or so just to soften up.

# Chocolate-Tahini Tart
# with Crunchy Salt

*Serves 8 to 10*

**CRUST**
¾ cup all-purpose flour
¼ cup unsweetened cocoa powder
¼ cup confectioners' sugar
½ teaspoon kosher salt
½ cup (1 stick) unsalted butter, melted

**FILLING**
10 ounces bittersweet chocolate,
　　at least 68% cacao, chopped
⅔ cup tahini (almond butter and peanut
　　butter also work here)
Pinch of kosher salt
1 cup heavy cream
¼ cup honey
Flaky sea salt, such as
　　Jacobsen, for sprinkling

**DO AHEAD:** Chocolate tart crust can be made 2 days ahead and refrigerated. Tart can be made 1 day ahead. Unless your kitchen is unseasonably hot, you do not need to refrigerate here; it can be stored at room temperature.

I like my chocolate in small, concentrated amounts, preferably with some form of salty peanut butter on the inside and in a serrated cup shape. This tart, while decidedly more refined than anything that comes out of a shiny orange wrapper, satisfies me in a similar fashion. With its intensely chocolatey filling, it's meant to be eaten a small sliver at a time, but the nuttiness from tahini, light sweetness from honey, and addicting saltiness from a generous sprinkling of the crunchiest, flakiest salt you can get your hands on might make that challenging.

Chocolate is the star of the show, so spring for a bag of the good stuff meant for baking. This can be baking chips (not to be confused with chocolate chips), coins found in a specialty baking supply store, or high-quality bars or chunks. Cheaper chocolate meant for tossing into cookie dough or eating as a bar often contains additives (and more sugar), which means it never quite behaves the same way as chocolate made specifically for melting and baking.

**1 MAKE THE CRUST:** Preheat the oven to 350°F.

**2** Combine the flour, cocoa powder, confectioners' sugar, and kosher salt in a medium bowl. Drizzle in the melted butter and mix until well combined (it'll have a sort of Play-Doh-type texture). Press this into the bottom and up the sides of a 9-inch tart pan (or you can use a 9-inch springform pan), using a measuring cup or your hands to flatten it and make sure it's all packed and even.

**3** Bake 15 to 20 minutes. It's difficult to tell when this is done because it's already brown, so there is no color indicator to rely on. Test by pressing the center: it should be firm and opaque, not squishy or greasy looking. Remove from the oven and let cool.

**4 MAKE THE FILLING:** Combine the chocolate, tahini, and kosher salt in a medium bowl. Heat the cream and honey in a small saucepan over medium heat. Once it starts to simmer, remove it from the heat (do not let it boil or the cream will be too hot, and you'll have to wait too long for it to cool down) and pour it over the chocolate and tahini. Let it sit for a minute or two to melt the chocolate.

**5** Using a spatula, mix until well blended and no bits of chocolate remain. Use quite a bit of elbow grease here—really commit. After a minute or so, the mixture should look thick, glossy, and well emulsified.

**6** Immediately pour the filling into the cooled crust and smooth the top. Sprinkle with flaky salt. Let sit for at least 1 hour before slicing.

# Jen's Key Lime Pie

*Serves 8*

## CRUST
**10 graham crackers (about 1¼ sleeves, depending on the brand)**

**4 tablespoons coconut oil, melted**

**2 tablespoons (¼ stick) unsalted butter, melted**

**1 tablespoon granulated sugar**

**¾ teaspoon kosher salt**

## FILLING AND TOPPING
**4 large egg yolks**

**1 (14-ounce) can sweetened condensed milk**

**2 teaspoons finely grated lime zest, plus more for garnish**

**1 cup fresh lime juice (from 8 to 10 limes)**

**Pinch of kosher salt**

**1 cup heavy cream**

**¼ cup confectioners' sugar**

**1 cup full-fat Greek yogurt or sour cream**

**DO AHEAD:** Key lime piecrust can be baked 1 day ahead. Key lime pie with filling (sans whipped topping) can be made 1 day ahead. With topping, it can be made 5 hours ahead.

Perfectly in-season fruit pies aside, I think we can all agree that key lime pies are the best. And this key lime pie just might be the most perfect one I've ever had. There's coconut oil in the crust for a slightly nutty, tropical vibe, and the filling is light, fluffy, and maybe too tangy for some people—just how I like it. Plus, it's made with sweetened condensed milk—perhaps the greatest ingredient of all time—for a slight caramel flavor and ultra-creamy texture.

The yogurt topping was born from necessity during a time I was serving this as my cousin Jen's "birthday cake" and I ran out of cream, and no bodega in a five-block radius carried it. I had to supplement with Greek yogurt. Not only did it do the job, but it did it better than heavy cream, delivering something that is both lighter and richer, if you can imagine.

**1 MAKE THE CRUST:** Preheat the oven to 350°F.

**2** Smash the graham crackers with your hands until you've got coarse crumbs. You can also use a food processor, but I like to do this with my hands to control the size of the crumb. Be sure you've got a few larger crumbs in there for some good texture, but nothing should be bigger than a lentil. Mix these crumbs with the coconut oil, butter, granulated sugar, and salt until you've got really moist crumbs, almost like wet sand. Press the crumbs into a 9-inch pie plate and bake until the crust starts to lightly brown around the edges, 12 to 15 minutes. Remove from the oven and set aside to cool. Leave the oven on.

**3 MAKE THE FILLING:** In a large bowl, vigorously whisk the egg yolks until they're pale and fluffy, just a few minutes. Add the sweetened condensed milk and whisk a few more minutes, until the mixture is light and airy. Using a spatula or wooden spoon, fold in the lime zest and lime juice (if you use a whisk, all the bits of lime zest get caught in there, and I hate that). Add the salt for good measure. Pour this into your partially baked crust and return it to the oven to bake another 20 to 25 minutes. The center should barely jiggle; FYI, the top should not brown, so keep an eye on it.

**4** Remove the pie and let it cool completely—like, so completely you might want to put it in the refrigerator. Actually, just put it in the refrigerator.

*recipe continues*

# Cocoa Banana Bread

*Makes 1 loaf*

Nonstick cooking spray, for the pan
½ cup Demerara sugar
1½ cups all-purpose flour
½ cup unsweetened cocoa powder
1 teaspoon baking soda
1 teaspoon kosher salt
6 tablespoons (¾ stick) unsalted butter,
    at room temperature
⅓ cup granulated sugar
¼ cup lightly packed light brown sugar
1 teaspoon vanilla extract
1 large egg
5 extremely ripe bananas, 4 coarsely
    mashed and 1 sliced lengthwise
½ cup mascarpone, full-fat sour cream,
    or full-fat yogurt  (4 ounces)

**NOTE:** This bread will sink slightly from the weight of the banana on top—don't worry, that's okay. If that gives you anxiety, skip the banana on top.

**DO AHEAD:** Banana bread can be made 5 days ahead, wrapped tightly, and kept at room temperature.

This version of banana bread is more cake than bread, and I wouldn't be able to get away with saying "There's banana in it, so it's basically breakfast!" because no, this is not breakfast. This is a chocolatey, buttery, almost decadent thing and probably not appropriate for anyone to eat first thing in the morning. While mascarpone will give you the richest, moistest cake with the best flavor, sour cream or yogurt will get the job done; just make sure they are full-fat.

**1** Preheat the oven to 350°F. Spray a 9 x 4-inch loaf pan with nonstick spray. Sugar the inside of the pan with ¼ cup of the Demerara sugar (or regular sugar if you don't have Demerara), tapping out any excess.

**2** In a medium bowl, whisk the flour, cocoa powder, baking soda, and salt together; set aside.

**3** Using an electric mixer and a separate medium bowl or a stand mixer fitted with the paddle attachment, beat the butter, granulated sugar, light brown sugar, and vanilla on high speed until the mixture is super light and fluffy, 3 to 5 minutes. Using a spatula, scrape down the sides of the bowl and add the egg. Beat until well combined and the mixture returns to that previously light, fluffy state, about 2 minutes. With the mixer on low, slowly add the dry ingredients and beat just to blend. Using a spatula, fold in the mashed bananas, followed by the mascarpone, mixing just to blend.

**4** Pour the batter into the prepared loaf pan, smoothing the top. Place the banana halves, cut-side up, on top of the batter. Sprinkle with the remaining ¼ cup Demerara sugar and bake until the sides start to pull away and the cake is baked through in the center (it's a very dense, moist cake, but it should still spring back slightly when pressed in the center), 90 to 100 minutes.

**5** Let cool completely before slicing.

# Honey-Yogurt Pound Cake with Raspberries

*Serves 8*

**Nonstick cooking spray or softened butter, for the pan**
**1½ cups all-purpose flour**
**2 teaspoons baking powder**
**1 teaspoon kosher salt**
**½ cup sugar**
**¼ cup honey**
**¾ cup whole-milk Greek yogurt**
**⅓ cup grapeseed or vegetable oil**
**2 large eggs**
**2 cups fresh raspberries, blackberries, or blueberries**

**DO AHEAD:** This cake can be baked 3 days ahead, wrapped in plastic wrap, and kept at room temperature.

I've attended a lot of potlucks, dinner parties, baby showers, going-away parties, backyard barbecues, crab boils, and general gatherings in my day, and I know which kinds of desserts travel well and which ones do not. For example, pies that have not had the chance to properly cool do *not* do well in canvas tote bags in a fast-moving cab. Galettes that are too large to fit onto your largest plate are not good candidates for mass transit. A wonderfully delicate chocolate tart seems like a great idea to bring upstate for a trip with friends, until someone puts their overnight bag directly on top of it, ruining your entire weekend. Or at least the dessert part.

Point being, when traveling, the type of dessert must be thoroughly considered, and I can tell you that this cake was born to travel.

**1** Preheat the oven to 350°F. Prepare a 9 x 4-inch loaf pan with nonstick spray or grease with softened butter.

**2** In a medium bowl, whisk the flour, baking powder, and salt together; set aside.

**3** In a large bowl, whisk the sugar, honey, yogurt, oil, and eggs together. Using a spatula, gently fold in the dry ingredients until all the floury bits have disappeared (do not overmix—that's how you get an enthusiastically domed pound cake, which we do not want), followed by the raspberries (try to evenly distribute without squishing them).

**4** Pour the batter into the prepared loaf pan and smooth the top. Bake, rotating halfway through, until the cake is golden brown, pulling away from the sides of the pan, and springs back when pressed in the center, 60 to 70 minutes. Let the cake cool completely before removing it from the pan.

# Caramelized Honey
# with Figs and Ice Cream

Serves 4

¾ cup mild honey

2 tablespoons (¼ stick) unsalted butter

1 tablespoon white wine vinegar or
    fresh lemon juice

Kosher salt

1½ pounds fresh figs, halved
    lengthwise (I leave the stems on,
    but you can snip them if they
    bother you)

Lots of the best vanilla ice cream you
    can find

Flaky sea salt, such as Jacobsen,
    for sprinkling

**NOTE:** This technique is also very good with peaches, nectarines, or apricots.

I like to use honey in lieu of granulated or brown sugar in desserts when I'm going for a deeper, more complex flavor and I don't have to worry about compromising texture (honey adds quite a bit of moisture, whereas sugar does not). Ideal candidates include cakes, pie fillings, and frozen desserts (it especially shines like the sweet little star it is in the Frozen Blackberries and Labne with Honey on page 266). To me, honey is so good on its own that I would be more than happy to just eat it straight from the jar.

But then there's caramelized honey. Caramelized honey is like taking regular honey up to eleven. It's Honey, Part 2. It's "Honey, Now with 90 Percent More Honey." The flavors mature and grow, going from something vaguely sweet with delicate floral notes to an insanely sticky substance with slightly bitter, darker, almost wild flavors. Because caramelizing the honey really does intensify the flavors, start with something a little more mild, like alfalfa or clover honey.

Often, desserts are far more complicated than they ought to be. This dessert was originally supposed to be a tarte tatin situation, but after eating some of the softened figs and that caramelized honey with a pint of vanilla ice cream, I thought, Nah. We're good here.

**1**  Cook the honey in a large skillet over medium heat, stirring occasionally, until it's bubbling furiously and starting to caramelize, 4 to 6 minutes. If using a cast-iron skillet, test the color of the honey by spooning some onto a white plate; it should be dark amber, the color of good maple syrup.

**2**  Stir in the butter, vinegar, and kosher salt. Once the butter has sizzled and melted, add the figs, cut-side down, and cook until they're just glazed and slightly softened, a minute or two. Remove from the heat and flip the figs just to coat the other side. Serve the figs in the caramelized honey syrup with lots of vanilla ice cream and flaky sea salt sprinkled over.

# Everyone's Favorite Celebration Cake

*Makes one 9-inch three-layer cake*

### YELLOW CAKE

**Nonstick cooking spray or softened butter, for the pans**
**3¼ cups all-purpose or cake flour**
**2 teaspoons baking powder**
**1½ teaspoons kosher salt**
**1½ teaspoons baking soda**
**1½ cups buttermilk**
**¾ cup vegetable oil**
**2 teaspoons vanilla extract**
**1 cup (2 sticks) unsalted butter, at room temperature, cut into 1-inch pieces**
**2 cups granulated sugar**
**½ cup lightly packed light brown sugar**
**5 large eggs**
**3 large egg yolks**

### CHOCOLATE FROSTING

**12 ounces bittersweet chocolate (chocolate chips are fine)**
**8 ounces sour cream, at room temperature**
**1 cup (2 sticks) unsalted butter, at room temperature**
**1½ cups confectioners' sugar**
**Generous pinch of kosher salt**

**Lots of sprinkles**

While this may look deceptively like a birthday cake, I know from personal experience that this is the perfect cake for when there is anything to celebrate or, sometimes even more, the tragic absence of anything to celebrate. It's a holiday cake, a baby shower cake, a wedding cake, and a just-because cake. It's a cake you make when you have a bit of extra time on your hands and lots of people to feed.

While I never really stress about using cake flour versus all-purpose when baking, cake flour will give you a more delicate, ethereal crumb, which is definitely a good thing. That said, you can certainly use either with great success.

For the most even three layers, use measuring cups (or, even better, a scale) to measure the batter into each pan. Yes, that is sort of type A personality overboard crazy, but it's also the best way to make sure each layer is the same, if you're not so confident in your batter distribution abilities.

**1 MAKE THE CAKE:** Preheat the oven to 350°F and position one rack in the top third of the oven and one rack in the middle of the oven. Prepare three 9-inch cake pans with nonstick spray or grease with softened butter.

**2** In a large bowl, whisk the flour, baking powder, salt, and baking soda together; set aside. In a medium bowl or a measuring cup, combine the buttermilk, vegetable oil, and vanilla; set aside.

**3** In a large bowl, combine the butter, granulated sugar, and brown sugar. Using an electric mixer or a stand mixer fitted with the paddle attachment, beat everything together on high speed until it's super light and fluffy, about 4 minutes. Add the eggs and egg yolks one at a time, incorporating each one before adding the next. Beat the batter until it's almost doubled in volume and very light and fluffy, about 5 minutes. (Don't forget to scrape down the sides of the bowl periodically.)

**4** With the mixer on low, gently beat in one-third of the flour mixture. Before it's fully combined, add one-half of the buttermilk mixture. Repeat with remaining flour and buttermilk, ending with the flour, until everything is well blended and no lumps remain.

**5** Divide the cake batter evenly among the three cake pans and place two pans on the upper rack and one pan on the middle rack. Bake 35 to 40 minutes, rotating the pan on the middle rack to the upper rack halfway through baking, so they all get even oven love

*recipe continues*

(one of the cakes won't see the middle rack, but that's okay). You'll know the cakes are done when they are golden brown, pulling away from the sides of the pans, and the tops spring back ever so slightly when you press them.

**6** Remove the cakes from the oven and let sit for 5 minutes to cool slightly before inverting them onto a wire rack to cool completely. (If you don't have a wire rack, let them cool in the cake pans on the counter.) I avoid using a sharp knife to run around the edges (that's how you ruin a cake pan), but if you notice the cake sticking at all, use something a little duller, like a butter knife, to coax it out of the pan.

**7 MAKE THE FROSTING:** Place the chocolate either in a bowl in the microwave, heating it in 30-second intervals until melted, or in a double boiler—or a makeshift double boiler (a bowl set over a saucepan of barely simmering water, but not touching the water)—stirring occasionally until it's melted. The melted chocolate should be warm but never hot, with no visible chunks left.

**8** Add about one-third of the sour cream to the melted chocolate and, using a spatula, combine them until no white streaks remain. Repeat with another third, and finally the last third. The chocolate will stiffen a bit as you add the sour cream, and this is okay.

**9** In a large bowl, combine the butter, confectioners' sugar, and salt. Using an electric mixer or a stand mixer fitted with the paddle attachment, beat everything together on high speed until it's fluffy and almost pure white, about 5 minutes. With the mixer on low, slowly add the chocolate mixture and blend. Increase the speed to high and beat until everything is combined and the frosting looks super fluffy and delicious, as if it came from a can (but it didn't), about 2 minutes.

**10 ASSEMBLE THE CAKE:** Once the cakes are cooled, transfer one layer, top-side up, to a large parchment-lined plate. Use an offset or regular spatula to spread frosting on the first layer of cake. Place a second layer on top, bottom-side up (layering the rest with the flat bottoms on top makes a cake with a straight rather than domed shape) and frost. Repeat with the remaining layer.

**11** Once all the layers are assembled, apply a thin layer of frosting all over, making sure to cover the whole cake. This is a "crumb coat," and it's just the base layer, so don't worry about making it perfect. Chill the cake for 30 minutes to 2 hours, but keep the remaining frosting at room temperature.

**12** Remove the cake from the fridge and, using either an offset spatula or a butter knife, give it another coat of frosting, doing whatever decorative patterns or swirls your heart desires. Super smooth, peaks and valleys—your cake, your call.

**13** Finish and decorate with sprinkles however you please!

**NOTE:** To get the sprinkles onto the sides of the cake, you can put some in your hand and kind of simultaneously toss and pat them onto the sides. Do this on a rimmed baking sheet to contain the sprinkles.

# How to Casually Frost a Cake

The great thing about frosting a cake is that by the time you're ready to do it, all the hard work has been done. You already know the cakes survived their trip to the oven, because you're about to frost them, and you've just made the frosting, which I'm assuming tastes amazing. If you don't own an offset spatula or other fancy cake-decorating tools, that's fine, because I know from experience that you can definitely use a butter knife to do this job.

Before you do anything, take a deep breath. You're about to frost a cake, not perform oral surgery. Remember, this is supposed to be fun. Isn't this fun? Then clear off your countertop so you have plenty of space to work and won't get frosting everywhere.

Okay, so start by placing one of the cakes on a large plate lined with parchment (even if you did have a cake stand, chances are it wouldn't fit in the refrigerator, so use a plate). Dip your offset spatula or butter knife into that glorious bowl of frosting and dollop about a cup of the frosting right in the middle of the cake. Spread it evenly all over the top of the cake, just like you're spreading peanut butter onto toast.

Place your second cake on top and repeat just like the first layer with the flatter, bottom side up. Press the third cake on top and press lightly. Doesn't it look great already? Stand back a second and admire it. Make sure it's (mostly) straight, adjusting a little to the left or a little to the right if it's looking a tad crooked.

Using the offset spatula or butter knife, spread a really thin layer all around the sides of the cake, making sure to get the frosting into every nook and cranny, patching up any gaps in the cake layers, as if you're caulking tile or something (this is the crumb coat, but this is a casual frosting job, so let's not get technical). This is just to trap any crumbs in the frosting.

Put this cake in the fridge and let it chill out there for 30 minutes to 2 hours. All this is doing is creating a firm, smooth, crumb-free surface for you to frost upon. Pat yourself on the back, maybe have a glass of wine. Don't think about what the cake is doing in there, because the answer is nothing; it's just hanging out, so you don't need to check on it.

After the cake is as chilled and relaxed as you are, take the frosting and, using the offset spatula or butter knife, just kind of smear it all over the sides of the cake from top to bottom. Smear and swoosh until you can't see any cake left.

Now for the final act: Dump any remaining frosting on top of the cake and spread it, swoosh it, smear it, smooth it. This is the top of your cake and the thing everyone will ooh and ahh over, so make it count. Congratulations! You just frosted a cake casually, as if it was no big deal.

# Rhubarb-Almond Galette

*Serves 8*

**1 large egg, lightly beaten**
**½ recipe (1 disk) The Only Piecrust**
**(page 256)**
**All-purpose flour, for dusting**
**¼ cup almond paste**
**2½ pounds rhubarb, halved lengthwise,**
**then cut crosswise into 4- to 6-inch**
**pieces**
**½ cup sugar**
**Vanilla ice cream (optional)**

**DO AHEAD:** Galette can be baked 1 day ahead.

Too tart for some, too stringy for others, rhubarb is a vegetable struggling to find its place in a fruit world, and for whatever reason, I can relate to that. And sure, it's not really an eat-out-of-hand type of deal, but when you give it just the right amount of sugar and cook it till just softened, it definitely competes for the title of Most Delicious Fruit.

Often just thrown to the strawberries and cooked to an indistinguishable mush, I think the long, elegant stalks deserve their own show. When baked in a galette, they maintain their lovely shape, showing off that vibrant pink color for all to admire, no longer hiding behind seedy raspberries or just-in-season strawberries.

Even in the early spring, when it is in season, rhubarb can be tricky to find. It likes colder climates, which is why you can get it in Maine until late July, but sometimes it never appears in California. When you can find it, go for the deepest, reddest stalks you can get your hands on, buy it all, chop it up, and freeze it. While defrosted rhubarb isn't spectacular for galettes (it will give off too much liquid as it defrosts), you can make some pretty fantastic jam later on with the thawed stuff.

**1** Preheat the oven to 375°F.

**2** Beat the egg with 1 teaspoon water and set aside (this is your egg wash, and it will help the crust get super golden brown on top).

**3** Roll out the pie dough on a lightly floured surface to a round 14 to 16 inches in diameter, more or less.

**4** Transfer the dough to a parchment-lined baking sheet.

**5** Flatten large bits of almond paste between your palms until they are super thin (about ⅛ inch) and place them on top of the dough, leaving a 2-inch border. Arrange the rhubarb pieces on top of the almond paste. Don't worry about placing them in any sort of pattern or anything; just kinda Lincoln Log them onto each other.

**6** Fold the edges of the dough up and over the rhubarb. Brush the edges of the dough with the egg wash and sprinkle the whole thing with sugar, throwing most of it on top of the rhubarb (remember, the almond paste is pretty sweet, so you don't need as much sugar as you think you might).

**7** Place the galette in the oven and bake until the crust is golden brown (think the color of a roasted cashew), 50 to 60 minutes. Let it cool slightly before eating with the best vanilla ice cream you can find.

# Pistachio-Plum Crisp

*Serves 8*

## TOPPING

1 cup all-purpose flour (gluten-free or
    almond flour works well here, too)
¼ cup lightly packed light brown sugar
1 teaspoon ground cardamom
½ teaspoon kosher salt
1 cup shelled pistachios, walnuts,
    almonds, or pecans, finely chopped
6 tablespoons (¾ stick) unsalted butter,
    cut into 1-inch pieces, at room
    temperature

## FILLING

4 pounds red plums, black plums,
    or apricots, pitted and sliced
    1 inch thick
¾ cup granulated sugar
3 tablespoons cornstarch
1 tablespoon fresh lemon juice, white
    wine vinegar, or unseasoned rice
    vinegar
1 teaspoon rose water (optional)

If there were a dessert hierarchy in order of perceived complication, crisps would sit beneath galettes, which sit beneath pies. It's the kind of dessert invented for people who always say, "I can't make dessert." Crisps are nearly impossible to mess up, and even if you do, nobody will notice (I promise).

Oh, and I realize shelled pistachios can be challenging to find, so just know I would never ask you to shell all those pistachios one by one just for this dessert, because I am not a monster; feel free to use almonds, walnuts, or pecans instead. In fact, swap the plums for apples or strawberries, if you like (the optional rose water goes exceptionally well with both), and use cinnamon in place of the cardamom. Go ahead, make this your own. Be free—express yourself!

**1** Preheat the oven to 350°F.

**2** **MAKE THE TOPPING:** In a medium bowl, combine the flour, brown sugar, cardamom, salt, and ¾ cup of the nuts. Using your hands, work the butter into the dry mixture until it's completely incorporated (it will be soft and slightly sticky); set aside.

**3** **MAKE THE FILLING:** Toss the plums, granulated sugar, cornstarch, lemon juice, and rose water (if using) together in a 3-quart baking dish. Scatter the topping over the plums and scatter the remaining ¾ cup nuts on top.

**4** Bake the crisp until the fruit is bubbling and cooked through and the topping is crisp and golden brown, 55 to 65 minutes.

**5** Let cool slightly before eating.

# Blueberry Cake with Almond and Cinnamon

*Serves 8*

Nonstick spray, for the pan
1 cup almond flour
¾ cup all-purpose flour
1 teaspoon baking powder
1½ teaspoons ground cinnamon
¾ teaspoon kosher salt
¾ cup (1½ sticks) unsalted butter,
    at room temperature
½ cup light brown sugar
¼ cup plus 3 tablespoons granulated
    sugar
2 large eggs
1 teaspoon vanilla extract
2 cups blueberries

**DO AHEAD:** The cake can be baked 4 days ahead, wrapped tightly in plastic wrap, and stored at room temperature.

Whenever I have a muffin, my first thought is generally, "Why aren't muffins better?" Butter, sugar, eggs, flour—I mean, by all accounts, it should be at least an 8/10 every time. And yet I find myself wishing that most were even a tenth as good as the ones from Costco that I grew up eating, which we all know are just cakes baked in muffin cups. After giving it a lot of thought, I realized that instead of making a muffin that just tastes like cake, what I wanted was a cake that tasted like a muffin. So here it is, basically one giant muffin top, now in sliceable cake form.

You'll notice that after baking it's a bit more shallow than a classic cake, but since it's so rich (thanks, almond flour!), the portion size remains the same. Another added bonus from the fatty nut flour is that this cake stays fresh as the day it was born for a few days, even if you forget to wrap it tightly every time you sneak a bite, which is my signature move.

I prefer the tinier late-summer blueberries for this because they tend to be juicier and tangier (and cuter). Use whatever you can find, because even an okay blueberry, when baked, is a pretty spectacular blueberry.

**1** Preheat the oven to 375°F. Spray a 9-inch fluted tart pan or round cake pan with nonstick spray.

**2** Whisk together the almond flour, all-purpose flour, baking powder, cinnamon, and salt in a medium bowl.

**3** Using an electric mixer, in a medium bowl, beat the butter, brown sugar, and ¼ cup of the granulated sugar together on medium-high speed until the mixture is super light and fluffy, 3 to 4 minutes.

**4** Scrape down the sides of the bowl and with the mixer on medium, add the eggs one at a time, beating until each one is incorporated, followed by the vanilla. Increase the speed to medium-high and beat until the mixture is pale and nearly doubled in volume, 4 to 5 minutes. Fold in the almond mixture until no dry spots remain. Gently add 1½ cups of the blueberries by hand, making sure you don't totally smush them.

**5** Transfer the batter to the prepared tart pan and, using a spatula or the back of a spoon, smooth the top. Sprinkle the remaining 3 tablespoons granulated sugar on top and bake until the cake is deeply golden brown and pulls away from the edges slightly, 30 to 35 minutes. It should start to crackle a bit on top (what you're looking for).

**6** Remove from the oven and let cool completely before slicing.

# Strawberry Shortcake Cobbler

*Serves 6*

**SHORTCAKES**

1¼ cups all-purpose flour, plus more for the work surface

½ cup coarse yellow cornmeal

2 tablespoons light brown sugar

2 tablespoons granulated sugar

1 tablespoon baking powder

¾ teaspoon kosher salt

½ cup (1 stick) unsalted butter, cut into 1-inch pieces, at room temperature

½ cup heavy cream

**FILLING**

5 cups strawberries (about 2 quarts), hulled and halved

½ cup granulated sugar

2 tablespoons cornstarch

1 tablespoon fresh lime or lemon juice

2 tablespoons heavy cream

2 tablespoons light brown sugar

**DO AHEAD:** Cobbler can be baked 4 hours before serving and kept at room temperature.

Strawberry shortcake: great in theory, a little annoying in practice. I'd better like you a *lot* if I'm going to make you an individually assembled dessert. But this cobbler gets at the point (tender, buttery shortcake; juicy, lightly sweetened strawberries), and it gets at it in a more efficient and, dare I say, delicious way. The shortcakes get baked right on top of the strawberries, so by the time they're golden brown and perfect, the strawberries have given up a bit of their juices, which roast with just enough sugar to create a gloriously delicious, syrupy sauce. Two birds, one cobbler.

**1** Preheat the oven to 350°F.

**2 MAKE THE SHORTCAKES:** In a large bowl, combine the flour, cornmeal, brown sugar, granulated sugar, baking powder, and salt. Using your hands, rub the butter into the flour mixture until no large chunks remain. Add the cream and mix with your hands just until blended. Turn the dough out onto lightly floured work surface and knead the dough just until it's no longer super sticky, about 2 minutes.

**3** Using your hands, form the dough into a circle about 1 inch thick. Using a 2-inch cookie cutter (or an approximation thereof—I use water glasses, mason jars, whatever), punch out as many shortcakes as you can. Re-pat the scraps to 1 inch thick and repeat until all the dough is used. Set the shortcakes aside while you prepare the filling (transfer to the refrigerator if they feel too soft).

**4 MAKE THE FILLING:** In a medium bowl, toss the strawberries with the granulated sugar, cornstarch, and lime juice. Transfer the berries to a 9-inch cast-iron skillet, pie dish, or cake pan (a 9 x 13-inch baking dish will also work in a pinch) and top with the shortcakes.

**5** Brush the tops of the shortcakes with the cream and sprinkle with the brown sugar. Bake until the shortcakes are golden brown and the juices of the strawberries have thickened and bubbled up around the edges of the skillet, 25 to 30 minutes.

**6** Remove from the oven and let cool slightly before digging in (this will not only prevent unnecessary mouth burns, but letting it cool a bit will help set the juices so it's not too runny).

# Brown Butter–Buttermilk Cake

*Makes one 9-inch cake*

## CAKE

Nonstick cooking spray or softened
   butter, for the pan
½ cup (1 stick) unsalted butter
1 vanilla bean, split and seeds scraped,
   or 1½ teaspoons vanilla extract
2 cups all-purpose flour
½ cup granulated sugar
½ cup light brown sugar
1½ teaspoons baking powder
½ teaspoon baking soda
¾ teaspoon kosher salt
1 cup buttermilk
2 large eggs

## ICING

2 tablespoons (¼ stick) unsalted butter
1¼ cups confectioners' sugar
2 to 3 tablespoons buttermilk
Flaky sea salt

**DO AHEAD:** The cake can be made
2 days ahead, wrapped tightly,
and kept at room temperature.

   The cake can be iced 8 hours ahead
and kept at room temperature, loosely
covered with plastic wrap or covered
with a cake dome.

Cooking electric-yellow butter low and slow, until the milk solids begin to caramelize, turning the color of perfectly toasted brioche with a smell to match, is like spinning gold into ... something even better than gold (still working on this metaphor). While I've tried just drinking the stuff straight, I can say it's also great when spooned over roasted carrots, used to dress steamed fish, or tossed with whole-wheat pasta (especially with mushrooms, as on page 148).

   But should you want to harness the full power of this life-changing ingredient, look no further than this cake. Brown butter and all the bits (the dark brown caramelized parts at the bottom of the pot) get swirled into a thick buttermilk batter and then iced with even more brown-butter business. It's doubling down on perfection, and the result is something that tastes like an old-fashioned donut, in cake form. I could go on, but after hearing that, I'm assuming you've already committed.

   If icing isn't your thing, this recipe makes an excellent last-minute birthday cake (go ahead and make the frosting on page 281) or base for an upside-down cake (page 296).

**1**  Preheat the oven to 350°F. Prepare a 9-inch round cake pan with nonstick spray or grease with softened butter. Line with parchment paper, leaving a bit of overhang, if you like (I do this if the cake pan is old and has lost all its nonstick mojo, but also because visually, I like the ridges it makes on the sides of the cake).

**2**  In a small saucepan, melt the butter with the vanilla bean seeds and pod (if you're using vanilla extract, wait to add it when you mix the wet ingredients). Cook, swirling the pot every so often, until the butter is foamy and starting to brown on the bottom, about 5 minutes (it should smell like hazelnuts and marshmallows and everything good in the world). Use a whisk to scrape up the bottom bits, then remove the pan from the heat and set it aside to cool slightly.

**3**  Whisk the flour, granulated sugar, brown sugar, baking powder, baking soda, and salt in a large bowl.

**4**  Whisk the buttermilk, eggs, and vanilla extract (if using) in a medium bowl until no visible bits of egg remain. Add the buttermilk mixture to the flour mixture and whisk just to blend (a few streaks of flour are fine). Remove the vanilla bean pod from the butter and pour the butter into the batter, whisking just to blend (do not

*recipe continues*

overmix; this cake is particularly sensitive to becoming tough). Save the pot used to make the brown butter; you'll use it again for the glaze.

**5** Pour the batter into the prepared pan and bake until the edges are golden brown and the top springs back when pressed slightly, 35 to 40 minutes (if you're using a cake tester, insert it into the center of the cake; it should come out clean).

**6** Remove the cake from the oven and let it cool completely before icing.

**7** **MAKE THE ICING:** Melt the butter in the same small saucepan over medium heat. Cook, swirling the pot every so often, until the butter is foamy and starting to brown on the bottom, about 4 minutes. Use a whisk to scrape up the bottom bits, then remove the butter from the heat and set aside to cool slightly.

**8** Whisk the confectioners' sugar, buttermilk, and brown butter together until you've got a smooth, shiny, pourable, frosting-like icing. Pour the icing on top of the cake, using an offset spatula, if needed, to spread it to the edges and letting it drip down in spots. Sprinkle with flaky sea salt and let sit 10 to 15 minutes to set.

---

**For Upside-Down Cakes**

This Brown Butter–Buttermilk Cake is especially well suited for an upside-down cake because (*a*) it requires no mixer to throw it together, whereas most recipes do, and (*b*) it sort of mimics that boxed yellow cake flavor (I mean that as the highest compliment, of course). That way, all you're really left to do is figure out what fruit you want. I don't advise using berries or overly ripe fruit, because they tend to fall apart and just turn to mush (no thanks).

For something like pineapple upside-down cake, all you need to do is scatter an additional ½ cup lightly packed light brown sugar onto the bottom of the cake pan, dot it with 2 tablespoons (¼ stick) unsalted butter, and place sliced pineapple (about ¾ inch thick) on top. The maraschino cherries are optional but very cute and make me feel like I'm living in a tiki bar, so maybe just go for it.

Pour the batter on top of the pineapple and bake as per the instructions above. When the cake has been out of the oven for about 10 minutes (it should still be a bit warm), place a large plate on top of the cake pan and, using a kitchen towel to hold it, flip the cake out on top of the plate.

Remove the cake pan and peel away any parchment, revealing the rings of juicy, caramelized pineapple. This will also work with peeled, cored, and sliced apple rings as well, although they are arguably not as iconic.

# acknowledgments

Thank you to my editor, Doris Cooper, who took me out for pizza and convinced me I should write a book. Aside from your sharp, thoughtful edits, I will be forever grateful for your cheerleading, real-talk guidance, and general hand-holding; your patience with me has been immeasurable. I heard you were the best, and now I know for certain you are.

To Aaron Wehner for believing in this project and loving the cover as much as I did, and to the rest of the team at Clarkson Potter, especially the brilliant Stephanie Huntwork, Jana Branson, and Kate Tyler: Thank you for your overwhelming support and generous flexibility. And to Amy Boorstein, Kim Tyner, and Danielle Daitch for all your help along the way.

To my agent, Nicole Tourtelot. Choosing to work with you was one of the best decisions I've ever made. Thank you for your candor, your time, and for always responding to my manic late-night e-mails, texts, and phone calls. You truly deserve a medal.

To Michael Graydon and Nikole Herriott, two of the kindest, hardest-working, most creative people I know. Thank you for your willingness to take on this project, do things in an insanely unconventional way, break literally every rule (are there rules?), and still like me afterward. This book is as much yours as it is mine, and I hope you're as proud of it as I am.

To Amy Wilson, this book would have been half as good without your props, your styling. and your calming energy. Thank you for all you gave to this project, and I'm sorry about the raccoons.

To Elizabeth Spiridakis-Olson: When I knew I was going to do a book, I didn't know what it was going to be, but I knew I wanted to do it with you. Your eye for impeccable design, ridiculous fashion sense, and think-outside-the-box approach to everything in life made this book truly special.

To Anna Billingskog, Lauren Shaefer, and Julia Callon: Thank you for your insanely hard work, long hours, delightfully upbeat attitudes, and fantastic talent. The shoots would have been half as fun and twice as hectic without you all. Thanks for making me look good.

To Adam Rapoport, Carla Lalli-Music, Christine Muhlke, Alex Grossman, and the rest of my family at *Bon Appétit*

magazine, past and present. Thank you for teaching me, editing me, pushing me, and drinking with me. I wouldn't have made this book if it weren't for you all.

To Hunter Lewis for taking a chance and giving me a job. It was my lucky day, truly.

To Ron Mendoza and William Werner, the two guys who basically taught me everything I know about making dessert, working hard, and good music.

To all the amazing humans who helped test recipes, organize spreadsheets, separate receipts, grocery shop, and wash dishes to help me with the making of this book: Kendra Vaculin, Mariette Mayerson, Yewande Komolafe, Jena Derman, Emily Fleischaker, Mollie Chen, Shannon Mulcahy, and Ariel Brodey.

For the ceramicists that lent their gorgeous wares, especially Ariela (ANK Ceramics), Nina and Jennifer (MONDAYS Projects), Nate (Felt + Fat), and Caroline (TOOOLS).

To Katie Mayerson, Clayton Blaha, Eva Scofield, Michael Wooten, Mercedez Perez-Garcia, Julia Kramer, Lilli Sherman, and Eric Sullivan: I feel wildly blessed to have you all in my life. Thank you for the pep talks, emergency phone calls, group texts, reality checks, unconditional support, and abundant love. I admire you all and I would be a shell of a woman without you.

To my family in California (Mindy, Carleigh, Ethan, Grandma, Kimmy, Art, and Jesse), thank you for being my biggest fans. And to my family in New York (Jen, James, Julia, Ben, Yosef, Finny, and Theo), you are my favorite people to cook and eat with. Thank you for making New York my home.

To Mom and Dad, hi! I love you! Thank you for always trusting in me to make the right choices (even when I didn't), for teaching me how to be independent, speak my mind, and listen to my gut. And for always encouraging me to do what I love–your support while I "figure it all out" has meant everything to me.

To BHB. Your strength, humor, kindness, resourcefulness, optimism, patience, and love allowed me to start, write, shoot, edit, and finish this book. I'm so glad you had to bake those biscuits. ILYSM.

# index

**ALISON ROMAN** is a contributor at *Bon Appétit*. Formerly the Senior Food Editor at *Bon Appétit* and *BuzzFeed*, her work appears regularly in the *New York Times* and has been featured in *GQ, Cherry Bombe,* and *Lucky Peach*. The author of *Lemons,* a Short Stack Edition, Alison has worked professionally in kitchens such as New York's Momofuku Milk Bar and San Francisco's Quince. A native of Los Angeles, she lives in Brooklyn.